Woodworking
FAQ

The Workshop Companion

Build Your Skills and Know-How
for Making Great Projects

Spike Carlsen

 Storey Publishing

*To my extraordinary kids
Tessa, Kellie, Zach, Maggie, and
Sarah, as well as Paige, Morgan,
Anna, and others who will
someday call me "Poppy."*

*A huge thanks to Kat, the love
of my life and partner
in all things.*

*In the immortal words of that
great philosopher,
Randy Newman, you all . . .*

*"give me reason to live,
you give me reason to live,
you give me reason to live!"*

The mission of Storey Publishing is to serve our customers by publishing practical information that encourages personal independence in harmony with the environment.

Edited by Nancy D. Wood and Lisa H. Hiley
Art direction and book design by Cynthia N. McFarland

Cover photography by Marcelino Vilaubi, except for author's photo by Kat Carlsen
Technical assistance for photography by Nick Noyes
Illustrations by Melanie Powell

Indexed by Nancy D. Wood

Storey Publishing
210 MASS MoCA Way
North Adams, MA 01247
www.storey.com

Printed in China by R.R. Donnelley
10 9 8 7 6 5 4 3 2 1

Library of Congress Cataloging-in-Publication Data on file

CONTENTS

A NOTE ABOUT SAFETY

Woodworking is both intrinsically rewarding and inherently risky. The same tools that cut and shape the wood can do the same to you. Read and follow the instructions and guidelines that come with the tools and materials you use and, above all, use common sense. There's always more than one way to tackle a task; if you're uncomfortable using a certain tool or performing a certain procedure, find an alternative way of getting the job done. Remember, with the proper tools, attitudes, and work habits, woodworking can be a safe, enjoyable, lifelong pursuit.

Introduction

When you hear the word "woodworking," what image springs to mind? That of some bearded old gent toiling away with a hand plane? Or some brawny soul standing in front of a large, complicated machine? The world of woodworking does encompass those scenarios, but it includes more than that. In fact, there's a good chance it includes YOU. If you've ever built a birdhouse, repaired a wobbly chair, or installed shelves in your closet, you're already a woodworker. You may not be Norm Abram of *The New Yankee Workshop* fame, but you (like 15 million others in America) still get to call yourself a woodworker.

Woodworking is a bit like cooking: Even though some people may be more experienced at it, spend more time at it, or have fancier equipment than you, that doesn't prevent you from rolling up your sleeves and cooking away. The more you cook, the better you get. You might have a few soufflés that fall, but you have plenty of victories, too. You buy higher quality equipment as you need it and more cookbooks as you forge into new territories. So it is with woodworking: You start with the basics, build your arsenal of tools and skills, then move on to more challenging projects as you improve. This book will help you do just that.

In days gone by, woodworking wisdom was often passed down through the generations, or at least from shop teacher to student! As this happens less and less, the need for a book that addresses your basic woodworking questions arises more and more. This book is packed with practical information for all skill levels. If you're a beginner, it will help answer the most fundamental questions: Which wood should I use for this bookcase? Which direction do I move my router? Why do I need three different grits of sandpaper? How do I clamp a picture frame? If you're an intermediate woodworker, you'll find lots of information to help you improve your woodworking skills. And even if you're an advanced craftsperson, there's still plenty of useful information in the answers, tips, charts, and projects herein.

This book does not attempt to answer every woodworking question ever asked, nor does it attempt to answer every question completely. If it did, it would take a forklift to move around. Rather, our goal is to address the most common questions and misperceptions about woodworking, present the basics so you can decide whether or not to move forward, then direct you to other sources for more information. While the book is broken down into 13 chapters, most questions could fit in more than one category. For instance, the information on edge-gluing boards could easily fall into three or more chapters. So we encourage you to use the index and table of contents to track down the information you're looking for.

The realm of woodworking is chock-full of opinions regarding which woods, tools, and techniques are best. That's part of what makes things interesting! If you want to spark a lively debate among a roomful of woodworkers, just ask them about the best way to mount adjustable shelves in a bookcase, install trim around a window, or finish a dining room table. Every woodworker, wood, and project is different. But we've drawn upon the experience and know-how of some of the best woodworkers in the field to help sort out fact from fiction. So carve ahead, and good luck in all of your projects.

―――――――――――― ACKNOWLEDGMENTS ――――――――――――

I've been working with, writing about, and learning about wood and woodworking for over 30 years. Yet in the process of writing this book, I realized how much I had yet to learn.

Thus I owe a great deal of gratitude to a group of exemplary woodworkers and teachers who were willing to share their experience and knowledge. Thanks to Dave Munkittrick, for his deft woodworking and reviewing skills; Tom Caspar, of *American Woodworker* magazine, for his insights on hand tools and sharpening; Allan Lacer, woodturner extraordinaire, for his expertise on turning; Mitch Kohanek, instructor of the National Institute of Wood Finishing at the Dakota County Technical College; Ken Collier and Travis Larson, of *The Family Handyman* magazine; Bruce Kiefer, Tim Johnson, Dick Thorngren, and Jim Adami — woodworkers extraordinaire; and others too numerous to name.

And a great deal of thanks to the team at Storey Publishing: a group that both talks the talk and walks the walk.

Setting Up Shop

Use what talents you have; the woods would have little music if no birds sang their song except those who sang best.
— REVEREND OLIVER G. WILSON

Your workshop doesn't have to be a 500-square-foot building full of $500 tools. In fact, most woodworkers do well with far less. The corner of a garage, a room in the basement, or an unused outbuilding will work just fine for most people. Don't have even that much space? Well, perhaps you can take heart from this apartment dweller: a fellow who loved woodworking so much he set up his lathe on the kitchen counter so he could turn pens and small bowls. He disposed of his waste in the garbage disposal and played polka music whenever he worked, so his landlord downstairs couldn't hear the thumping of the lathe. The main thing is to have a space that's safe to work in and conveniently organized, and there are lots of ways to do that. Here are some of the basics.

Your Workspace

Organization, safety, and comfort are three important objectives you should keep in mind as you plan your workspace. Here are some tips on reaching those goals.

Q We're moving, and I finally have room for my own small workshop. How can I make the most efficient use of my new space?

A Often, workshops just "happen," and the way tools, materials, and everything else are arranged is inefficient. The beauty of your situation is that you can start from scratch. As you set up your new shop, keep the following thoughts in mind.

⊙ Create workstation "clusters" to save space and minimize distances between tools frequently used in conjunction with one another. Your "wood preparation" cluster may consist of your table saw,

7

jointer, and planer. Your "wood shaping and dimensioning" cluster may consist of a miter saw, bandsaw and drill press. Your "assembly area" may consist of your workbench, clamp rack, and assembly platform.

⊙ Plan so that your stationary tools (especially your table saw) and work surfaces are at the same height within each cluster. It may mean raising some tools on blocks or wheels, or cutting an inch or two off the legs of your workbench, but you'll find this makes working with large panels and long stock much easier. The surfaces around you can lend a helping hand by supporting loose ends.

⊙ Use mobile bases with locking wheels for big tools, allowing you to store them against the wall and roll them out when needed. While drill presses, table saws, and planers can easily go mobile, it's best to leave your lathe and workbench grounded, solid, and vibration-free.

⊙ Work "out of the box." Since final assembly consumes lots of space and can be relatively free of mess, use nearby spaces for that task. Keep on hand a pair of collapsible sawhorses and an old door to create a temporary worktable. If you cut lots of long materials in a short shop, arrange tools so the material can extend through a door, a window, or even an access hole cut through the wall.

tip: Look Up for a Helping Hand

If you work in a small shop where it's hard to position outfeed tables or rollers to hold the ends of long boards as you work, try looking up. Build a "dogleg" out of ¾" plywood, and use a bolt and wingnut to secure it to a ceiling joist. Position the horizontal leg at the right height for supporting the boards you're working with. To use the dogleg, swing it into place and tighten the wingnut. When you don't need it, swing it back up and secure it to the side of the joist with a hook and eye or clamp.

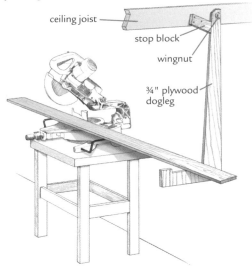

ceiling joist

stop block

wingnut

¾" plywood dogleg

Q What kind of fire extinguisher should I have in my shop, and where should I store it?

A Purchase a 10-pound, dry chemical ABC-rated fire extinguisher. Class A extinguishers are for ordinary combustibles, such as wood and paper; class B extinguishers can handle flammable liquids, such as solvents and oil-based paints; class C extinguishers are for fires involving energized electrical equipment, things like wiring and electrical motors. The materials and equipment in your shop can generate all three types of fires, and an ABC extinguisher is designed to handle all three.

Keep your extinguisher mounted by the door of your shop, and check it periodically to make certain it's fully charged. If a fire breaks out, evacuate the home and call the fire department. If the fire looks manageable (this is no time for heroics), stand eight feet away, pull the extinguisher's ring, aim the hose at the base of the flame, and squeeze the handle. Sweep the stream in a side-to-side motion, and advance on the fire as you make headway. Don't let the fire get between you and your escape route.

Q I don't have room for a dedicated workshop but would like to set up half of the garage for when I need it. What are a few simple things I can do?

A Workspaces are like carp: they'll grow to the size of their surroundings. So the first thing you should do is find some way of physically dividing the space in two. One technique is to purchase a roll of 6-mil polyethylene sheeting and set it up as a gigantic roller shade that you can easily raise and lower to cordon off your area. Attach a 1×2 to the top and bottom of a sheet of poly that is 6" longer than your garage is tall. Secure the top of this to the ceiling, and let the other 1×2 rest on the floor to create a temporary wall. When it's time to pull the car back in, clean up, roll up your giant shade, and use wire or a few Velcro straps to hold it to the ceiling.

Then the trick is to use every nook and cranny for storage and to make everything as portable as possible so you can set up and break down shop quickly. Here are a few other things to consider:

⊙ Install a hideaway workbench. You can make a simple version by mounting a solid-core (preferably slab-style) door with attached jamb lengthwise on the wall. The door can swing down to create a work surface; pegboard installed inside the jamb frame can hold a surprising number of tools. Use ¾" steel pipe flanges and pipes to create removable, screw-on legs.

⊙ If the walls are unfinished, install 2×4s or 2×6s between the studs to create mini-shelves. You can also use those cavities to store lumber vertically.

⊙ If the ceiling is unfinished, install 1×2s perpendicular to the joists or trusses to create storage space for longer moldings and pieces of lumber.

tip: Take Note

Keep a stack of sticky notes on your workbench and next to your table saw and miter saw for jotting down measurements, angles, and odd shapes. You'll quickly recoup your $2 investment by making fewer mistakes.

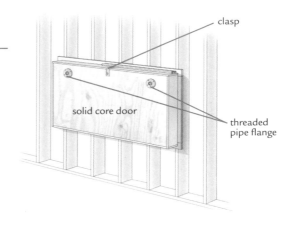

clasp

solid core door

threaded pipe flange

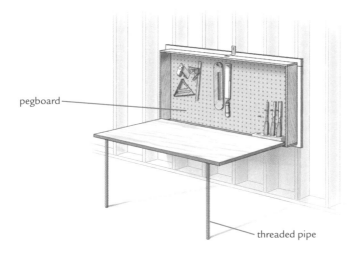

pegboard

threaded pipe

6 REASONS WE LOVE WOODWORKING

Humorist Dave Barry once wrote, "The only really good place to buy lumber is at a store where the lumber has already been cut and attached together in the form of furniture, finished, and put inside boxes." But the fact that you're reading this book indicates that you feel otherwise. Here are six reasons we love working with wood:

1 Your goals are clear — and you get to decide how to reach them. Some woodworkers love following step-by-step directions exactly; others like to improvise as they go. There's plenty of room for both approaches.

2 Woodworking offers the "just right" level of challenge. It's not so simplistic as to be boring yet not so complex as to be off-putting. It's like golf: The only person you have to compete against is yourself. And you get instant feedback; if the miters don't meet (or the ball is in the sand trap), you know right away.

3 Woodworking is a process and a product, the proverbial journey and destination. Creating sawdust is fulfilling, but seeing, using, or giving away the final product is just as rewarding.

4 Woodworking can be both a solitary and a communal endeavor. Most woodworkers work alone, but once the chisels are put away, the camaraderie begins. Woodworking clubs, guilds, tool swap meets, friends, stores, and websites provide lots of opportunities to share and learn (see Resources for more information).

5 Woodworking knows no age, gender, or other bounds. There are 95-year-old woodcarvers and 5-year-old toymakers. There are specialty groups, such as Woodworking for the Blind and Wheelchair Woodturners. All are welcome to the table.

6 When your spouse says, "The _____ is broken," or "We could sure use a ____ around here," you can respond, "I can build (or fix) that!"

The popularity of woodworking was perhaps best summed up by woodworker extraordinaire James Krenov when he explained, "People are beginning to look for something to do where they can say the things that they cannot say in the bank or at the office, to people who haven't got the time to listen."

Q I've been bitten by the woodworking bug, but my enthusiasm is outrunning my know-how, leaving me a bit frustrated. How do I find courses that will educate my inner woodworker?

A There are a number of excellent schools across the country that are designed to help enthusiasts just like you. Search "Woodworking Schools" on the Web and you'll find dozens of opportunities ranging from schools that offer two-day seminars to those that offer two-year degree programs (see Resources). Also, many community colleges and adult education programs offer classes in woodworking, and most larger metropolitan areas have woodworking clubs and guilds.

Q My shop has a concrete floor, which is great for cleanup but a killer on my back. Are there any solutions for easing the pain?

A Start by wearing a good pair of work shoes or boots, then purchase antifatigue floor mats for areas where you stand a lot. They'll not only reduce stress on your knees, back, and feet, they'll also provide a slip-resistant surface and a cushioned area to prevent damage to dropped tools. You can even buy heated mats for added comfort in unheated spaces. Be sure to choose heavy mats with beveled edges so they don't create a tripping hazard.

Q I'm going to convert part of our basement into a workshop. Our daughter's bedroom is next to this space, and our bedroom is directly above it. What can I do to keep the noise contained?

A Use a two-pronged approach: 1) soundproof the space, and 2) minimize the amount of noise and vibration your tools emit. If your wall-stud and ceiling-joist cavities are open, begin by packing the spaces with fiberglass or rock wool insulation. This will help somewhat, but contrary to popular opinion, the real keys to soundproofing a space are adding mass to walls and blocking air gaps, rather than using lots of soft, absorbent materials. Sound travels through air, so blocking air gaps cuts off the travel path. Increasing mass helps dampen and suppress vibration, reducing the amount of vibration that's transferred to adjacent rooms.

Other things you can do include:

- ◉ Replace any hollow-core doors with solid wood doors. Install a tight-fitting sweep at the bottom and foam weatherstripping around each door to prevent noise from escaping through air gaps.
- ◉ Add a second layer of drywall to the walls. If the existing drywall is ½", install ⅝" drywall (and vice versa). Stagger the seams of the two layers so you completely eliminate cracks and gaps.
- ◉ Add resilient channels (available from any drywall supplier) perpendicular to the joists of unfinished ceilings, then secure your drywall to the channels. These inexpensive metal strips help suppress vibration through the ceiling of your shop. Install one or preferably two layers of drywall.
- ◉ Seal gaps around outlets, pipes, and ducts with silicone caulk or expanding foam.

As for methods of keeping your tools quieter, try some of these ideas:

- ◉ Add cork or rubber feet to the bottoms of tool stands to isolate vibration and noise. (One woodworker crafted his own from hockey pucks!)
- ◉ Tool stands can both transmit noise and create noise. To prevent rattling, periodically tighten the bolts. Add weight to stands, in the form of sandbags or concrete blocks, to help stabilize them.
- ◉ Pay attention when buying new tools. Belt-driven tools are usually quieter than gear-driven tools. Unbalanced pulleys and "lumpy" belts can create a racket. Closed tool stands block more noise than open stands.

Workbenches and Tool Storage

Building even a simple piece of furniture may require planing boards, routing edges, carving details, gluing joints, and cutting tiny trim pieces. All of these tasks require a secure way of holding onto the pieces and a solid surface to work on. A cabinetmaker's or woodworker's workbench fits the bill exactly. It can be one of the most important tools in your shop and — by employing a system of vises, bench dogs, and holdfasts — will allow you to work safer, faster, and with more precision.

Q I'm going to build a workbench and want to make sure it's at a comfortable working height. Are there any rules of thumb?

A One common guideline is to measure from the floor to the crease of your wrist and use that as the right working height. However, there are too many variables — including how tall you are and what you like to work on — to give one right answer. If you do lots of work with planes, you might like a lower bench. If you do lots of assembly work or work with small objects, you might favor a higher bench. Most benches are in the 32" to 36" range. For a point of reference, most bathroom vanity tops are 32" high, while most kitchen countertops are 36". Pretend to perform some of your favorite woodworking tasks on these surfaces to see which height is most comfortable.

Q When I look at photos of professional woodworkers' shops, they usually show the workbench in the middle of the room rather than against the wall. Doesn't that waste space?

A Freestanding workbenches take up more space — that's why you're more likely to see them in big shops — but they offer several advantages. You have access to all four sides of the project without having to reposition it. It's also easier to accommodate and clamp down projects that are bigger than the benchtop. You can make the workbench any width you like. Built-in workbenches are normally 24" or less in width; any greater depth makes it difficult to reach across to access wall-mounted tools.

But built-in workbenches are fine. They allow you to mount tools, cabinets, and lighting conveniently on the wall behind the bench. Whichever type of bench you decide on, be sure to have at least 30" of unobstructed floor space on the open sides.

Q The jaws on my workbench vise are angled, so they meet at the top first. How do I adjust them so they're square?

A The jaws of most vises are purposely designed to angle in slightly at the top. There's usually a little play in the screw mechanism, so angled jaws actually wind up parallel and deliver even pressure as they're tightened. If the jaws started out square, they would apply more pressure at the bottom than the top.

THE WONDROUS WOODWORKER'S WORKBENCH

There are a hundred possible variations to a woodworker's workbench. Some are open-bottomed, while others contain a wealth of doors and drawers for storage. Many woodworkers craft their own and consider it to be one of the most satisfying projects of all. Here are the standard parts:

- ◇ **Bench dogs.** These are small cylinders or rectangular blocks that fit snugly into holes in the benchtop. In conjunction with the vises, they can help hold boards of nearly any shape and size.

- ◇ **Holdfasts.** These L- or J-shaped devices, installed through openings in the workbench, "pinch" pieces of any shape and size against the work top. Some work via simple friction, while others employ a screw-clamp mechanism. A workbench may have provision for just a single holdfast or for multiple ones.

- ◇ **Face vises.** Normally located on the left front side, these vises grip boards during planing and other procedures. Some have bench-dog holes, while others have pop-up tabs that can be used in conjunction with surface bench dogs for gripping boards.

- ◇ **Tail vises.** These screw-operated vises can grip a board between their jaw and the cutout at the front of the workbench. They can also be used to clamp parts between bench dogs set in the benchtop and bench dogs set in the moving jaw of the vise.

- ◇ **Tool tray.** This provides a well for storing frequently used tools. Ramped ends allow for easy clean-out.

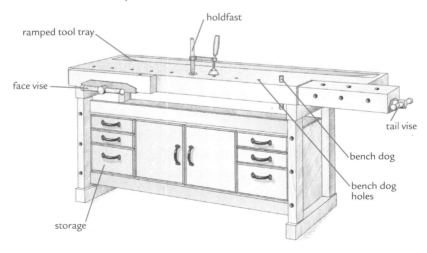

ramped tool tray

holdfast

face vise

tail vise

bench dog

bench dog holes

storage

tip: Table Saw Work Top

If you need more assembly or working space but can't find room because your table saw takes up so much space, make the best of a crowded situation: Remove the rip fence from your table saw, unplug it, and lower the blade. Cut a piece of ¾" plywood a few inches wider and longer than your table saw, then secure cleats to the bottom edge so they snug up to the sides of the table. Now whenever you need a work surface, lay your temporary plywood top on your table saw and cut, glue, paint, or drill away.

Storing and Handling Lumber

Q Right now, I use the space between the studs in my unfinished garage as a place to store lumber. But I'm running out of room. Got any simple lumber rack ideas?

A You can put the studs to work, but in a different way. Use them as the vertical supports for a simple lumber rack. Here are two versions:

Threaded pipe. Snap horizontal lines every 15" across your studs, then bore holes at a 5-degree angle (slanted upward) where the chalk line crosses each stud. Take 18" or 24" lengths of ½" or ¾" threaded iron pipe, and twist and shove one into each hole. Screw a pipe cap on the end of each "arm" to cover the sharp ends.

Slanted spars. Cut several dozen 2×4 blocks with 5-degree angles on each end. Snap lines across the exposed studs at the spacing where you want your cross arms. Nail the blocks to the sides of the studs so there's exactly 3½" of space between each block (use a 2×4 scrap for a spacer as you work). Nail a full-length 2×4 on the other sides of the studs to sandwich the blocks in place, then cut and insert your 2×4 spars (arms) to hold your lumber.

tip: Let's Roll

If you need a spur-of-the-moment outfeed roller (for catching the end of a long board as it comes off your jointer, sander, or table saw), try a paint roller. Slip a paint cover over the roller cage, then clamp the handle to a sawhorse at the correct height to catch the emerging ends of thin or lightweight boards.

LUMBER RACK OPTIONS

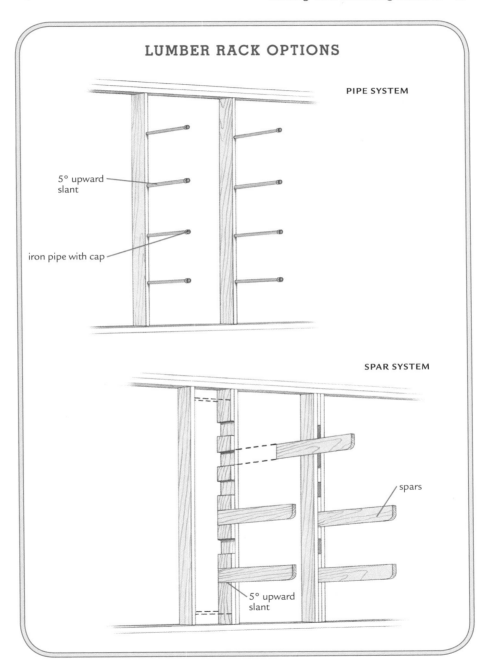

PIPE SYSTEM

5° upward slant

iron pipe with cap

SPAR SYSTEM

spars

5° upward slant

PAINLESS PLYWOOD TRANSPORT

Moving plywood into and around the shop can be a back-breaking, knuckle-banging chore. Here are three simple ways to ease the task:

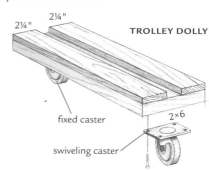

TROLLEY DOLLY

2¼" 2¼" 2¼"

fixed caster

swiveling caster

2×6

1 **Trolley dolly.** Secure a fixed caster near one end of a 2'-long 2×6, and install a swiveling caster near the other end. Nail 2¼" strips of wood along each edge to create a channel. Set the plywood in the channel and wheel away. Or, if there's an old skateboard lying around. . . .

2 **Loopy lugger.** Tie the ends of a 20'-long rope together. Place opposite ends of the loop under the corners of a sheet of plywood, then stand the plywood up, grab the rope in the middle, and haul away. Adjust the length of your loop until you find the right hauling size. To increase comfort, slide a length of garden hose over the loop to create a handle.

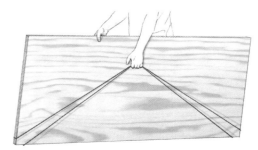

LOOPY LUGGER

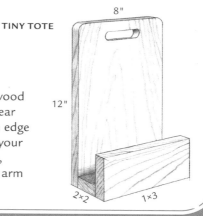

TINY TOTE

8"

12"

2×2   1×3

3 **Tiny tote.** Cut a scrap piece of ¾" plywood to 8" × 12", then cut out a handhold near the top. Screw a 2×2 along the bottom edge and a 1×3 cleat on top of that. To use your tote, slide the plywood into the trough, lift, and carry. You can use it with your arm either over or behind the plywood.

tip: The Easy Way to Cut Plywood

Wrestling a full sheet of plywood onto sawhorses and supporting the parts while you cut them with a circular saw can be a hassle. An easier way is to cut your plywood while it's resting on a 1" × 4' × 8' sheet of extruded foam on the floor. Adjust the depth of your blade so it cuts into your foam base only ⅛" or less. If you have limited space for storing your foam cutting platform, cut it in half, duct tape the halves together on one side to create a hinge, then fold it before storing it.

Dust Collection

Q **I use a shop vacuum connected to my miter saw for dust collection, but it's a hassle to walk to the other side of the workbench to turn it on every time I make a cut. Are there any step-savers?**

A You have a few options:

- Buy a tool-triggered shop vacuum. Plug your tool into this specialized vacuum, and whenever you pull the tool trigger, the vacuum automatically starts. Most offer disposable bags, beefed-up motors for long run time, high-efficiency filtration, easy-to-clean filters, and low noise levels. The vacuum also can stay on a few seconds longer than the tool to clear the hose and tool of debris. Most models include adapters that make them easy to connect to routers, belt sanders, and other portable tools, but you may need to improvise or use duct tape for a few connections. Many vacuums have amperage limits that restrict the size of the tool you can use them with.

- Install a vacuum-triggering outlet. These inexpensive "smart" sensors plug into the wall and have two outlets — one for your tool and the other for your vacuum. When you pull the tool trigger, the sensor automatically switches on the vacuum. Many keep the vacuum running a few extra seconds after the tool is powered off.

- Use a remote control transmitter and receiver. These include a special adapter that the vacuum plugs into, and a small remote control. Pressing the remote signals the adapter to turn the vacuum on. Some remotes can transmit through walls.

- Improvise. Plug your vacuum into a switched multiple-outlet strip. Keep the strip close to your saw, and manually switch your vacuum on and off when you work.

Q I'm finally at a point where I need a dust collection system that's more efficient than a broom and dustpan. How do I sort through the bewildering array of dust collectors out there?

A There are lots of shapes, sizes, and price points, but dust collectors can be broken into two primary categories.

Single-stage collectors. These are usually configured as one large cylindrical bag perched atop another with a snail-shaped motor separating them. They're the least expensive and are excellent for the small shop. Sawdust, chips, and shavings are sucked through an impeller or fan into the unit, where they fall into the lower bag. The upper bag acts as a gigantic filter, collecting the fine sawdust as air passes through it and back into the shop. Since these collectors are limited in the amount of suction they create, most are mounted on a dolly that can easily be wheeled about to collect sawdust from one machine at a time. But they can be permanently installed in one location with short lengths of ductwork running to a few tools.

Two-stage collectors. This type of collector is configured so the dust and chips entering the unit are pulled into, and settle within, a chamber or barrel before the air is drawn through the impeller and filter. Many are typified by a single-filter bag or a funnel-shaped cyclonic chamber perched upon a barrel for collecting chips and shavings. They're more expensive and many are permanently installed with rigid ductwork leading to them, though portable versions are available. These collectors can move a tremendous amount of air, measured in cubic feet per minute (CFM), and are often used in large-scale operations where dust collection from more than one tool at a time is required.

Q The dust collectors I've looked at all list the cubic feet per minute (CFM) they can move. But that doesn't help me decide which one to buy without knowing the airflow requirements of different tools. What are some common requirements?

A CFM listings tell only part of the story. Air movement is greatly affected by the type of ductwork used, its length and diameter, and how many turns the air has to make between the tool and the collector. When in doubt, err on the large side.

Basic requirements for common tools are:

◉ Scrollsaw: 200 CFM
◉ Drill press: 300 CFM
◉ 10" table saw or bandsaw: 350 CFM
◉ 12" planer or jointer: 400 CFM
◉ 15" planer: 600 CFM

Q What are some basic guidelines for designing a dust collection system?

A You're right on track when you talk about "designing" a system; dust collection is something that should be planned, not just evolve. Construct your system as you would a good freeway, so dust can flow with a minimum of congestion: create wide lanes (using ductwork at least 5" in diameter), install smooth pavement (using smooth or special spiral ductwork), and include gentle entrance ramps (installing large-radius Y-fittings and elbows instead of sharp-angled ones.) Other basics to remember include:

◉ Position the tools requiring the highest CFM closest to the collector.
◉ Make duct runs as short as possible, and use as few bends and elbows as possible to minimize air resistance. Each 90-degree bend creates as much airflow resistance as approximately 9' of straight ductwork.
◉ Minimize the number of branches by aligning tools along a single straight run of ductwork.
◉ Minimize the amount of flexible "accordion" duct used. Each foot of flexible duct creates as much air resistance as 3' of rigid duct.
◉ Install blast gates to close off ports to machines or branches not being used.

Some suppliers offer assistance in helping you design the optimum collection system for your shop (see Resources).

Q Is it okay to use standard sheet metal ductwork (the stuff I can buy at a home center) for my dust collection ductwork?

A Standard sheet metal ductwork is fine. It's inexpensive, readily available, and easy to install, but there are a couple of things to watch out for. First, make sure to use the heavy-duty stuff. Light-gauge ductwork, such as the type used for dryers, bath fans, and vent hoods, can collapse due to the suction created by the dust collector.

Create gentle curves; use two 45-degree elbows instead of a single 90-degree fitting to create a more gradual sweep. Also, use large-radius Y-fittings instead of tight-radius T-fittings when transitioning from the branch duct to the main duct. The more gradual the bend, the less it restricts the flow of air and debris. One rule of thumb when making 90-degree turns is to use fittings that create a radius at least 1.5 times the diameter of the pipe.

Q I have an elaborate dust collection system. Why would I need a separate air cleaner?

A Air cleaners or air scrubbers — the box-shaped devices you see mounted on the ceilings of some shops — capture what your dust collection system can't collect at the source or dust that is propelled from bits and blades as you work. Power hand-sanding is a *big* culprit. This fugitive dust can wreak havoc on your finishes, but more importantly, it can affect your health. Over 125 woods contain some type of chemical that can irritate your respiratory system, eyes, and skin, and can contribute to asthma and emphysema problems. Long-term exposure to certain wood dusts has been linked to nasal cancer.

Air scrubbers can capture particles as small as one micron. This is important because these particles are hard to see, leading you to believe the air is clean when it's not. They're the hidden enemy. To put this in perspective, a speck of dust needs to be 10 microns across before the human eye can even see it. Most air cleaners are rated based on the size of particle they can filter and amount of air they move. For the sake of your health and finishes, consider purchasing a scrubber. The best place to install one is as close as possible to where the fugitive dust is created. This is often over your workbench where you hand-sand or use routers and other handheld power tools.

DIY DUST COLLECTION

Some tools, such as planers and table saws, have built-in dust ports that make them easy to connect to a dust collection system. But other tools and situations aren't quite as convenient. Here are a few seat-of-the-pants dust collection solutions.

Floor sweeps. You can never put away the broom in a workshop, but you can do away with the dustpan and lots of stooping. Notch out the long flat side of a 4" × 12" angle boot and mount it at floor level. When it's time to clean up, simply sweep dust and debris into the open chute. Beware of sweeping in screws or other metal items that could produce a spark as they bang and clang against the ductwork.

Drill presses. Secure a PVC reducer coupling to a section of vacuum hose to create a mobile dust collection port for drill presses and benchtop sanders. Secure a magnet to the reducer so you can easily mount it to the cast-iron tables of tools.

Lathes. You'll never catch all the chips from a lathe, but you can capture some of them. Modify a "ceiling box" or section of square ductwork to create a wide-mouth port for collecting wood chips. You can make a similar port for miter saws and other tools.

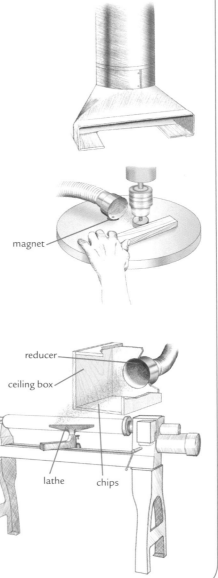

magnet

reducer

ceiling box

lathe

chips

Electrical, Lighting, and Heating Systems

Q I've heard it costs half as much to run tools at 220 volts than 110 volts. Is that true?

A No. There are advantages to 220 wiring, but saving on your electric bill isn't one of them. A tool running at 220 volts uses half as many amps, which means you can run smaller wires to your tools. The lower amp load also means there will be less line-voltage drop, supplying more power to the tool so it can develop higher torque. Most tools with motors 2 hp and larger or those that are located a long distance from the circuit breaker will operate better at 220.

Q I'm converting our two-car garage into a workshop. The studs are exposed, so I can wire the space any way I want. What are some things to consider?

A Lucky you. Being able to wire your space from scratch means you can provide excellent lighting for working, have fewer extension cords to trip over, and install the right circuitry so you're not constantly tripping breakers. Here are a few guidelines:

Lighting. Put your lights on their own circuit. Then, if the table saw breaker trips while you're ripping a board, you won't be left in the dark with a saw blade spinning at 4,000 RPM. Provide one 15-amp circuit for every 1,500 watts of lighting you wish to install. You may want to have one circuit for general lighting (the lights you flip on whenever you enter your shop) and another circuit for task lighting in areas where you do detailed or finishing work.

Outlets. Install 20-amp circuits for all your outlets; each can handle a load of up to 2,400 watts, versus 1,500 watts for a 15-amp circuit. Install one dedicated circuit for your air compressor and another for your dust collection system, since these will often be used in conjunction with other tools. To avoid cord clutter, install outlets every 4' along your workbench. Put the first outlet on one circuit, the second outlet on another circuit, and alternate as you go down the line. In a garage setting, outlets should be ground fault circuit interrupter (GFCI)–protected to minimize the chance of shock; this can be done with GFCI-protected circuit breakers or GFCI-protected outlets.

RECIPE FOR GOOD WORKSHOP LIGHTING

Kitchen designers know the importance of a thoughtful lighting plan. They know their clients spend hours every day doing detailed work, often with sharp tools in their hands. Sound familiar? Here are a few tips you can take out of the kitchen and into the workshop:

◇ **Provide both general and task lighting.** *General lighting* broadcasts light throughout the entire room for easy and safe navigation. In the kitchen, this is usually done with a grid of recessed lights; in the workshop, with rows of fluorescents. *Task lighting* focuses on individual areas and workstations. In the kitchen, this typically is accomplished with track and under-cabinet lighting. In the workshop, it can be done with onboard lights (such as those attached directly to drill presses) and spotlights focused on stationary tools.

◇ **Minimize shadows and glare.** Position task lighting so your head or body doesn't cast a shadow over your work area and bulbs don't glare directly into your eyes.

◇ **Check the bulb.** Sometimes improving lighting conditions can be as simple as screwing in a lightbulb. Fluorescent lights dim over time, so consider replacing those over five years old with new ones. Beam spread varies greatly with incandescent bulbs: Floodlights broadcast light in a 70-degree arc, while spotlights focus it in a much tighter 20-degree arc.

◇ **Paint ceilings white.** White ceilings help reflect and "even out" both natural and artificial light. White ceilings also make light fixtures less obtrusive.

Stationary power tools. Install a separate circuit for each large tool. If the motor runs on 220 to 240 volts (or can be set up to do so), wire the circuit accordingly. Check the tool's instruction manual or data plate to determine its amperage requirements.

Convenience and safety. If you have a workstation in the middle of your shop, install a hanging pendant-type outlet from the ceiling to eliminate foot-tangling extension cords. Now is also the time to install a phone line, along with a flashing-light indicator to tell you when your phone is ringing. For safety, install a heat-detecting fire alarm; standard units can be set off by sawdust.

Traffic control. Consider adding a subpanel (an auxiliary electrical service panel, or breaker box) inside your garage to simplify and consolidate all your electrical needs.

Q I stained a coffee table to match some other furniture, but when I brought it from my shop into the living room it was a much different shade. How do you explain that?

A It's probably because most shops are lighted with fluorescent fixtures and most living rooms are lighted with incandescent fixtures and natural light. Most shop light fixtures contain "cool white" bulbs that cast a predominantly bluish-green light, while incandescent bulbs accentuate yellows and reds. The result? If you're working with red stain under fluorescents, you're more likely to use a deeper shade to compensate for the lack of red in the light.

It's always best to make color test samples, using the actual wood, stain, and topcoat you'll be using in the project. View them in the room where the finished project will reside. If that's impossible, view your test samples under natural light or, in a pinch, under halogen light. Replacing your shop's cool white bulbs with warm white bulbs will also help bring the lighting there closer to that of your home.

tip: Curtains for Better Lighting

To create easy-to-move lighting, mount a drapery track to the ceiling over your workbench, then suspend several incandescent reflector lights by their cords from the sliding carriers that normally hold the curtain hooks. When you need task lighting over a specific area, just slide the lights over.

Q Is there a formula for figuring out how many fluorescent lights I need in my shop and how far apart I should space them?

A There's no single right answer, but there is a formula to use as a guideline:

1 Measure the distance between the work surface and the ceiling (or the planned height of the light fixtures). If you have an 8' ceiling and a standard 3'-high workbench, your working number is 5'.

2 Multiply your working number by 1.5 (in our example, 5 × 1.5' = 7.5'). This gives you the recommended distance between continuous rows of standard two-lamp fluorescent fixtures.

3 Divide your working number in half to determine the suggested distance between the wall and first row of lights (in our example, 5' ÷ 2 = 2.5').

If you're over 40 or do highly detailed work, consider spacing your fixtures closer together.

tip: Right-Height Switches and Outlets

Install all of your electrical boxes 50" off the floor. That way, no matter where you lean a 48"-tall piece of plywood, you'll still have access to your switches and outlets.

Q During the winter, I use my garage workshop for an hour here and an hour there. What's the most economical way to heat the space?

A It's expensive to heat up an entire room for a short stint, so consider installing electric radiant heat. Radiant heaters emit infrared radiation that warms objects within the room, such as you and your tools, rather than the room itself. Radiant heaters run quietly and work quickly. A wide variety of ceiling-mounted units are available.

Safety Gear

Some accidents, such as the slip of a chisel or the kickback of a board, can take place in a split second. Others, such as hearing loss or respiratory problems, can develop over a matter of years. Both types are preventable and it's up to you to prevent them. Here's how.

Q Which type of hearing protector is best: earmuffs or earplugs?

A The NRR (noise reduction rating) number you see on hearing protector packages indicates how many dB (decibels) they cut the noise level by; the higher the number, the better. Compressible foam earplugs — the type you twist and insert directly into the ear, where they expand — offer the very best hearing protection, with an NRR of around 30. Earmuffs that cover the ear have an NRR in the 20 to 25 range.

That said, the "best" protector is one you'll actually wear. Earplugs are inexpensive and small, but many people hate the sensation of

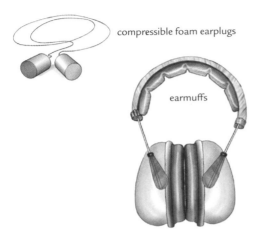

compressible foam earplugs

earmuffs

something stuck in their ears. They're also easy to misplace and can collect gunk easily. Earmuffs are bulky and more expensive but can be easily perched on top of the head when not in use, making them ideal for when you're using tools intermittently.

Fine Woodworking magazine recently surveyed woodworkers and found that 60 percent preferred earmuffs, 30 percent preferred some type of plug, and 10 percent wore nothing at all. You can also wear both types for maximum protection.

Q Do earmuffs with built-in radios offer as much protection as standard muffs?

A Some offer excellent hearing protection. But if you crank up the music, you're right back where you started — with noise that will hurt your hearing. If you wear them, keep the volume at a low level.

Q How much noise do various tools make, and at what point do they start damaging hearing?

A You should don hearing protection when sound levels exceed around 85 dB. The decibel scale is misleading, since it's logarithmic, not linear; for every 3 dB increase there is a doubling of the noise hitting your ears. Here are a few representative noise levels:

- 60 dB, normal speech
- 75 dB, random orbital sander, drill press
- 85 dB, shop vacuum
- 95 dB, table saw, router
- 105 dB, pneumatic nailer, circular saw
- 120 dB, chainsaw

If you're using a 105-dB circular saw and want to bring the noise level down into the 85-dB or less safe range, you'll need a hearing protector capable of lowering the dB level by at least 20 dB.

Q I wear prescription glasses with polycarbonate lenses. Do they offer adequate protection for shop work?

A Your frames and lenses may be able to pass the standard safety test (the ability to withstand the impact of a ¼" pellet moving at 150' per second), but there's more to eye protection than that. Safety glasses need to block dust and debris from the side, top, and bottom. Standard glasses fall short in those areas.

Q What offers the best protection: safety glasses, goggles, or a face shield?

A Like hearing protectors, the best sight protector is the one you'll actually wear. Some experts recommend keeping all three types in the shop. Use *safety glasses* with adequate side protection for tasks where small chips may fly. Wear *goggles* when generating large volumes of dust or working with chemicals and finishes that could splash. Wear a *face shield* when bigger chips and airborne debris may be involved, such as when working with a lathe or grinder. **NOTE:** Since face shields are open at the bottom, you should wear them in conjunction with safety glasses or goggles.

You should actually wear safety eyewear any time you're in your workshop. The wood shavings from a plane might not threaten your eyes, but the dowel dangling over the shelf above your workbench may. If you have trouble reading, consider purchasing a pair of reading safety glasses, available at specialty woodworking stores.

tip: The Eyes Have It

Every year around 15,000 people visit hospitals and ERs with eye injuries stemming from workshop accidents. This is an absurd statistic, since you can buy a basic pair of safety glasses or goggles for under $5. Clean your eyewear with an antistatic, antifog solution; stash an extra pair of safety eyewear in your pneumatic nailer case; and keep an extra pair of safety glasses in your shop for visitors or helpers to wear.

Q Does the little "snout" on the front of some dust masks help filter the air better?

A The snout is actually an exhaust valve. It doesn't filter air but offers other benefits, such as allowing you to exhale more easily, keeping your face cooler and preventing your safety glasses from fogging. The masks cost a little more, but if you're more comfortable, chances are you'll wear them more often.

HIDDEN HAZARDS OF WOOD AND SAWDUST

Working with wood is a safe, pleasurable pursuit, yet there are hidden dangers. Sawdust in general has been classified as a nasal carcinogen. While actual confirmed cancer cases are rare, many other problems have been associated with sawdust exposure. Some woods and sawdust cause immediate reactions, while others are *sensitizers*, meaning they may not produce an initial allergic reaction, but repeated exposure over time can. Here are a few common woodworking woods and their associated dangers:

WOOD	POTENTIAL HAZARDS	DEGREE
Rosewood (wood and dust)	respiratory problems, sensitizer, irritant	highly toxic
Satinwood (wood and dust)	eye, skin, respiratory irritant	highly toxic
Red cedar (bark and dust)	sensitizer	highly toxic
Yew (dust)	eye and skin irritant	highly toxic
Iroko	eye, skin, respiratory irritant	very toxic
Cocobolo (wood and dust)	sensitizer and irritant	very toxic
Spalted maple	respiratory irritant	very toxic
Beech (bark and dust)	eye, skin, respiratory irritant	moderately toxic
Teak (dust)	sensitizer	moderately toxic
Black walnut (wood and dust)	eye and skin sensitizer	moderately toxic

Q What do the NIOSH and "N" numbers on a dust mask indicate?

A NIOSH stands for National Institute for Occupational Safety and Health, the agency that sets standards for dust exposure limits. The "N" numbers, such as N95 and N99, indicate the percentage of airborne particles that the mask will filter out.

Q What's the lowdown on those Darth Vader-looking masks I've seen some woodworkers wear?

A You're referring to powered or supplied-air respirators. Most combine a full-face shield with a battery-operated fan and filter that continuously deliver fresh air. On some models, everything is contained in the helmet; with others, an air hose connects the helmet to a belt pack that contains the battery, fan, and filter. They're an excellent choice if you have a beard or have trouble using more conventional dust masks. The very best ones include hearing protectors, so your sight, hearing, and respiratory protection are all in one neat package.

Q Whenever I use my fingers to hold boards against the table and fence of my table saw or router table, I get paranoid about cutting my hand, or worse. What's the solution?

A You need strong, fearless fingers that can help keep your boards safely pressed against the fence and table as you work — in other words, you need featherboards. Featherboards have dozens of wood or plastic slats that are strong enough to apply top and side pressure to a board, yet flexible enough to allow you to push the board past the cutter or blade. They not only keep fingers safe, but, because of the consistent pressure they apply, they also help you create straighter cuts and more accurate rabbets, dadoes, and profiles.

Q Where do I put a featherboard in relationship to the blade or bit?

A Position your featherboards about ½" in front of the blade or bit. Positioning them directly across from, or behind, a blade can cause possible pinching and kickback.

2" to 3"

½"

⅛" to ¼" feathers

Q Can I make my own featherboards?

A Yes. Make some short ones that you can mount to the fence to apply downward pressure, and make longer ones for applying side pressure. Begin by cutting a 30-degree angle on the end of a 1×4 or 1×6 (see previous page). Draw a line parallel to this angle, 2" to 3" inches away. Then draw a series of side-by-side cut lines at ¼" intervals. Cut the feathers with a bandsaw, jigsaw, or handsaw.

Use a strong, flexible wood, such as ash or hickory, with straight grain and no defects. You can use pine, but the fingers need to be a hair thicker. Avoid plywoods or MDF, since the fingers of these materials break too easily. Experiment with material, feather width, and feather length until you create featherboards that produce the right amount of pressure for the work you do.

Q How do I secure featherboards to the tool I'm working on?

A There are three mounting options. The simplest is to just clamp them to the table or fence. You may need two clamps or some kind of cross brace to keep them positioned at the correct angle and distance. Many homemade and store-bought versions are designed to be secured using a standard miter slot. There are also magnetic versions that can be positioned anywhere on the tool table, as long as it's iron.

MAKE YOUR OWN PUSH STICKS AND SHOES

A good woodworker can never have too many of three things: project ideas, clamps, and push sticks. If you're tired of shelling out money after accidentally throwing out or cutting through your store-bought versions, consider making your own.

The best material to use is ½" or ¾" plywood. It's inexpensive and lightweight, and it won't snap along the grain like solid wood can. Paint your homemade helpers bright yellow so they're easy to find and don't wind up in the scrap heap. To create full-size patterns, enlarge the ones here on a photocopier until they measure 11" from heel to toe.

First Aid

Q It seems like every time I head into my shop, I head back out with a sliver. What's the easiest way to remove one?

A This is an area where old wives' tales abound. Tips range from using a good old tweezers to wrapping bacon around the finger over-night to lubricate the splinter so it comes out more easily. Always wash the area before and after removing the sliver. If the skin is particularly tender, you can dull the pain with a bee-sting swab. Then try one or more of the following:

⊙ Use a sterilized needle to lift the end of the sliver far enough above the skin so the tweezers can grab it. Sometimes you get only one chance, so grab the sliver firmly and pull in the direction it entered.

⊙ Lightly press packing tape or duct tape over the sliver, then remove the tape, pulling in the same direction the sliver entered.

⊙ Fill an empty plastic pop bottle with hot tap water, rest your sliver finger over the opening until the vapors soften the skin, then pull with a tweezers.

⊙ Cover the sliver with white glue, wait for it to dry, then remove the glue — and hopefully the sliver. You can also try using a dab of a wax-based hair removal product. Since it has enough gusto to remove a hair follicle from the root, it may be able to do the same thing with your sliver.

Q What's a good basic first aid kit to keep in the shop?

A Keep the following items in a wall-mounted box in your workshop:

⊙ Sterile gauze pads, gauze rolls, and adhesive tape

⊙ Assorted adhesive bandages, including fingertip and knuckle varieties

⊙ Butterfly bandages (for closing large cuts)

⊙ Scissors

⊙ Splinter tweezers and needles (stored in small jar of alcohol)

⊙ Elastic bandage

⊙ Antiseptic cream for burns and cuts; alcohol prep pads

⊙ Instant ice packs (to reduce swelling and transport severed parts)

⊙ Plastic bag for severed parts

⊙ Eyewash and cup, and a small mirror for inspecting eyes

- ⊙ Latex gloves
- ⊙ Asthma inhaler (to counteract allergic reactions to fumes, dust)

Safety equipment companies offer a wide array of assembled kits (see Resources).

BASIC WORKSHOP FIRST AID

Accidents always happen to someone else, right? Well, if you ever happen to be that "someone else," here's what to do. But remember, first aid is just that — the initial action you take. Visit the emergency room if there's any doubt regarding the severity or treatment of your injury.

- ◇ **Eye injuries.** For embedded foreign matter, go to the emergency room. For surface matter, flush with lukewarm water (the shower works well) or use an eyewash and cup. For chemical splashes, flush eye with running water for at least 5 minutes.
- ◇ **Abrasions.** Clean affected area with soap and water, check for embedded debris, apply antibiotic cream, then apply a bandage. Check daily for signs of infection (redness or red lines emanating from wound).
- ◇ **Cuts.** Clean affected area with soap and water, apply pressure to stop bleeding, use a butterfly bandage to close the cut. Seek emergency help for deep cuts or those spurting blood.
- ◇ **Contusions.** Apply ice packs. Take pain reliever that contains ibuprofen to combat swelling.
- ◇ **Amputations.** Raise the wounded area above the heart. Apply direct pressure to the wounded area with a clean cloth. Place the amputated part in a plastic bag and keep it cool (but not frozen).
- ◇ **Swallowed poison.** Drink a few sips of water or milk. Call the Poison Center at 1-800-222-1222. Do not induce vomiting.

The 4-hour, 2×4 Workbench

Here's a workbench you can build in an afternoon. It's sturdy and inexpensive, and it can be freestanding or set against the wall. The legs are made from doubled-up 2×4s, with the inner 2×4s cut into blocks to help support the upper framework (for the top) and the lower framework (for the storage platform). You can add vises, holdfasts, and bench-dog holes (see page 15) to customize your workbench.

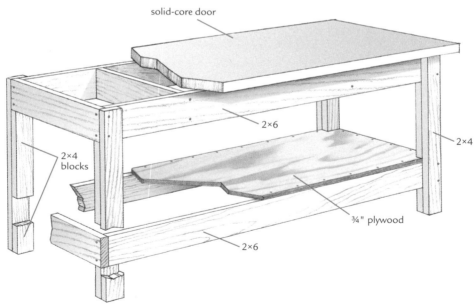

solid-core door

2×6

2×4

2×4 blocks

¾" plywood

2×6

2 Wood & Plywood

*Wood evolved as a functional tissue of
plants and not as a material designed to
satisfy the needs of woodworkers.*
— BRUCE HOADLEY

Take a minute to ponder the wonders of the board you're about to cut into. It's made quite a journey. Even a 24'-long, 8" × 8" timber started life as a seed no larger than the tip of your thumb. That seed took three essentially "invisible" components — sunshine, water, and air — and combined them to create one of the most versatile natural resources ever known.

While it grew, its roots prevented erosion, its leaves converted carbon dioxide into oxygen, and its branches provided shade for houses, animals, and you. It may have kicked out delicious fruit, syrup, or nuts in its day. And now you're about to create something beautiful with it. Wood is a living thing. One of the qualities that make it both a wondrous and sometimes frustrating thing to work with is that it keeps moving, growing, and "living" long after it's been run through the sawmill.

Lumber Basics

Q I've heard that some "hardwoods" are actually softer than some "softwoods." Can you explain the real difference between the two?

A The words "hardwood" and "softwood" are essentially nicknames. Like most nicknames, the words are *pretty* descriptive, but not *perfectly* descriptive. The truth is, there are some "hardwoods" that are softer than some "softwoods" and vice versa.

Here's the story: The world of trees is divided into two main groups: gymnosperms and angiosperms. Gymnosperms, or softwoods, are the type of tree most people refer to as evergreens or "trees with needles." This group includes trees like fir, pine, and cedar — woods that are often used in construction. Angiosperms, or hardwoods, are commonly referred to as broadleaf trees. This group includes maple, oak, cherry, walnut, and other woods often used for cabinetmaking and furniture building. The confusion comes in with some hardwoods, such as balsa and basswood, which are lighter and more easily dented than softwoods like yew or pitch pine.

Q I was shopping for thick wood for a chair seat, and the guy at the hardwood store steered me toward the "eight-quarter" material. I found what I was looking for but still don't know what he was talking about.

A Hardwood lumber is normally sold in quarter-inch increments, such as 5/4, 6/4, and so on. To convert that fraction into a whole number (think back to grade school math), divide the numerator by the denominator. Therefore 4/4 material is 1" thick, 5/4 material is 1¼", 8/4 wood is 2", and so on. Typically these actual thicknesses are reduced by ¼" when the board is surfaced on both sides. Therefore, if you buy lumber that's ¾" thick after being planed on both sides, you'll pay for 4/4 material. If you buy directly from a mill, you can often specify an exact thickness. For example, you could specify 25/32" boards so that after sanding or planing your final board will be 24/32" (or ¾").

Q I made my first trip to a hardwood dealer and found lumber priced by the board foot. What is that and how do I calculate it?

A Picture a piece of wood 1" thick, 12" wide, and 12" long, and you'll have your board foot. But you'll find very few boards of that size at the lumberyard. To determine the number of board feet in a slab of lumber, multiply thickness (in quarters) by width (in inches) by length (in feet), then divide by 12. If you have a board that's 6/4 × 7" × 6', it contains 5¼ board feet. Price is calculated on the volume of the board before it's planed; if the board has been planed to ¾" thickness, you'll be charged for the full 1", or 4/4, rough-sawn thickness.

LEGENDARY QUARTERS

Legend has it that old water-powered sawmills had blades that could only be adjusted in ¼" increments, thus the system of selling boards by "the quarter."

Q What's the difference between plainsawn, riftsawn, and quarter-sawn boards?

A The differences have to do with how they're cut from the log, how they look, and how they behave. Looking at the end of a board and studying the grain orientation is a good place to start.

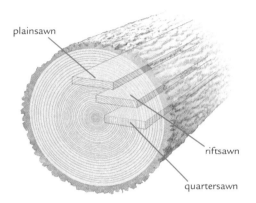

plainsawn

riftsawn

quartersawn

Plainsawn (also called flatsawn) boards have growth rings that run, for lack of better words, parallel to the face of the board. They often have an owl-eye, U-shaped, or cathedral pattern to the grain. Compared to the other cuts, plainsawn boards shrink less in thickness but more in width, and are the most likely to cup and twist.

Riftsawn (also called riftcut) boards have growth rings oriented at 30 to 60 degrees to the face of the board. The grain pattern is often clear and straight. These boards are more stable and less likely to warp than plainsawn boards.

Quartersawn boards exhibit growth rings that are, for the most part, perpendicular to the face of the board. They have the straightest grain and exhibit lively and attractive rays in some woods, especially white oak. They're the most stable in terms of width and command a premium price.

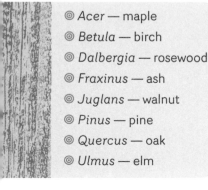

◎ *Acer* — maple
◎ *Betula* — birch
◎ *Dalbergia* — rosewood
◎ *Fraxinus* — ash
◎ *Juglans* — walnut
◎ *Pinus* — pine
◎ *Quercus* — oak
◎ *Ulmus* — elm

Q When I see wood or trees with names like *Acer saccarum,* it doesn't really tell me much. What do these names mean?

A Woods and trees have both botanical and "street" names. The first word of the botanical name (which is always capitalized) is the genus. The second word (which is lowercase) is the species. In the botanical world, white oak would be called *Quercus alba*. There usually are many species of trees within any given genus.

Oak, for instance, has well over 200 species. On the previous page are some common woods and the genus to which they belong.

Q What woods are on the endangered species list?

A The Convention on International Trade in Endangered Species of Wild Fauna and Flora (CITES), formed in 1973, lists three different levels of protection or appendices. The most restricted woods in international trade include Brazilian rosewood and monkey puzzle. Woods that are at risk, but not as closely regulated, include Cuban, Honduran and Mexican mahogany; lignum vitae; brazilwood; and ramin. While hardwood dealers rarely sell these woods, you'll occasionally encounter boards for sale that were taken from downed trees or imported prior to being listed by CITES.

Q What are the different grades of hardwoods, and what exactly do these grades mean?

A In order for woodworkers, dealers, and mills to compare apples to apples (or apple wood to apple wood) and speak a common language, the National Hardwood Lumber Association established guidelines over 100 years ago for grading lumber. The equations used can be perplexing, but the results are what you really need to know. Here are the basics for the four most common grades of lumber. (**NOTE:** With the exception of select lumber, boards are graded from their poorer side.)

⊙ **FAS (firsts and seconds)** is the highest grade. The minimum board size for grading is 6" × 8', and the yield of clear (knot- and defect-free) lumber must be 83 percent or more. It must be able to yield clear boards that are at least 4" × 5' or 3" × 7' in size.

⊙ **Select** is the next highest grade. The minimum board size is 4" × 6'. This grade is a bit of a hybrid; the good face must grade like an FAS board, and the poorer side like a No. 1 Common board.

⊙ **No. 1 Common** is next in line. The minimum board size is 3" × 4', and the yield of clear lumber must be at least 66⅔ percent. The board must yield clear boards that are at least 3" × 3' or 4" × 2'.

⊙ **No. 2 and No. 3 Common** are the lowest grade. Minimum board size is 3" × 4', and the yield of clear lumber must be at least 50 percent for No. 2 and 33⅓ percent for No. 3 boards. It must be able to yield a clear board at least 3" × 2'. Both sides are likely to have defects, such as splits or missing knots.

One important fact to take away is this: Clear lumber cut from a No. 2 Common board is often just as high in quality as that cut from an FAS board; the pieces will just be smaller. With careful planning and cutting, you can often save money by using lower grade lumber to produce high-grade pieces. Another thing to bear in mind is that "defects" often can be gorgeous and add to, rather than take away from, the character of a piece.

Q What's the difference between heartwood and sapwood?

A To a tree, the difference has to do with the job each performs. Sapwood, located in the outer layers of the tree, is actively involved in conducting sap upward. As a tree ages and adds growth rings, new sapwood takes on the job of feeding the tree, while the older sapwood is retired and transformed into heartwood. Extractives that form in the cell wall (see the next question and answer) produce the deeper, richer color of heartwood and are the reason why it is usually the part of the tree most sought by woodworkers.

DEMYSTIFYING SOFTWOOD DIMENSIONS

You've surely noticed that the 1×6 pine boards you bring home from the lumberyard aren't really 1 by 6 of anything. They started their lives as boards that were thicker and wider, but by the time they've been sawn, planed and kiln-dried, their dimensions have been reduced. Below are the nominal and actual dimensions of common boards. In any case, it's always a good idea to measure your lumber; a 2" × 10" board can run anywhere from 9⅛" to 9⅝" in width.

NOMINAL WIDTH	ACTUAL WIDTH		NOMINAL THICKNESS	ACTUAL THICKNESS
2"	1½"		1"	¾"
3"	2½"		5/4 boards	1" to 1⅛"
4"	3½"		2"	1½"
6"	5½"		4"	3½"
8"	7¼"		6"	5½"
10"	9¼"			
12"	11¼"			

10 WACKY TIDBITS ABOUT WOOD

Next time you're gathered around the workbench with some fellow wood nuts, impress them with these wacky facts about your material of choice:

1 Lignum vitae, an extremely dense, oily tropical hardwood, was used for submarine and hydroelectric generator bearings right up through World War II.

2 The Spruce Goose contains only 5 percent spruce. The dominant wood is birch.

3 A company calling itself the Ancient Kauri Kingdom is dredging up 50,000-year-old kauri logs from the bogs of New Zealand, then milling and selling the wood for $35 and up per board foot.

4 Old Ironsides got its nickname when cannonballs fired by the Brits during the War of 1812 bounced off the 4"-thick live oak planks sheathing the hull.

5 Red cedar, the preferred wood for making pencils, became so scarce in the 1920s that manufacturers bought barns and fence posts from farmers for raw materials.

6 A water system constructed from 400 miles of hollowed-out elm logs was unearthed in England after 400 years and found to be in amazingly sound condition.

7 St. Mark's Cathedral in Venice, Italy, is supported by 1 million wood pilings driven into the boggy soil below over one thousand years ago.

8 A blimp hangar constructed by the U.S. Navy in the 1940s covers 5.6 acres, contains 2 million board feet of yellow pine, and was built in 27 working days.

9 Livio De Marchi, considered by many to be the world's finest woodcarver, crafted a life-size version of a Ferrari F50 in wood — then "drove" it in the canals of Venice.

10 Baseball Hall of Famer Joe Sewell used only one bat during his 14-year career, racking up over 2,200 hits.

Q What makes some woods naturally rot-resistant? Is it all or only part of the tree that's rot-resistant?

A As a tree ages, chemicals known as extractives migrate toward the center of the tree and make a home in the cells. These extractives help protect the tree by inhibiting rot and fungi growth. For woodworkers, two nice qualities evolve: the wood is more rot-resistant and much more colorful. Some boards will contain both dark heartwood and the lighter-colored sapwood, which isn't rot resistant. For outdoor projects, use the heartwood.

Q What are some common rot-resistant woods to use for outdoor projects?

A There are dozens of woods that are rot-resistant, but some make more sense to use outside than others. For example: walnut, oak, and chestnut are rated by the U.S. Forest Products Laboratory as woods having heartwood with a "high" resistance to decay, but they are rarely used outside because of cost, weight, availability, and other factors. The most commonly used softwoods are cedar, redwood, cypress, and pressure-treated pine. The most commonly used hardwoods are teak, Ipe, mesquite, and white oak.

Q Are there any reasons I can't use construction-grade lumber for building fine furniture?

A You can use boards from your lumberyard or home center and save an appreciable amount, but you need to do a few extra things first:

⊙ Check the growth rings on the end of the board. If you see bullseyes, it's been cut from the center of the tree and is more likely to twist and warp. Look for boards that have nice even growth rings running at a 45- to 90-degree angle to the face of the board.

⊙ Remove large knots and defects by ripping your boards narrower or crosscutting them shorter.

⊙ Square up the edges, since most construction lumber has "eased" or slightly rounded edges. You can do this using a jointer, planer, or table saw.

⊙ Let it dry. Most construction-grade lumber has about a 20-percent moisture content; you want your wood at about 8 percent. Stack and sticker your wood (place thin strips of wood between each layer to improve airflow, as shown on page 48.) Store in a dry, heated environment for a few weeks before using it.

DEALING WITH LUMBER "CHARACTER FLAWS"

Legendary woodworker George Nakashima became legendary by turning cracked, "defective" lumber into beautiful masterpieces. "Just short of being worthless, a board often has the most potential," he once explained. But some boards have defects that make them difficult to deal with, and you wind up fighting them the whole way. Here are some common lumber "character flaws" and ways to make the best of them:

◇ **Cupped** refers to a board that's concave (or convex) across its width. The wider the board, the more likely it is to cup. Make the best of a bad situation by ripping cupped boards into narrower strips.

◇ **Bow** refers to a defect where the board is so curved that it teeter-totters when you try to lay it flat. The best way to deal with bowed boards is not to buy them.

◇ **Crook** refers to a defect where the board lies flat, but is curved along its length like a rainbow. You can create usable lumber by cutting straight boards from it with a straight-cutting jig (see page 97) or a simple table saw sled (see page 110).

◇ **Wane** describes rough, barky edges of boards. These uneven areas can nearly always be removed with a table saw.

◇ **Shake** refers to long, loose flaps of wood on the face of a board. Difficult to fix or work with, it's best to cut out and remove the defective areas.

◇ **Chatter, chipped grain, and burn** are defects created by poor machining. Most can be removed through sanding and planing.

◇ **Twist is** a situation where the ends of a board are out of plane with each other. Slightly twisted boards can be flattened using hand planes, jointers — and lots of patience. A planer can make a twisted board thinner, but not flatter (unless you use the special jig explained on page 120).

Movement in Wood

One challenge all woodworkers face is dealing with wood's predisposition to shrink and expand in response to changes in humidity and temperature. This may eventually result in cracks, gaps, and weak joints. This section offers some tips for meeting that challenge.

Q Why is it so necessary to use dry wood?

A Wood shrinks and changes shape as it dries. You want the bulk of that shrinkage and change of shape to occur *before* you start working with it. Freshly cut wood is also extremely heavy — in some species, over twice as heavy as when it's dry. Plus, wet wood is more susceptible to decay and rot. That said, there's an entire field of woodworking called "green woodworking" that focuses on building furniture and other items with wet or unseasoned wood. This furniture is often "rustic" in nature.

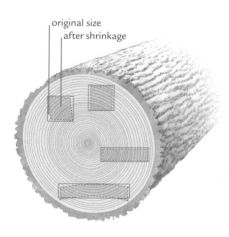

original size
after shrinkage

Q Does wood shrink and expand equally in all directions?

A No. The amount of shrinkage varies from species to species, but generally wood shrinks 8 to 10 percent tangentially, 4 to 5 percent radially, and close to zero percent lengthwise. In other words, the surface of the board where the grain intersects it perpendicularly, or close to perpendicularly, shrinks the most. This means woods of different shapes will shrink differently based on how they're cut from the tree.

Q A friend told me I should use quartersawn boards for a tabletop because they're more stable than flatsawn boards. Is that true?

A Yes. Due to the orientation of the grain, the boards will tend to expand and contract less across their width and be less prone to cupping.

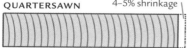

FLATSAWN   8–10% shrinkage

QUARTERSAWN   4–5% shrinkage

Q How much can wood expand and contract?

A Some kiln-dried wood can change ⅛" to ¼" in width for every foot. This may not seem like much, but when you add it up, a 4'-wide table can vary in width by as much as an inch from dry season to wet season.

Q I've heard wood dries out in stages. What does that mean?

A Picture wood as a bundle of paper drinking straws filled with water. If the water is emptied from the straws, the bundle will remain the same size. That's the first drying stage. If you were to extract the moisture from the straws themselves, the bundle itself would start shrinking. That's the second stage. In stage one, the moisture held in place by the cell walls dries out, bringing the wood down to a moisture content of about 30 percent. In stage two, water leaves the cell walls themselves. This is when noticeable differences start occurring. The wood shrinks, and as it shrinks it becomes denser, harder, and stronger.

Q How long does it take for wood to dry thoroughly enough to stop shrinking and expanding?

A Wood never stops moving. It's always trying to reach its equilibrium moisture content (EMC), the point at which moisture is no longer entering or exiting the wood. A board's EMC changes as the relative humidity changes. So unless wood is kept in a controlled environment where temperature and humidity never fluctuate — and even museums have difficulty doing that — the EMC is constantly changing, and the wood shrinks and expands accordingly.

Q How much fluctuation can there actually be?

A In dry areas, environments, or seasons where the relative humidity is as low as 20 percent, the EMC can be as low as 4 percent. In damp areas where humidity levels reach 80 to 90 percent, the EMC can reach nearly 18 percent. As a compromise, most kiln-dried lumber has a 6 to 8 percent moisture level.

Q How can I tell if my wood is dry enough to build with?

A The best way is to check it with a moisture meter. There are two types. *Pin-style* meters have pins that you push into the wood to measure electrical resistance, which in turn is expressed as a percentage of moisture. *Pinless* meters use radio frequencies to measure moisture levels. Pinless meters generally are more expensive, but they don't leave pinholes in your wood and often can give more accurate readings in dense woods that are difficult to penetrate with pin-style meters. Prices range from $50 to $200 and more.

tip: A Scrap Wood Hygrometer

Throughout the year, the humidity in your workspace, and therefore the dimensions of the wood you're working with, can vary appreciably. One way to know how much to compensate when you're building is to use "moisture boards." Glue up 12"-wide planks of your most frequently used woods, measure their widths during both the driest and the most humid months of the year, and write those measurements on each board. When it's time to perform an exacting task, such as fitting an inset door or drawer, consult the moisture board made of that type of wood to see how much it's expanded or contracted, and adjust the fit of your pieces accordingly.

From Log to Board

Q What's the advantage of buying wood that hasn't been milled on all four sides?

A Lower cost is one advantage, since running a board through a saw and planer fewer times creates less work for the mill. But there are other pros to buying rough lumber. For starters, it gives you control over the exact thickness of the wood. If a project calls for material that's ⅜" or ⅞" thick, you can purchase the raw materials accordingly and generate less waste.

Second, when a board is milled straight on both sides, then cut square at the ends, there's a chance that the most highly figured, attractive wood will wind up in the scrap heap. By purchasing lumber that's rough-milled, you have an opportunity to plan your project around these beauties if you wish.

Finally, some woodworkers feel they can create a smoother surface than a mill can. Production mills feed boards through their planers at fairly high speeds, which can compromise smoothness. If you own your own planer and jointer, you can run boards through your machines at a slower speed, creating smoother surfaces. This, of course, presumes your machinery is accurate and properly adjusted.

Q I know that S4S refers to a board that's smooth on all four sides. What about S2S and all those other lumberyard numbers and letters?

A Yes, S4S refers to a board that's been surfaced (S) on all four (4) sides (S). Other alphanumeric descriptions mean the following:

- ⊙ S2S: planed or surfaced on two sides
- ⊙ S1S: surfaced on just one side
- ⊙ S1S1E: surfaced on one edge and one side
- ⊙ S1S2E: surfaced on one side and both edges
- ⊙ S2S1E: surfaced on both sides but just one edge

You can also order wood "hit or miss," which flattens the board, but leaves some rough areas. This provides more options by allowing you to fine-tune the final thickness based on your needs.

Q I just cut a fallen oak in our backyard into 8' lengths with the hope of eventually having it milled into flooring. What steps should I take to keep the wood sound?

A Your best option is to have the logs milled into boards ASAP to prevent possible discoloration from fungus or mold. If that's not possible, prop up the logs on scrap wood to get them off the ground. Leave all the tight bark in place, but remove any loose stuff to prevent decay. More importantly, seal both ends of the log. Wood dries out rapidly through the end grain, and the logs will check and split along their length if left untreated. Brush on a thick coat of ordinary latex house paint or a wax-emulsion coating manufactured just for that purpose.

Q Some of those 8' sections of oak weigh 600 or 700 pounds. When I'm ready to have them sawn into boards how will I get them to the sawmill?

A Let the sawmill come to you. There are plenty of individuals and companies that can custom-cut your boards with a portable chainsaw, bandsaw, or circular saw mill. Each type has their pros and cons. *Chainsaw mills* are the most portable and easiest to set up, but because of the wide kerf, they waste a fair amount of material with each cut. *Bandsaw mills* are larger but cut a smaller kerf and leave a smoother surface. *Circular saw mills* work quickly but are bulkier, harder to set up, and require more skill and caution to operate.

Look on the Internet or in the Yellow Pages for "Sawmills, portable." Some operators will charge by the hour, some by the bid, and others by a "cut of the proceeds" (a percentage of the wood that's cut).

Q Once the boards are cut, how do I dry them?

A Patience is the first requirement. The rule of thumb is to allow one year of air-drying per inch of thickness (oak can take substantially more time; alder and poplar less). The key steps are:

⊙ Select a location that's flat, shielded from direct sunlight, and away from buildings so air can circulate well.

⊙ Lay down a pair of long 4×4s to create a base. Position them so they're 3' apart, parallel to each other, and level to the ground and to each other. On top of these, position 4'-long 4×4 crosspieces every 2' to create a flat grid.

⊙ Seal the ends of your boards with latex paint or endgrain sealer to prevent them from drying out too quickly, which can lead to end checks and cracks.

⊙ Lay your first layer of boards perpendicular to the crosspieces, with the ends even to one another and the boards spaced about ½" apart. Some people use lower-grade boards for the first layer, since it's the most susceptible to damage from ground moisture.

⊙ Place ¾" × ¾" spacers (called stickers) perpendicular to the first layer of boards, positioning them directly above the 4×4 crosspieces. Continue to stack and sticker your wood until the stack is complete.

⊙ Cover the stack with treated plywood that extends past the stack in every direction. Slant it an inch or two to promote water drainage. Weight it down with cinder blocks or sandbags.

⊙ Wait and wait and wait.

Too much air circulation on a breezy fall or spring day can dry out your boards too fast and create problems. Many people will place tarps over their stack and roll them up or down to control drying rate. One excellent reference for further information is "Drying Hardwood" from the USDA Forest Service (see Resources).

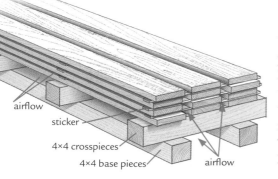

airflow
sticker
4×4 crosspieces
4×4 base pieces
airflow

Q Once my lumber has been air-dried, can I use it as flooring or to build furniture?

A Not yet. Even wood that's been air-dried a full year still has about a 20-percent moisture content. Bring the boards into an unheated garage or outbuilding, then restack with stickers in between. This will bring the moisture content down to 12 to 15 percent — better, but still not dry enough for flooring, furniture, or cabinetry. Getting lumber down to the 6 to 8 percent moisture content required for stability involves bringing (and again, restacking) your wood into a heated environment, such as a spare room or heated workshop, and letting it dry and stabilize for as much as a month. To assure your wood is ready to use, check it with a moisture meter (see page 45).

Q I was using my table saw to rip some thick boards and they started warping immediately. Did I buy defective boards?

A No, chances are you bought defectively dried boards. Your lumber was case-hardened, a condition that arises when the outer fibers or shell of a board have dried too rapidly and attempt to shrink, but are prevented from doing so by the moist interior. Even after the interior dries, uneven tensions and pressures remain within the board. When the board is cut open, the tensions are released and the wood can twist, turn, and pinch in unpredictable directions, creating a dangerous situation on the table saw. One telltale sign of case-hardening is the presence of surface checks or cracks on the board.

The situation can be remedied only by drying the boards more slowly so the entire piece is at equilibrium. Large commercial kiln operators often steam their lumber after drying (called "conditioning" the wood) to lightly swell the outer fibers to minimize the tension and create a board of uniform dryness.

Q I've read about companies reclaiming logs that have sat on the bottoms of lakes, rivers, or bogs for over 100 years. Is the wood usable, and is it any different from the wood I can buy from my hardwood dealer?

A As long as the wood is sound and properly dried — which can take years — you can use it. There's actually one company in New Zealand that's hauling up perfectly sound 50,000-year-old kauri logs from peat bogs and converting them into gorgeous slabs of lumber.

What's different about wood from these sinkers? Most of these logs, many of which sank while floating down rivers and across lakes on their way to the mill, are from old-growth trees. This is significant, since they typically grew slower, producing wood with a tighter grain structure. Some of these logs can be massive in size and yield very wide boards. And some woods take on a particular hue from minerals in the water. It can be beautiful stuff. Just be prepared to pay three or four times as much as you would for standard lumber of the same species (see Resources for some companies that sell reclaimed sinker logs).

tip: Clean Wood for Sharper Cuts

Rough-sawn boards can harbor lots of dust and grit in their raised grain and kerfs. This debris can quickly dull saw blades, planer and jointer knives, and other tools. Before milling the boards, scrub them with a stiff wire brush and blow away the debris with a few good blasts of compressed air. In extreme cases, give them a quick power wash, then let them dry before milling.

Wood Selection: Grain and Figure

The "grain" of a board relates to the way its growth rings are displayed; "figure" relates to variations in those growth rings and other surprises. Paying attention to grain and figure can make the difference between a project that looks ho-hum and one that looks spectacular. Here are some tips on making the most of the boards you have.

Q Is the main difference between red oak and white oak the color of the lumber they yield?

A There is a difference in color between the two, but they differ more in performance than looks. The heartwood of white oak ranges in color from tan to straw, while that of red oak tends toward reddish brown. But there is so much variety within each species that some white oaks are actually redder than red oaks.

The primary difference has to do with their pores. Those of white oak are plugged with microscopic structures called *tyloses*, making the wood water-resistant and the ideal candidate for barrel making, boatbuilding, and outdoor projects. The pores of red oak are so open you can actually blow through them, and they often need to be filled before finishing. That said, both are ideal for furniture, cabinetmaking, and millwork.

10 GREAT WOODS FOR WOODWORKING

There are over 50,000 different species of trees on this planet, yet given this vast number, a handful of woods rise to the top of the woodworking pile. Below are ten popular woodworking woods and some of their unique characteristics. (Price: $ = lowest, $$$$ = highest)

WOOD	CHARACTERISTICS	USES	PRICE
Ash	Gray-brown; straight, pronounced grain; coarse texture; heavy and strong	Bats, hockey sticks, tool handles, furniture, curved boat parts	$$
Butternut	White to light brown; soft; straight, coarse grain	Carving, cabinets, turning, kitchen utensils	$$
Cherry	Light to dark reddish brown; straight, faint grain; moderately hard; finishes well	Cabinets, architectural woodwork, furniture, pipes	$$$
Hard Maple	Light, reddish brown; beautiful blistered, fiddleback and curly figure; lightweight, yet hard	Furniture, cabinets, flooring, butcher blocks, baseball bats, piano actions	$$
Mahogany	Light to deep reddish brown; straight, interlocked grain; coarse texture	Fine furniture, office furniture, decorative veneers, stairways, boatbuilding, caskets, pattern making	$$$
Pine	Pale yellow to light brown; soft and lightweight; stains poorly; good workability	Construction lumber, millwork, window sashes, doors, musical instruments, cabinets, paneling	$
Rosewood	Chocolate brown to violet brown; amazing figure; heavy, hard and dense (barely floats); oily; rare	Stringed instruments, turning, fine furniture, decorative items	$$$$
Teak	Golden brown; resists rot and moisture; oily; abrasive on tool edges; sawdust is an irritant	Outdoor furniture, boat decks, flooring	$$$
Walnut	Light gray-brown to purplish brown; highly figured grain, burls and crotches; polishes well; strong and stable	Furniture, carving, gunstocks, cabinets	$$$
White and Red Oak	Reddish brown to tan; strong grain figure; hard and heavy; stains well	Cabinets, flooring, furniture; cooperage and boatbuilding (white oak only)	$$

tip: The 25% Rule

When you head out to purchase lumber for a project, buy at least 25 percent more than your actual estimate. That 25-percent cushion will allow you the luxury of setting aside defective pieces of lumber instead of struggling to make them fit. You'll also have more options when it comes to selecting "show pieces" for the visible parts of your project. And you'll have more material for trying out tool settings and testing stains and finishes. If your shop starts overflowing with leftover odds and ends, start making breadboards!

Q At a recent woodworking show, I encountered a gorgeous table made from a redwood burl. What exactly are burls and what other trees have them?

A Burls are the large, knob-like growths that project from the trunks and limbs of some trees. Within the burl are clusters of buds that have been stunted and distorted. The result is a wood structure that is highly unpredictable and (usually) highly attractive. Most sawyers equate sawing open a burl with cracking open a geode — no two are the same, and what's inside is a surprise. Because of their rarity, many burls are sliced into veneers or used for small turnings. In addition to redwoods, other trees that frequently sport burls include walnut, elm, amboyna, and, occasionally, oak and ash.

Q What is spalted maple? Can I create my own?

A Spalting occurs when certain woods are attacked by rot and decay. During the process, the fungi generate thin waves of brown and black stain. These are often very attractive waves. Left to its own devices, the wood will eventually rot. But if harvested at the right time, the wood can be dried and used to create one-of-a-kind turnings and decorative items. Care must be taken when working with it, since there are soft, spongy pockets interlaced with hard wood. Some people have allergic reactions to the fungi-laden wood. To create your own spalted wood, set a newly cut section of hard maple on the ground, pile damp dirt on top of it, and cover it with a black garbage bag. The ideal temperature is 60 to 80 degrees. Check it every few weeks and repeat the process until the right amount of spalting has occurred. Mill the log into boards and let it dry as you would any other wood — then go to work.

SAVE $$$ WITH WOOD IMPOSTERS

Some woods are expensive, some are difficult to obtain, and some are hard to match if you're repairing an existing piece. What to do? Try using imposters — less expensive, more readily available woods that, with a little work, can mimic the look of more expensive species. Below are a few examples. Always experiment on scraps before using stains and dyes to "convert" your wood.

◇ **Mimic ebony with maple.** Maple has a density and tight pore structure similar to that of ebony. Cut your maple pieces to their final size and shape, then sand with 360-grit paper, paying special attention to the end grain. Flood the surfaces with India ink, and wipe off any excess.

◇ **Mimic cherry with poplar.** The grain of carefully selected poplar boards can mimic that of cherry. Experiment with water-based cherry dye. You can lighten areas while the dye is wet using a damp cloth and, after it's dry, with fine sandpaper. If absorption is erratic, try sealing the poplar first with dewaxed shellac or sanding sealer.

◇ **Mimic walnut using willow or red alder.** Select heartwood pieces that mimic the grain and color of walnut. Apply a light-colored stain to "push" the willow closer to the color of walnut.

Plywood Grades, Types, and Cuts

Q Why do some plywoods look like they're made from one big sheet of veneer, while others look more like boards that have been glued up edge-to-edge?

A It has to do with how the veneers are cut from the log. The type that looks like one big sheet is *rotary-cut*. The log is mounted on a gigantic lathe and the veneer is sliced off as if it were a giant roll of paper towels. This makes extremely efficient use of the log and creates huge sheets of veneer.

The second type of veneer is *plain-sliced*. The log is cut into individual slices in the same manner you'd cut slabs of wood from a log. This results in stacks of narrower veneers that must be glued side by side to create a panel wide enough to cover a 4'-wide plywood core. The slices can be quartersawn or plainsawn (see page 38).

VENEER CORE

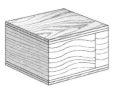

LUMBER CORE

PARTICLEBOARD OR MDF CORE

Q I read that not all plywoods are made out of plies of wood. Can you explain that?

A The term "plywood" seems to apply to all veneered panels regardless of how they're made. One of the main differences is in the core material used.

Veneer core plywood is made of three or more layers of veneer glued together with the grain of alternate layers running perpendicular to one another. The result is a strong, stable panel with excellent screw-holding and glue-bonding qualities.

Lumber core plywood is made of softwood or hardwood strips glued side-by-side, covered by face veneers. There are three different grades: clear, sound, and regular. It has excellent screw-holding and glue-bonding qualities.

Particleboard core or MDF core plywoods have composite-panel cores. The resulting panels are inexpensive and extremely flat and have excellent surface uniformity, but they are extremely heavy and offer only fair screw-holding and bonding qualities. They can also be slightly less dimensionally stable than other plywoods.

Q Why do some sheets of plywood look so much better than others?

A It has to do with how the veneer slices are arranged after they've been plain-sliced.

book-matched

Book-matched patterns are created by arranging successively sliced veneers edge-to-edge so they mirror one another. This can create an extremely pleasing and consistent pattern.

slip-matched

Slip-matched patterns are created by arranging veneers in order just as they're sliced from the log. This creates a panel uniform in color and sheen, but the resulting pattern may be distracting.

random-matched

Random-matched patterns are created by joining veneer slices of varying widths and appearance that may not even be from the same log. Sometimes this yields a panel that looks like attractively edge-glued boards; other times it can look chaotic.

Q Why are some MDF and particleboard panels 49" × 97" instead of the more standard 48" × 96"?

A Some MDF and particleboard panels are oversized because the edges of these materials are weak and prone to damage. The extra inch in each direction allows you to remove edge damage and still wind up with the equivalent of a standard-size panel.

Q No matter how careful I am, the veneer on the face of some plywoods chip when I cut them on the table saw, especially on the bottom. How do I prevent this?

A Try using a 60- to 80-tooth melamine or laminate saw blade and a zero-clearance insert in your table saw (see page 111). If a new blade isn't in the budget, try putting masking tape over the cut line before flipping the piece over to make the cut. The tape will help minimize splintering.

Q What is "bending plywood"?

A Bending plywood is plywood with two thick outer veneers running in the same direction, with a thinner layer of inner veneer running perpendicular to them. They can be manufactured to bend in either the long or short direction (but not both). They're manufactured in ⅛", ¼", and ⅜" thicknesses and are intended only for decorative purposes. Most hardwood specialty stores either stock or can order bending plywood in a limited number of species.

Q How is plywood graded?

A The good face of a sheet of plywood is graded much like we were in high school, except the marks run AA through E. In general, plywoods graded B and higher have excellent appearance and are intended to be proudly exposed. Those graded C and lower should be used only when appearance is not important. The cores and backs of some hardwood plywoods are also graded or ranked.

Q I'm making card tables for the couples in our bridge club. I'd like to use ¾" plywood instead of solid wood for the tops, but I'm not sure how to cover the edges. What are my options?

A It depends on how you want your tables to look, how durable you want them to be, and how much time and money you'd like to spend.

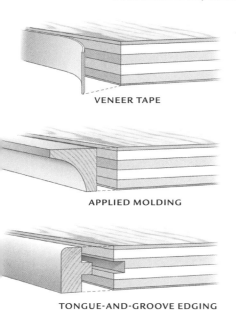

VENEER TAPE

APPLIED MOLDING

TONGUE-AND-GROOVE EDGING

Preglued veneer tape is inexpensive and easy to install, but it's the least durable option. Use your iron on a low setting to activate the glue and press the veneer in place. Once it's on, go back with a sanding block to knock off any high spots or overhanging edges.

Applied moldings are a sturdier option. You can use simple strips of solid wood or decorative moldings, such as base cap or cove. Miter the corners, and glue and nail the pieces to the plywood and at the corners. These will stand up to most abuse save a glancing blow.

Tongue-and-groove edging is the most labor-intensive but most durable option. Use a router with a slotting cutter bit to cut a groove around the edge, then create a T-shaped molding with a tongue that you glue into the groove.

Q How do I read the stamp on a sheet of construction plywood?

A Stamps can yield a lot of information if you know how to read the numbers and letters. Here are some clues:

⊙ Letter combinations, such as A–C and C–D, refer to the grades of the front and back face plies. A is smooth and paintable, while D allows knots and knotholes up to 2½" in diameter.

⊙ Exposure classification relates to type of glue and veneer used. *Exterior plywood* uses waterproof glue and C-grade or better veneers. *Exposure 1 plywood* is similar but can use D-grade veneers; it's best used in construction situations where long delays and exposure to the elements are expected. *Exposure 2 plywood* has glue with moderate moisture resistance and is intended for protected construction situations. Plywood rated as *Interior* is constructed with glues and veneers that should remain high and dry.

⊙ Pairs of numbers, such as 32/16, refer to the span rating. The first number relates to the maximum distance in inches it can span between support members when used as roof sheathing. The second number relates to the span when used as flooring.

⊙ Fractional measurements, such as 15/32", relate to actual thickness.

Other codes relate to grading agency, mill number, and other things you probably don't need to know about.

Composite Panels

Plywood panels are composed primarily of thin sheets of wood; composite panels are made up of particles and pieces bonded together to create a sheet. Both types have their pros and cons. Here's the lowdown.

Q What's the difference between particleboard and medium-density fiberboard?

A They look similar, contain the same basic materials, and, at 100 pounds per ¾" sheet, both require the strength of the Incredible Hulk to lift. But there are major differences. *Particleboard* is made by com-bining sawdust-size particles with glues and resin, then formed into a panel using heat and pressure. *Medium-density fiberboard* (MDF) is made by first "cooking" the particles to break them down into tiny fibers that are then coated with adhesive and pressed into a finished panel.

Think of particleboard as Rice Crispy bars, where the cereal and marshmallows have simply been mixed together. Think of MDF as fudge, where the ingredients have been melted together to create a more uniform dessert.

One main advantage of MDF over particleboard is that the surface is flat and ultra-smooth, making it the ideal surface for applying paint. MDF is also uniform throughout, meaning edges cut with saws, and profiles cut with routers, are crisper and cleaner. Finally, most MDF panels are 1" longer in each direction than particleboard, giving you more options and a wider margin of error when working.

tip: MDF vs. Particleboard

It takes a mat of sawdust and resin 5" thick to form a ¾" panel of particleboard. To manufacture an MDF panel of the same thickness requires almost 24" of material.

Q Do I need to use any special tools or techniques when cutting or shaping MDF and particleboard?

A The glues and resins used are tough on cutting edges, so it's best to use carbide-tipped saw blades and router bits. It's also a good idea to slow down the feed rate so your blades and bits stay cooler, which in turn will reduce wear and friction. Finally, do everything you can to keep the sawdust out of your shop and lungs. It's superfine and will infiltrate every nook and cranny, including the narrow opening around your dust mask. Use your dust collector (and air cleaner, if you have one) and wear a dust mask rated for fine particles. A cheap mask won't do the job.

Q Which is better, plywood or oriented-strand board (OSB)?

A In terms of weight, strength, nail-holding ability, and the distance they can span between support members, plywood and OSB are nearly identical. OSB typically is less expensive, and since one face is usually textured, it is less slippery to walk on — a factor to consider if you're sheathing a roof. One of the biggest differences is their reaction to moisture or standing water. While plywood remains stable, the edges of OSB tend to swell and remain swollen. Keep your OSB high and dry and you shouldn't have any problems.

Moldings

Moldings can be functional (covering gaps or exposed plywood edges), decorative (adding some pizzazz to a fireplace mantel) or both. Either way, they can be one of your best friends when you're building furniture, remodeling a room, or tackling other woodworking projects.

Q I bought some long baseboard moldings and later discovered they were made from lots of shorter pieces finger-jointed together. Are these moldings as strong as solid wood ones?

A As clear, straight lumber becomes increasingly rare, finger-jointed material is becoming increasingly common. The actual glued joint isn't quite as strong as solid lumber, but since the finished piece is free of knots and defects, the overall piece is most likely just as strong. Since appearance usually trumps strength for millwork anyway, the material you have will work just fine.

Q A friend made cherry quarter-round molding using a table saw and router. I tried doing the same thing but had trouble balancing my router on the skinny strips of wood. What did I do wrong?

A You did things in the wrong order. Instead of ripping your material to width and then routing it, you should rout the edge of a wide board and then rip it to width. That way, you have a wide, flat surface for stabilizing your router base as you work.

Q I'm restoring an old house and need to replace a missing piece of painted chair rail molding in the dining room. No one makes it anymore and I can't find it at architectural salvage yards. What should I do?

A If you needed hundreds of feet of the molding, it might be worth it to have a bit custom-made for mass-producing the pieces. But for a single piece, you may be able to improvise. Take a look at a cross section of the chair rail and see if there's a combination of stock moldings and profiles you can cut with conventional router bits that will approximate the size and shape you need.

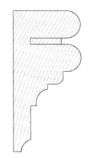

ORIGINAL MOLDING

Q My basement is usually damp, and every once in a while water sneaks in through a window well. Can I use MDF for the baseboard molding I want to make and install?

A No. MDF will wick up water and expand if the edges are subjected to moisture, and it won't shrink back to normal size when conditions dry up. Moisture can also affect paint adhesion. You're better off using polyurethane or synthetic moldings.

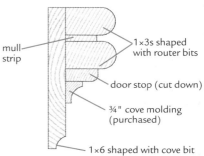

mull strip

1×3s shaped with router bits

door stop (cut down)

¾" cove molding (purchased)

1×6 shaped with cove bit

DO-IT-YOURSELF REPRODUCTION

Two Simple Plywood Storage Racks

Plywood is a wonderful material to have around. The problem is, many woodworkers have too much plywood and too little storage space. Here are two simple storage ideas:

Swing-out rack. Build an L-shaped frame from 2×4s or 2×6s, then sheathe both sides with ½" plywood as shown. Secure a heavy-duty caster to one end and two hinges to the other end, then screw the hinges to a wall stud. The swing-out feature allows you to position the rack anywhere — even in a corner — since you can swing it out, slide out the material you need, then roll it back out of the way.

Ropes and weights. Secure beefy screw hooks to two studs, 52" off the floor, then tie sections of rope to them with old window sash weights or weightlifting weights tied to the other end. Place skids on the floor to keep your plywood high and dry, then stack your material against the wall and drape the weighted ropes across the face to hold the sheets in place. Use the stud cavities for stashing narrow scraps.

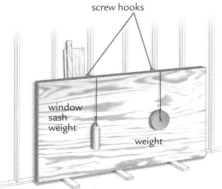

screw hooks

window sash weight

weight

ROPES AND WEIGHTS

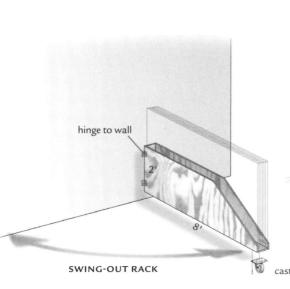

hinge to wall

2'

8'

SWING-OUT RACK

caster

Hand Tools

3

*Using a hammer is easy. You pick it up and
keep hitting things until you've built something.*
— RED GREEN

Every year in Japan, a contest is held to determine which artisan can create the thinnest hand plane shaving. In one recent year, the winning shaving was 3 microns thick: about one-tenth the thickness of a human hair. You may never create a shaving that fine, but you will become more adept at using hand tools with practice. Competency with hand tools involves not only learning what to do with them but also what not to do with them, how to sharpen and maintain them, and how to use them safely.

Some Basics

Q What's a good basic set of hand tools for someone getting started in woodworking?

A There's no single right answer, since there are so many different branches of woodworking. But there are a few across-the-board tools everyone should have:

- ⊙ 16-ounce claw hammer. This is small enough to drive finish nails yet beefy enough to drive larger ones.
- ⊙ 25' tape measure. A 1"-wide blade makes it easy to take long measurements without your tape going limp.
- ⊙ Triangle square for squaring off boards before cutting and for finding and transferring angles.
- ⊙ Utility knife for sharpening pencils, opening packages, marking precision cut lines, easing sharp edges, and dozens of other tasks.
- ⊙ Multi-bit screwdriver. One with Phillips, slotted, and square-drive bits stored on board will handle most situations and screws.
- ⊙ Sharp ¾" chisel for mortising, removing waste, and other tasks.
- ⊙ Three or four squeeze-type (one-handed) bar clamps for glue-ups, joining parts, and securing jigs.
- ⊙ Carpenter's apron or belt to keep the above tools close at hand and to minimize time spent searching for misplaced tools.

tip: Sharp Tools Are Safer

Contrary to popular belief, a sharp tool is safer than a dull one. You're more likely to force a dull chisel, plane, or utility knife, which increases their likelihood of slipping, ruining your workpiece, and throwing you off balance. With any tool, remember to keep your fingers and other body parts out of the projected path of the tool.

Q I live in a humid area, and my shop is in my garage. What can I do to prevent my tools from rusting?

A You have two options:

1 **Get the moisture out of the air.** If you have a space loaded with tools, you can run a dehumidifier (as a bonus, you'll feel cooler). If you just have a few tools, keep a container of silica desiccant in your toolbox (you can actually buy desiccants you can "recharge" in your oven). Some woodworkers also swear that a lump or two of charcoal in a toolbox will absorb enough moisture to prevent rust.

2 **Keep the moisture off the tools.** A cheap and effective method is to apply a coat of good old automobile paste wax. Rub it on, let it sit, then buff. As a bonus, your hand planes, table saws, and other tools will have a smoother glide to them.

CUTTING A KERF AND LOSING YOUR TEMPER

Woodworking — like most other pursuits — has a language all its own. Here are definitions for two "foreign" words you'll encounter over the next few pages:

◇ **Kerf** refers to the width of the slit or slot that a blade makes when making a cut. The kerf of a Japanese pull saw may be as narrow as 1⁄32", while that of a chainsaw can exceed 1⁄4".

◇ **Temper** refers to the process of using heat to strengthen or harden the metal of a chisel, blade, or other cutting tool. Overheating a tool during sharpening can cause it to "lose its temper" and its ability to stay sharp.

Measuring and Marking Tools

Q The little hook on the end of my tape measure wiggles back and forth a little. Will that affect the accuracy of my measurements?

A Yes, it affects your measurements, but in a positive way. The little hook that's perpendicular to the blade is about $1/16$" thick. It's no coincidence that the hook moves back and forth that same $1/16$". That way, regardless of whether you're taking an inside measurement (so the hook is compressed) or an outside measurement (where the hook is pulled outward), you'll get an accurate measurement.

Q Is there a fast way of dividing a board into strips of uniform width without doing a lot of math and conversions?

A Angle a tape measure across the width of a board until the tape reads as a multiple of the number of strips you want, then make your marks accordingly. For instance, if you want to divide a $7\frac{1}{4}$"-wide board into four equal strips, angle your tape measure across the board until it reads 8", then make tick marks on the board at the 2", 4", and 6" marks. Measure from the edge of the board to the first tick mark to get the width of each strip. If you're going to rip the board into strips, make sure to account for the kerf or width of the blade.

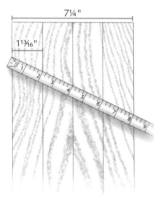

METRIC CONVERSIONS

From time to time, you'll need to convert standard measurements into metric or vice versa. To do so, follow these simple formulas:

TO CONVERT	TO	MULTIPLY BY
millimeters (mm)	inches	0.0394
centimeters (cm)	inches	0.394
centimeters	feet	0.0328
inches	centimeters	2.54
feet	centimeters	30.48
yard	meters (m)	0.914

tip: The Tape Measure in Your Wallet

A dollar bill is 6" long and 2½" wide. If you need to measure something but find yourself without a tape, reach for your billfold.

Q When I measure from the short side of an angled cut, I have trouble positioning the end of the tape. How do I improve my accuracy?

A Position the 1" mark of your tape on the short side of the angle, measure over, then add that inch back on when you make your mark. It's easier to align the tape's hash marks than the wiggly hook end.

Q How do I make sure the bookcase I'm building is square before installing the plywood back?

A Measure diagonally from one corner of the bookcase to the other in both directions, then compare measurements. If they're equal, your bookcase is square. If not, compress the corners that had the longer measurement, measure both diagonals again, and keep tweaking your bookcase until the readings are equal. Hold the piece square with cross braces or by clamping it down to the work surface.

Q How do I check to see if the wall I'm building in the basement runs square to the existing wall?

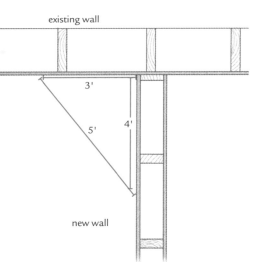

existing wall

3'

5'

4'

new wall

A We can thank the Greek mathematician Pythagoras for providing an easy solution. With the new wall set temporarily in place, measure 3' from the corner along the existing wall and make a mark, then measure out 4' along the new wall and make a mark. The diagonal measurement between the two marks should be exactly 5'. If it's less than 5', the end of your wall needs to move outward. If it's more than 5', it needs to move inward. Double your numbers for greater accuracy or for larger projects by measuring 6' and 8' along the walls, then checking for 10' diagonally.

tip: Masking Tape Memory

You measured how long that molding needed to be, but now you're in front of the miter saw and can't remember if it was 17 ⅝" or 15 ⅞". Save wasted footsteps, head scratching, and lumber by keeping a piece of masking tape stuck to the case of your measuring tape for jotting down numbers. When it's full, peel it off and replace it.

Q My neighbor built a wall-to-wall entertainment center in his garage, then installed it in his family room. He said he used a story stick to record the locations of the windows, outlets, heat vents, and light switches. What's a story stick and how is it used?

A It's simply a stick you use to record the locations of all the items just mentioned. Cut a stick to the same length as the wall, and position it along the wall. Then, mark the actual edges of all the features (windows, outlets, and so forth). Below the marks, write the distance off the floor for each feature. Back in your workshop, the story stick provides a foolproof record of every obstacle in or on the wall. It also gives you a visual reference and allows you to lay out horizontal and vertical dividers so they won't interfere with anything.

At first glance a story stick may seem primitive, but at second glance you'll realize it eliminates a lot of measuring, errors, and steps between the shop and the family room to double-check your measurements. Story sticks can also be used to transfer measurements when working on a lathe, as you make reproductions and build furniture.

STORY STICK

tip: Loopy way to subtract measurements

Let's say you've got a wall that's 83 7/16" long and you want to know how much space will be left after you install a cabinet that's 35 13/16" wide. Here's a fast, foolproof way of doing it without a lot of head scratching. Make a loop out of your tape so the tip rests exactly against the 83 7/16" mark. Find the 35 13/16" mark and read the number straight across from it (in this case, 47 5/8"). That's the distance you have left. You can do this to subtract any measurement from another.

tape   83 7⁄16"

35 13⁄16"

47 5⁄8"

Q When I use my chalk box to snap lines on plywood, sometimes the lines wind up so thick and fuzzy it's hard to tell where the real line is. How do I get a smooth, clean line?

A Before filling your chalk box, pull out 15 or 20 feet of string and then insert the chalk bottle nozzle in the opening and squeeze until the box seems full. Tap it a few times, close the sliding flap, then start reeling it in. As you roll in the string, the rotating reel helps distribute the chalk evenly along the string and throughout the case. If you load it while all the string is on the reel, you'll wind up with too much chalk on one end of the string and not enough on the other.

Once your box is loaded properly, use it properly. After hooking one end in place and reeling out the right amount of string, give it a light "twang" in mid-air to get rid of excess chalk before snapping the actual line. You'll get a crisper line.

tip: Different Chalks for Different Tasks

Not all chalks are created equal:

- ◆ Blue is for temporary use, such as snapping lines on floors for wall positions.

- ◆ Red is for more permanent or rugged applications, such as lines for laying shingles where moisture and rain may come into play.

- ◆ White is the most easily removed and should be used on surfaces that might later be painted (such as interior walls).

Q I used a pencil to number the pieces of a large oak floor grate. I sanded it, but I still can't get the pencil marks out of the deeper grain areas. Do I have to keep sanding?

A You can remove graphite marks with denatured alcohol. Dampen a rag with it and rub with the grain until the marks are gone. Wear rubber gloves and a respirator, and be certain to work either outside or in a well-ventilated area.

Squares, Levels, Curves, and Angles

Q How can I tell if my framing square is truly square? And if it isn't, can I adjust it?

A To check it, place the short leg of the square along the factory edge of a piece of plywood and draw a line along the long leg. Flip the square over, place the short leg along the same edge of the plywood and see if the long leg lines up with the line you drew. If it's more than ⅛" out of square at the end, buy a new one.

dimple here to "close" square

dimple here to "open up" square

For finer adjustments, try this: If the square is less than 90 degrees, it needs to be "opened up." Place the square on a solid surface and use a metal punch and hammer to make a dimple on the ¼" mark of the inside edge of the short leg. The dimple will slightly expand the inner edge and help "spring" the square to 90 degrees. If that doesn't help, repeat on the ½" and ¾" marks. To "close" a square that's over 90 degrees, dimple the outside edge of the short leg starting near the corner.

Q How can I tell if my level is level?

A Place your level on a flat surface and check the center bubble. If it isn't exactly between the lines, add playing cards or sheets of paper beneath one end until the bubble reads perfectly level. Rotate the level end-for-end and, with the other end resting on your paper shims, check the bubble. If the bubble is exactly between the lines, your level is true. If your level is out of whack, it's best to replace the tool.

Q Why are the vials in most levels slightly arched or barrel-shaped?

A The slight upward curve gives the bubble a resting place when the level is reading exactly level. Otherwise, it would be impossible for the bubble to stay exactly between the calibration lines.

Q The angles on tools and in illustrations don't jibe with angles as I learned them. For one project I needed parts "cut at 30 degrees," but the angle on the end of the board was 60 degrees. What's up?

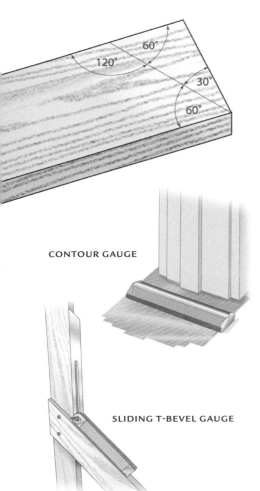

CONTOUR GAUGE

SLIDING T-BEVEL GAUGE

A You're right; what angles are called in the world of woodworking doesn't always jibe with the angles as specified in the world of geometry. Usually the angle mentioned in woodworking projects — and the angle listed on tool gauges — relates to how many degrees off of 90 degrees the cut is.

Q What's the difference between a contour gauge and a sliding T-bevel gauge?

A A *contour gauge* helps you transfer irregular shapes and curves from one object or workpiece to another. It consists of a housing that holds hundreds of small slats or pins. When pressed against an irregular shape, the pins hold their position so you can transfer that shape. A contour gauge is good for cutting flooring to fit around doorways or copying the shape of a spindle you want to reproduce on a lathe.

A *sliding T-bevel* helps you transfer or determine irregular angles. It consists of a handle and blade that can be adjusted to any angle. A wingnut holds the two together so you can transfer that angle to a workpiece or use it to determine the angle of a saw cut.

Q I can use a compass for drawing small circles, but what's the best way to draw large ones?

A The fastest method is to drive in a drywall screw at your center point, hook the end of your tape over the head, then hold the tip of your pencil at the desired radius measurement while you slowly draw the circle. Don't forget to take into account the diameter of the screw head. It's sometimes more accurate (and less of a hassle) to use a string with a loop in it (or a board with a hole drilled in) it to hold your pencil, instead of trying to press the pencil against the side of your tape as you swing the arc.

Planes, Chisels, and Scrapers

Q What do woodworkers mean when they talk about "cutting with the grain?"

A Cutting with (or against) the grain refers to how the cutting edge of the tool is moving in reference to the grain of the wood. When a chisel or plane blade cuts *with the grain,* the fibers shear off cleanly, creating a smooth surface. When it cuts *against the grain,* it digs into the fibers and lifts them up, creating a rough surface (this is called tearout). Taken to an extreme, cutting against the grain can gouge large slivers of wood from the surface, ruining your workpiece.

When you think about the right direction to work, think about petting your cat's back. When you stroke her fur with the grain, she purrs; against the grain, she hisses.

CUTTING WITH THE GRAIN

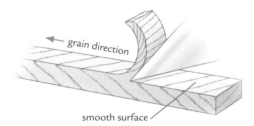

grain direction

smooth surface

CUTTING AGAINST THE GRAIN

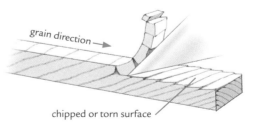

grain direction

chipped or torn surface

Q Do I apply the same amount of pressure to a hand plane the entire time I'm making a pass?

A No. As a general rule, start by pressing the nose of the plane down slightly with one hand as you push the handle forward with the other. As you approach the center of the board, press down and forward evenly with both hands. As you finish your cut, slightly press down on the heel of the plane with one hand while taking pressure off the nose with the other. This procedure will vary depending on what you're trying to do, but if you're just getting started using hand planes, it's a good basic method to practice.

Q Solve an argument. My brother-in-law swears the bevel on all hand plane blades should face down, but I'm pretty sure the bevel on a block plane blade faces up. Who's right?

A You are. Block planes are unique in that the bevel faces up. This means the blade can sit in the plane at a lower angle and that the plane itself can be designed with a lower profile, making it easier to operate with one hand. Why all the fuss over the need for a one-handed plane? Field carpenters who hang doors and windows and install cabinets

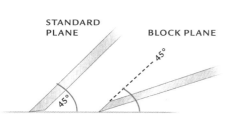

STANDARD PLANE

BLOCK PLANE

45°

45°

need something small they can fit in their pouch for fine-tuning components. Since a block plane is so petite, a carpenter can work overhead and in tight places, while easily holding the workpiece with one hand and planing with the other. Woodworkers love them in the shop for fitting doors and drawers, cleaning up saw marks, and dozens of other uses.

Q Sometimes I'll retract the blade in my plane to take a shallower cut. After a few swipes it stops cutting. Why?

A Adjusting mechanisms have a little play in them — usually way less than $\frac{1}{16}$" — but it's enough to make the difference. Always make your final adjustment by adjusting the blade downward (not upward like you've done.) This may mean retracting the blade farther up than you need to, then readjusting it back downward. But by doing this, the parts will be set so they prevent the blade from backing up.

Q Even after carefully sharpening my plane blade, I get grain tearout and a choppy surface. What am I doing wrong?

A There are two other components of the plane that, if not adjusted correctly, can contribute to grain tearout. First, the chip breaker on the topside of the blade should be set no further back than ¹⁄₃₂" from the cutting edge. This forces the shaving to rise at a steeper angle, which reduces the length and amount of the grain run. Second, the plane's mouth should be reduced in size so the sole of the plane can push the fibers down just ahead of the blade to prevent tearout. This involves adjusting the frog adjustment screw on a standard plane or the mouth plate on a block plane.

tip: A Cool Plane Blade Saver

To prevent nicking or damaging your plane blade when not in use, retract it, then cover and protect it with a large, flat refrigerator magnet adhered to the sole plate.

COMPONENTS OF A BENCH PLANE

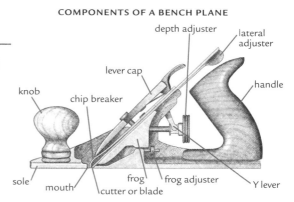

Q How thick should a good plane shaving be?

A Your goal should be to generate a long, consistent shaving about the thickness of a sheet of paper. Serious hand plane users shoot for tissue-paper thickness.

Q I was in an antique store the other day and found myself in a booth containing nothing but hand planes: 2" long, 2' long, and everything in between. How does one begin to understand what they all do?

A There are thousands of different planes out there. Before the advent of power planers, jointers, sanders, and routers, planes did it all. It's easiest to lump planes into groups and then look at what each group excels in (see the next page).

Block planes are compact in size and can easily be operated with one hand. While not as accurate for planing expansive surfaces as larger planes, they're perfect for fitting doors, drawers, and trim, and they're good for smoothing end grain.

Smoothing planes (often designated by numbers 3 to 4½) are around 10" long and excel at preparing board surfaces prior to finishing. They're short enough to work on slightly irregular or concave surfaces yet long enough to provide a stable platform for fine finishing cuts.

Jack or bench planes (often designated as number 5) are, well, jacks-of-all-trades. Usually about 15" long with a 2"-wide blade, they're good all-purpose planes that can level edges and smooth surfaces.

Leveling or jointer planes have soles ranging in length from 18" to 36". This long base makes them excellent for planing board edges square, straight, and true before edge-gluing.

There are hundreds of other planes designed for cutting decorative shapes, such as coves, rabbets, and moldings, as well as specialty planes used by coopers, coach makers, and other tradespeople.

Q I like to cut pieces a hair long, then shave them down to exact size with a block plane. How can I do this without tearing the end grain?

A Build a shooting board (or two). The stop block of this jig braces the workpiece and supports the end grain to minimize splintering. If you put a cleat along the back edge to hook over your workbench, you

SHOOTING BOARD

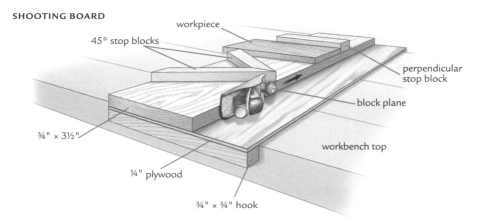

workpiece

45° stop blocks

perpendicular stop block

block plane

workbench top

¾" × 3½"

¼" plywood

¾" × ¾" hook

don't even need to clamp it down. For fine-tuning 45-degree miters, add angled stops, or build a separate shooting board with an angled stop.

Q I bought a chisel at my home center and wound up having to sharpen it after a few minutes. Shouldn't it stay sharp longer?

A The sharpness of new tools is so unpredictable that some wood-workers make a habit of sharpening every chisel and blade right out of the package. Some even think of them as "kits" — things that will need a lot of work before they're ready for use. Often the problem has to do with the non-beveled or back side of the blade not being totally flat. Place the back of your chisel flat on a waterstone (see page 76) or on a piece of super-fine sandpaper lying on a flat, solid surface. Hone it until the back is flat. It may take a while, but you should have to do this only once. Once the back is flat, sharpen the beveled side as well.

Q What's the difference between a mortise chisel and a bevel-edge chisel?

A They look similar until you examine them closely. They both have beveled tips, but the sides of a mortise chisel are square, while those of a bevel-edge chisel are beveled.

A *mortise* chisel, as the name implies, excels at chopping mortises. In order to stand up to the rigors of prying and the repeated blows of a mallet, the blade is square to increase heft.

A *bevel-edge* chisel is designed to be pushed with one hand and guided with the other. They're not as sturdy, but their beveled edges allow them to reach tight spaces and angles that a mortise chisel might have trouble reaching. Most home center chisels are of the bevel-edge variety.

Q What's a scraper and how does it work?

A A scraper is a piece of steel, usually rectangular or kidney-shaped, with a raised burr on the edge used for smoothing wood. In the right hands it will create a finished surface faster than sandpaper. To use a scraper, hold the tool in both hands, create a slight bow and tilt with your thumbs, then drag (or push) it across the surface of the wood, following the grain. It takes a while to get the motion down, but once you do you'll enjoy fast, clean results. The key is a sharp edge.

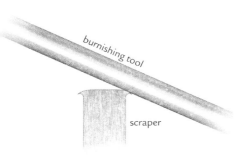

burnishing tool

scraper

Q How do I sharpen a scraper?

A Use a file and sharpening stone to create a square, crisp edge. Once this is done, place the scraper upright in a vise and run a burnisher or other hardened tool shaft across the edge at a slight angle to create a long, consistent burr on one side of the scraper. Angle the burnisher the other way and repeat to create a burr on the other side.

Sharpening

Q Can I sharpen my chisel with a file?

A Not easily, especially if it's an old file you pulled out of your grandpa's toolbox. The metal that files and chisels are made from are of similar hardness. Rather than cutting the metal, most files just bounce along the edge. Use a sharpening stone or grinder instead.

Q Is it true that the general-use bench grinders and wheels you buy at the hardware store or home center aren't really suited for sharpening woodworking tools?

A You can get by with a standard grinder, but they were really designed more for metalworking and heavy-duty grinding. A grinder designed for woodworking will cost more but offers these advantages:

Lower speed. Standard grinders operate at about 3,400 rpm; woodworking grinders work at about half that speed. Lower speed translates into better control and less likelihood of burning tool edges.

Friable wheels. You want a softer, somewhat crumbly wheel so the old, dull grits slough off faster, exposing new grits with sharp edges. An 80-grit aluminum oxide wheel with an "H" bond is good for most sharpening tasks.

Solid, adjustable tool rests. The tool rests on standard grinders tend to flex, making it difficult to sharpen wide chisels and plane irons accurately. The rests on grinders designed for woodworking tools are sturdier and can be adjusted for both angle and distance from the wheel.

You may want to look into one of the newer "dry" sharpening systems that looks a bit like an old 45 rpm record turntable. A clamping mechanism holds the plane blade or chisel at a consistent angle while the horizontal abrasive wheel sharpens the bevel. They can quickly sharpen damaged tools or hone those that need touching up.

tip: Sharpen Your Vision

When sharpening tools on a grinder, your viewing angle allows you to see the top and the shape of the tool but not the bevel that's being ground. To overcome this, secure a small, gooseneck bike helmet mirror to the side of your grinder (most are self-adhering), and adjust it so you can see the side of the tool.

Q I finally figured out how to sharpen my chisels and plane blades to create a crisp single bevel. Now one friend tells me he prefers double bevels, and another prefers hollow-ground bevels. What are these?

A When you create a *single bevel,* you sharpen and hone the blade so the entire cutting edge is one consistent angle.

A *double bevel* is when you grind the blade at an angle, then hone a portion of the tip at about a 2-degree higher angle. This creates a slightly thicker, "sturdier" bevel that doesn't require sharpening as frequently, which is especially important with hardwoods. Instead of having to resharpen the entire bevel when the blade dulls, you only have to sharpen the smaller honing angle.

A *hollow-ground bevel* is the natural result of shaping a blade on a round grinding wheel. As with a double bevel, you'll be able to restore a sharp edge faster when touching up a hollow-ground, since you have to remove less material compared to sharpening an entire single bevel.

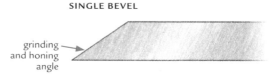

SINGLE BEVEL

grinding and honing angle

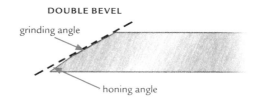

DOUBLE BEVEL

grinding angle

honing angle

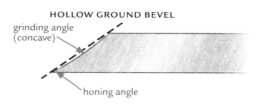

HOLLOW GROUND BEVEL

grinding angle (concave)

honing angle

Q What's the difference between a waterstone and an oilstone? And as a beginning woodworker, which should I buy?

A They're similar in that both are composed of abrasive grit held together by a binder. The liquid, whether it's oil or water, keeps the tool being sharpened cool and washes away the abrasive grit as it's ground away. Here are the primary differences:

Waterstones (also called whetstones) have a soft binder that allows the abrasive grit to be ground away relatively easily. This is a good thing, since this means new, sharp, abrasive particles keep being exposed. The downside is that the stones tend to become "scooped" or wear unevenly. However, they can be re-flattened by rubbing two stones together or by rubbing one stone across sandpaper secured to a flat surface (such as a piece of plate glass).

Oilstones have a harder binder, which means they last longer but work slower. The upside is that they remain flatter longer and aren't as affected by narrow chisels and gouges that might otherwise groove a waterstone.

Both work well. If you sharpen lots of wide, flat plane blades and chisels, your best bet might be a waterstone. If you sharpen lots of curved woodturning and carving tools, consider an oilstone. Whichever route you go, purchase medium-grit and fine-grit versions.

Q Should I leave my waterstone immersed in water all the time?

A Some stones don't require soaking, while others can deteriorate if left in water too long, so follow the manufacturer's directions. That said, most can be left soaking in water when not in use. It keeps them clean and saturated, so when you do sharpen with them they don't dry out as quickly. Keep your stones immersed in a plastic shoebox with a lid, and they'll be ready to go any time you are. Be sure to keep them out of below-freezing temperatures.

Q I read that when carbon steel tools are sharpened on a grinder, they lose their temper quicker than high-speed steel tools. I inherited some chisels from my uncle, and I'm not sure what type of metal they're made of. How can I tell?

A Take a look at the sparks as they come off the grinder. Tools made of carbon steel throw off multi-faceted sparks, like those from a sparkler. High-speed steel tools generate smaller, well-defined sparks. If your tools are carbon steel, quench them in water frequently to prevent them from overheating and losing their temper, or hardness.

Q Someone on talk radio was discussing sharpening tools with sandpaper. Is that possible?

A Yes, but it needs to be done on an absolutely flat surface. A good way to create that surface is by gluing a piece of ¼" glass to a piece of ¼" plywood. Once that's set, remove the backing from a sheet (or half-sheet) of pressure-sensitive sandpaper, and press it onto the glass with a rolling pin. While you're at it, make three sharpening plates — each with a different grit — so you won't be constantly swapping papers back and forth. (Or make a larger plate so you can adhere three different grits to it.) Which grits to use depends on how sharp your tools are to begin with. You may want to start with an 80-, 120-, 320-grit sequence of wet-or-dry silicon carbide paper, then adjust your grits to your situation.

tip: Sharper Tools with a Marker

Before sharpening a tool, run the tip of a felt pen across the bevel. Check the mark from time to time as you sharpen; it will let you know your progress and whether or not you're sharpening the edge evenly.

Hammers

Q Why do some hammers have curved claws and others straight?

A Generally speaking, *curved-claw* hammers are used for trimwork and other forms of "light-duty" carpentry. The head usually weighs 12 to 16 ounces. The curved claw has built-in leverage for pulling nails. *Straight-claw* hammers, with heads weighing 20 ounces and up, are used more for heavy-duty tasks, such as framing walls. The straight claw isn't as good at pulling nails — you often need to insert a block under the head to get the right leverage — but the straight claw comes in handy for cleaning out grooves in tongue-and-groove plywood and for prying boards apart.

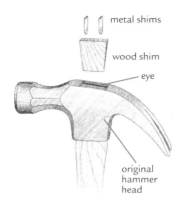

metal shims

wood shim

eye

original
hammer
head

Q My grandfather's hammer needs a new handle. How hard is it to replace?

A You sound like the old gent who mused, "I've had the same hammer for 45 years. Only had to change the handle four times and the head twice." Installing a new wood handle is simple. Saw off the old handle close to the head, then drill as many ¼" holes as you can through the remaining wood. Use an old chisel to pry and punch out the old wood. Purchase a handle that's the right length and fits snugly into the hammer's "eye," or opening. Sometimes you need to whittle it down a little.

The handle should come with one small, wedge-shaped wood shim and two small metal ones. Set the head in place and give the fat end of the handle several good raps on a hard surface so the head firmly seats itself. Saw off any part of the new handle protruding above the head. Drive the wood shim into the kerf in the top of the handle to expand the handle side to side, then drive the two metal shims in perpendicular to the wood shim to expand the handle even tighter into the eye.

Q I loaned a fiberglass-handle hammer to my brother-in-law and he somehow managed to break it. Is it replaceable (the handle, not my brother-in-law)?

A Yes, fiberglass handle replacement kits, which typically contain a handle, epoxy, and mixing equipment, are available. The basic procedure involves removing the old handle, cleaning the eye with a wire brush, inserting the new handle, then pouring the epoxy mixture into the eye to lock the new handle in place. Needless to say, it's critical that you align the new handle squarely to the head and keep it that way as the epoxy sets.

Q I went hammer shopping and became mystified by all the different handles. What are the advantages of one over another?

A The differences have to do with feel, durability, and shock-dissipating qualities. *Wood* handles rank high when it comes to shock dissipation (which can help prevent wrist and arm injuries) but low in durability. *Steel* handles are nearly unbreakable but rank low in shock-dissipation (though cushioned grips improve this.) *Fiberglass* and *graphite* handles combine durability with good shock dissipation, making them an increasingly popular, though more expensive, choice. Before buying any hammer, give it several practice swings to make sure the weight, balance, and grip feel right.

Q I've heard it's best to use a dead-blow hammer for assembling and disassembling tight joints. Why?

A A dead-blow hammer has a hollow head half-full of steel beads or sand. When the hammer makes impact, the beads move forward to eliminate any rebound and add a little extra oomph. The heads are wide to distribute impact evenly and are rubber-coated to prevent marring. They usually weigh more than a standard hammer, meaning you can deliver more force with a shorter swing. When you add up all these qualities, you can see why they're the woodworker's hammer of choice for "persuading" stubborn joints apart during furniture repairs or disassembling stubborn machinery and tool parts.

Handsaws

Q I have trouble with my handsaw jumping around when I start a cut and staying square as I cut. How do I perfect my technique?

A Use a starter block. Place a short 2×2 or 2×4 block directly next to your mark, snug your saw up next to it and give a few light, low-angle backstrokes. Keep the block in place to guide the blade until you've sawn a kerf deep enough (and square enough) to guide the blade for the rest of the cut. Another advantage of the starter block is that it keeps your thumb away from the blade so if it jumps, it will nick the block, not your thumb.

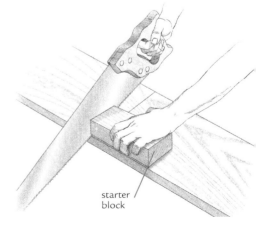

starter block

Q How do Japanese handsaws differ from Western saws?

A The most noticeable difference is that Japanese handsaws cut on the pull stroke, and Western saws cut on the push stroke. Since a Japanese blade is under tension from being pulled (rather than compression from being pushed) the blade can be thinner, creating a thinner kerf, which also cuts more efficiently. Thinner, more flexible blades also mean they excel at tasks such as cutting dowels flush and working in confined spaces. The metal used in Japanese saws typically is harder, requiring less frequent sharpenings. On the downside, Japanese saws are more expensive and nearly impossible for the average woodworker to sharpen. You can ruin them by bending the thin blades on the return stroke, and since you pull the sawdust toward you, your cut line can be obscured. It really boils down to personal preference. But if you've never used a Japanese saw, it's definitely worth a try.

There are dozens of different Japanese saws, including:

- *Ryoba* has two cutting edges; one with coarse teeth for ripping, the other with finer teeth for crosscutting.
- *Dozuki* has a stiff spine that allows it to be used like a backsaw.
- *Azebiki* has a convex blade that allows it to make cuts in the center of a board.
- *Mawashibiki* is a narrow saw used for cutting curves.

Q My grandfather used to sharpen his own handsaws. Is this a tradition I can carry on?

A Yes. It's time-consuming and requires special tools and skills, but some people get great satisfaction from sharpening their own tools or turning a flea market bargain into a usable tool. You'll need a saw vise for holding the blade securely, triangular-shaped taper files for the actual sharpening, and a saw set for slightly angling each tooth outward in an alternating pattern.

A full explanation on how to sharpen a saw could consume an entire chapter, but you can find many good articles on sharpening by searching online with keywords "handsaw sharpening" (also see Resources). Only you can judge what your time is worth. A new handsaw can be purchased for as little as $15 (though a good one will cost about three times as much), and a saw sharpening service will charge $10 to $20 for getting that old handsaw cutting like new.

Q I find it easier, safer, and more accurate to use a handsaw than a power saw when I cut small parts. But clamping or holding thin board in a vise can be a challenge. Is there a simpler way?

A Use a bench hook. It's a simple homemade jig that has a 1×1 cleat along the bottom edge that "hooks" over the edge of your workbench and a 2×2 backstop along the top for holding the wood as you saw. The push of the cutting stroke forces the cleat tightly against the edge of the workbench and the board against the backstop. This jig is simple to use, and it supports the wood fibers to minimize splintering during the cut.

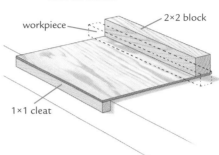

BENCH HOOK

workpiece — 2×2 block

1×1 cleat

Q I'm building dollhouse furniture and need to create cutouts that are too small and intricate for my jigsaw to handle. I don't own a scrollsaw. What are my options?

A Use a coping saw. Begin by drilling a small pilot hole in the scrap part of your cutout. Unscrew the handle of your coping saw far enough so you can remove one end of the blade from the slot in the retaining pin of the frame. Pass the blade through the starter hole, then reconnect the blade and tighten the handle until the blade is taut. Align the "ears" of the retaining pins so the blade is straight, then carefully make the cut.

You'll have the best control by clamping your parts to your workbench and using both hands — one on the handle, the other on the far end of the blade — to control the route of the coping saw blade. For really intricate cuts, some people reverse the blade so it cuts on the pull stroke. This keeps the blade in tension during the cut and offers better control.

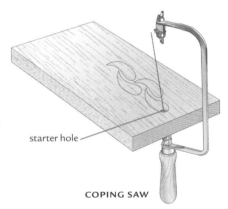

starter hole

COPING SAW

Screwdrivers and Wrenches

Q I have a drawer full of blunt, useless screwdrivers. Is there any way I can renew the tips?

A Yes. To sharpen a standard screwdriver, set your grinder's tool rest square to the wheel, then grind the tip until it's flat and all nicks are gone. Readjust the tool rest, and taper the faces and edges of the tip to the size you want. Sharpen a Phillips screwdriver by flattening the tip with a single-cut file, then using the square edges of the file to deepen the four grooves equally until the tip comes to a dull point. Square-drive tips can be restored by filing or grinding the tip flat, then lightly touching up the flat sides to restore the tip to its correct size. Don't overheat the tip or it will lose its temper (hardness) and become useless.

Q Is there a way to keep a screw from falling off my screwdriver, without using a magnetic-tip screwdriver?

A Use a square-drive screw and driver if you can. The tapered tip of the screwdriver and the tapered recess of the screw make them nest together tightly, so they stay on even at weird angles.

If you have to use a slotted or Phillips screw, put a dab of tack wax or glue stick on the tip, to hold the screw. If that fails, place the screw on the tip of your screwdriver, poke the tip of the screw through a piece of masking tape and wrap the ends of the tape around the screwdriver shaft.

Q Why do some box wrenches have 6 points in the opening, while others have 12?

tip: A 10-Cent Wrench

If you have an open-end wrench that's slightly too big for the job, fill the gap by slipping a dime or other coin between the opening in the wrench and the bolt head or nut.

A Since most nuts and bolts are six-sided, box wrenches with 6 points (or a hexagonal opening) are able to apply solid contact to all six sides of the fastener as you work. But you need to rotate the wrench 60 degrees to get the next "bite" as you tighten a bolt, which can be difficult in tight spaces. A 12-point wrench gives you twice as many positions to work from. They can also be used on 4-sided bolts and nuts. The downside? Since they can't grip as tight, you're more likely to round off the head of a stubborn bolt.

Clamps and Clamping

Clamps are some of the most important tools in your shop. Here are ten tips on getting the most out of them:

1 Always dry-assemble and "test-clamp" your workpiece before applying glue. This will help you avoid mistakes while giving you an opportunity to pre-adjust your clamps so you can position, install, and tighten them faster during the gluing-up process.

2 Mark your boards with masking tape, arrows, or chalk so the right components wind up in the right place and your boards are good-face-out or good-face-up. In the "heat of battle" it's easy to lose track of what goes where.

3 Don't use clamps to force ill-fitting parts together. Use a plane, jointer, or other tool to true up bowed or misshapen components.

4 Apply clamps like Baby Bear would: not too loose, not too tight, but just right. Over-tightening can starve a joint by squeezing glue out of it. It can also crush the wood fibers, weakening the area. With under-tightening, mating pieces don't make adequate contact. A properly glued and clamped joint will sport an even line of glue or small glue beads.

5 Pay heed to the "working time" or "open time" of your glue. If you don't have enough time, patience, or clamps to join everything in one shot, break the task down and do it in stages.

6 Evenly distribute clamp pressure over large areas by using multiple clamps or by placing scrap wood between the clamp jaws and workpiece.

7 Protect your workpiece from dents, grime, and glue stains. Place wood blocks between sharp jaws and the workpiece. Prop your workpiece up and off the work surface. Don't allow metal clamp parts to come into contact with glue.

8 Align your clamps so the centers of the jaws align with the centers of the boards you're gluing. This will prevent bowing, shifting, and other problems.

9 Keep the jaws of your clamps square to the workpiece to prevent throwing it out of square. Use a square or tape measure to check diagonals to make sure surfaces are meeting at 90 degrees.

10 Leave clamps in place for the recommended length of time (as specified by the glue manufacturer).

bungee cords hooked together

mousetraps

masking tape

V-blocks

scrap blocks

caulk gun

CLAMPING INGENUITY

Some of the best clamps aren't clamps at all. Here are six examples of seat-of-the-pants clamps you can use:

◆ **Bungee cords.** When you need to hold odd-shaped objects together, use bungee cords. Hook two together if you need extra length.

◆ **Mousetraps.** When you need light clamping pressure for small projects, try the spring-loaded mechanism of a mousetrap. Cut off the unused wood portion to make them even more compact.

◆ **Masking tape.** When gluing up small frames and small pieces of molding, masking tape often has enough oomph.

◆ **V-blocks.** When you need to hold a board on edge, try wedging it in place. Cut a V-shape from a block of wood, clamp this to your work surface, place the board along one edge of the V, then use the triangular cutoff to hold the board in place.

◆ **Scrap blocks.** Use small blocks and pieces of scrap wood to create an arm to extend the reach of a C-clamp.

◆ **Caulk gun.** The ratcheting action of a caulk gun's plunger is strong enough to apply pressure to small pieces of wood.

With fast-setting modern glues, some of the handiest, most accurate clamps of all are your fingers; just make sure you're gluing wood to wood, not wood to skin.

Q I like using wood hand-screw clamps, but they take forever to open and close. Are there any fast ways to adjust them?

A Grab a handle in each hand, then rotate your hands as if they were pedaling a bicycle. Once you have the jaws set at the approximate right distance, position the clamps and do the final tightening by twisting your wrists. **NOTE:** To prevent wood from sticking to wood clamps, place wax paper between the two.

Q I have a project that requires several 6'-long pipe clamps. Is there a way to use the shorter pieces of threaded pipe I already have?

A Buy pipe couplers that allow you to screw two sections of threaded pipe together to get the required length. They're inexpensive and easy to use and store.

Files and Rasps

Q With all the other tools out there, why would anyone use a file?

A Lots of people have bad first impressions of them because the files and rasps they've used were found at a garage sale or the bottom of a toolbox. Like any tool, they need maintenance and will eventually dull. Many old files are beyond their useful life span. But sharp files offer great speed and control when shaping curved objects or smoothing areas that are difficult to access with other tools. They'll allow you to start sanding at 180 grit rather than 60. And, since each tooth cuts rather than slices, there's less danger of grain tearout. Don't knock them until you've tried a good one.

Q What's the difference between a file and a rasp?

A A rasp has hundreds of individual cone-shaped teeth punched into a metal blank. They remove wood very aggressively with less clogging. Files have parallel grooves that have been cut into the face of the metal blank. *Single-cut* files have grooves running diagonally in one direction, *double-cut* files have grooves running in two directions to create a grid of diamond-shapes (and a smoother cut.) Generally, the teeth and grooves grow in proportion to the length of the tool, meaning the longer the tool, the coarser the cut.

Q How do you clean a file or rasp?

A A good rap against a block of wood will often dislodge sawdust and chips accumulated in the teeth. For clogged tools use a card file — a paddle-shaped tool with hundreds of short, stiff wires that will dislodge debris. When your tool starts sliding across wood rather than cutting it, it's time to clean it. If that doesn't help, it's time to replace it.

Q What's a 4-in-1 file?

A It's sort of the Swiss Army knife of the file and rasp world. As the name implies, it consists of 4 cutting surfaces. One side is flat, the other rounded. And one half of each side is a file and the other half a rasp. Most are about 8" long. It's a good all-purpose tool for rough shaping.

Q Is there a reason most files come without handles? How hard is it to install one?

A Most files do come handle-less, with just a pointed tang on one end. And you definitely should add a handle. Using a file with the tang exposed is uncomfortable and even dangerous. Store-bought handles are cheap, or you can make one in a few minutes by boring a hole in the end of a short section of dowel. A custom handle also makes a nice woodturning project. To install the handle, place the tang in the hole, then bang the end of the handle on a hard surface until the tang seats itself.

tip: Never Lose a Part

If you drop a small tool part or fastener on the floor, try this trick to find it: Hold a flashlight at floor level and sweep the beam back and forth. Even a small object will cast a big — and seeable — shadow.

Roomy Pegboard Tool Cabinet

Here's a woodworking project for stashing your woodworking tools. You can make yours any size or shape you want using the basic ideas shown here.

1 Build a box of 1×6s at the desired size. Nail a framework of ¾"×¾" spacer slats to the back inner edge, then inset ¼" pegboard.

2 Build two boxes of 1×3s (each half the width of your 1×6 box), then nail a framework of ¾" spacer slats to the center of each box. Cut and install pegboard on both sides of each slat frame.

3 Use long piano hinges to secure the 1×3 boxes to the edges of the 1×6 box.

The 1×6 box is deep enough to hold drills, planes and other large tools, while the 1×3 flaps are ideal for stashing and organizing hand tools. When you mount the box, screw it to the wall studs and set it on a 2×4 cleat bolted firmly to the wall to help support the weight; you could easily wind up with 100 pounds of tools in your new tool cabinet.

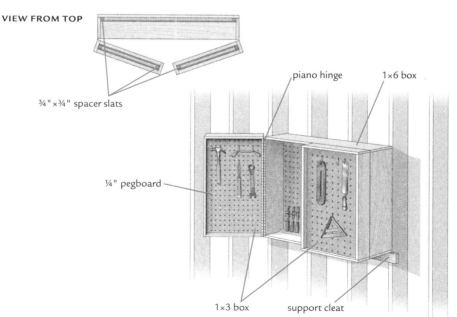

VIEW FROM TOP

¾"×¾" spacer slats

piano hinge

1×6 box

¼" pegboard

1×3 box

support cleat

4 Portable Power Tools

One thing separates humanity from its beastly origins: tool lust. That's the white heat that hits you behind the eyes when you see the perfect chainsaw or heft a heavenly hammer. And where does the lightning bolt strike? In a hardware store, of course.

— VINCE STATEN

Portable, or handheld, power tools are amazing helpmates. They're easy to store, easy to handle, and easy on the finances. And with the right know-how, they can help you work faster and more accurately, so you'll turn out better-looking projects. Sure, big stationary power tools can perform a multitude of tasks faster, but in many cases there's no substitute for the handheld version. You'll undoubtedly find routers, belt sanders, and cordless drills in even the most automated cabinet shops. Here we'll take a look at some of the basics of these little workhorses.

Drills

Q Whenever I drill holes with a spade bit, the backside of the wood or plywood splinters big time. What's the solution?

A If you look through the top of a hole you've drilled halfway, you'll notice there's no splintering at the bottom. That's because there's wood below the bit supporting or "backing up" the wood fibers as you bore through them. What you need on the exit side of your board is a backer board to support those last fibers as the bit exits. Firmly clamp a scrap piece of wood to the bottom side of your board, and you'll greatly reduce splintering.

Q A friend told me that, in a pinch, you can use a finish nail for a drill bit. Will that really work?

A Yes, especially in place of small bits that tend to break (or get lost) frequently. Find a finish nail that's the diameter of the hole you need. Grab a side cutter or end nipper, and put on your safety glasses. Nip the head off the nail (it may go flying — that's why you're wearing safety glasses), then chuck it into your drill just like a regular bit. The softer the wood, the better it works. Don't press down too hard; your improvised bit will easily bend.

Q I'm forever searching for my drill chuck key. Can I replace it with a keyless version?

A Probably, but before you start taking your drill apart, make sure the manufacturer offers a compatible keyless chuck, or that you can find a generic version that will fit.

To replace a keyed chuck with a keyless chuck:

1 Open the jaws of the chuck and remove the chuck screw that holds the chuck to the drill. It will be reverse-threaded, so turn it clockwise to loosen it.

2 Place the drill on a solid surface, position the key in the chuck and whap the chuck with a wood or plastic mallet so the chuck is forced to rotate counter-clockwise. You may need to do this more than once to jar it loose.

3 Remove the old chuck, thread the new keyless chuck onto the drill spindle (hand-tight will do), and firmly reinstall the chuck screw.

Q How do I sharpen a dull spade bit?

A Secure the bit vertically in a vise. Lightly rock a fine-tooth file on one of the beveled horizontal sections until you can feel the existing bevel, then give it five strokes. Do the same on the other side. Repeat this until these "flats" are sharp. (One seat-of-the-pants sharpness test is to run your fingernail across the edge; if it catches or shaves your nail a little, it's sharp.) Give a few quick strokes to the sides of the flats to square them up. Then sharpen the two sides of the point, again mimicking the existing bevel.

grinding wheel

59°

tool rest

Q Can I sharpen a twist bit?

A Yes. It's a little difficult because there are multiple edges and bevels on a typical twist bit, but you can at least get it cutting better than a dull bit. Before you start, study the tip of a large, sharp twist bit similar to the one you're going to sharpen to determine the angles that need sharpening. You'll note that it comes to a point, which is typically 118 degrees (59 degrees per side). Each side of that tip has a bevel to it, and as that bevel winds its way around the bit, there's usually another, secondary bevel right behind it. Concentrate on sharpening those two surfaces, and you'll be able to get the bit back in working order.

When you get down to doing the actual sharpening, set your drill bit on the tool rest of your grinder and "find" the 59-degree tip angle by feel. As you roll the bit clockwise, move the shaft downward and to the left to sharpen the secondary bevel. It takes practice, but you'll eventually get the hang of it. There also are a number of drill bit sharpening machines on the market (see Resources).

tip: Straight and True

To keep your drill straight and true when boring a horizontal hole with a spade bit, try this: Slip a washer over the shank of the bit, then tighten the bit into the chuck. Position the washer midway along the shaft and drill away. A moving washer will signal that you're tipping the drill up or down. You can keep the drill aligned side-to-side by eye.

Q My neighbor bought a new little cordless drill that works so well he never uses his big drill for driving screws any more. What did he buy?

A He most likely bought one of the impact driver/drills powered by a lithium-ion battery. Unlike a standard drill that has an adjustable chuck, the chucks on these accommodate only standard ¼" hex-shank bits. Impact driver/drills excel at driving screws: They drive them in like a standard drill initially but automatically convert to impact mode when the going gets rough. The impact feature provides better control, reduces the chances of stripping the screw head, and makes it so you don't have to push nearly as hard. The lithium-ion batteries are extremely lightweight and long-lasting, and most of the tools have built-in LED lights so you can see what you're doing. All said and done, it's the perfect tool for driving everything from drywall screws to lag screws.

Q Can I drill accurate 90-degree holes without a drill press?

A Yes. Make a portable drill press by securing two 1×2s together in an L shape. To use it, position the tip of the drill where you want it, snug your L-shaped jig against the sides of the bit to help you straighten it, then, keeping the jig in place, drill your hole. If you need to drill deeper than your jig allows, remove it and let the drilled portion of the hole guide the bit the rest of the way.

Sanders and Portable Power Planers

Whether it's a massive 36"-wide stationary belt sander or it's just you with a piece of sandpaper wrapped around a block of wood, the job of any sander is to replace large scratches with smaller and smaller scratches until the scratches disappear (at least to the naked eye).

Q How can I use a belt sander to sand the edge of a narrow board without the sander rocking and rounding the edges?

A Clamp a 2×2 or 2×4 along the edge of the board so that the belt sander has a wider surface to ride on. It will prevent rocking and also help you maintain an edge that's 90 degrees to the surface of the board. Remember to use scrap blocks between the clamps' jaws and the workpiece to prevent the jaws from leaving marks.

Q I make lots of toys with parts so small it's difficult to clamp them down to sand them. Any thoughts?

A If you don't have a stationary belt or disc sander, one of the best power sanders for small parts is a standard belt sander secured in an upside-down position. Some are designed with a flat top, so they can simply be flipped over; others require a store-bought or shop-made stand. Whichever you have, make sure the unit is clamped securely to your workbench. Note the direction the belt is moving, and take care not to catch any edges, lest your workpiece becomes airborne. You can grip small pieces with pliers or the jaws of a wooden block clamp.

Upside-down belt sanders also work well for sanding curves on larger pieces. You'll have better visibility and less arm strain moving a 2-pound piece of wood across a stationary belt sander versus wrestling a 12-pound belt sander across a stationary piece of wood. You can use the back part of the sander's case or cowl as a resting place for the curved part of the workpiece not being sanded; it will help keep the edge square to the sander and allow for better control.

Q When I'm sanding a large, flat panel, how can I make sure I'm not missing any areas as I progress from grit to grit?

A Draw a series of light squiggles across the face of the board with a pencil, then sand until all the marks are gone. Make a second set of squiggles, change your sandpaper to a finer grit, and sand again.

tip: A Belt Cleaner with Sole

You've probably seen the rectangular-shaped abrasive belt cleaner sticks you can buy for removing sawdust and gunk from sanding belts. But there may be a cheaper alternative right under your nose, or at least under your foot. Store-bought belt cleaners are made from natural crepe rubber, the same material used for making the soles of durable crepe-bottom shoes. The next time your sanding belt or disc gets clogged, try running the sole of an old crepe-bottom shoe across the moving belt in a side-to-side motion. It'll clean it up in a jiffy. Make sure to remove the laces first to avoid entanglement with any moving parts.

Q The Velcro hooks on my random orbital sander no longer grip. What's the cause of the problem and what's the cure?

A Your problem may have been created by applying too much pressure to the sander during the sanding process. Excess pressure can cause the hooks to degrade and lose their holding power. So, lighten up on the pressure and let the weight of the sander do the work. From time to time, use compressed air to blow the sawdust off the pad. Sawdust can contribute to excess heat and Velcro degradation. Always keep paper in place to protect the Velcro hooks. If your pad is completely shot, you can buy a replacement from an authorized dealer, online (see Resources) or at some home centers.

SELECTING A SANDER

A sander's function is simple. So why are there so many options, especially when it comes to handheld sanders? Here's a quick rundown:

Belt sanders excel at quickly removing stock, flattening large panels, and leveling uneven glue joints. The most common size is 3"×21" (3"-wide belt, 21" in circumference), but sizes ranging from 3"×18" to 4"×24" are widely available. Belt sanders are aggressive, and you can easily sand through veneers or gouge workpieces if you're not paying attention. They're also excellent for crude sharpening of chisels and other hand and garden tools.

BELT SANDER

Sheet, palm, and finishing sanders are designed for slow, controlled removal of stock through a back and forth vibrating motion with a slight orbital action. They're light enough to be used with one hand, making them ideal for sanding vertical surfaces, and their square bases make them easy to get into corners. Most accommodate either ⅓ or ¼ sheets of standard sandpaper.

Random orbital sanders combine a spinning disc with an orbital action. They're versatile: able to remove stock quickly with coarse paper or leave a smooth surface with fine paper. Since they minimize cross-grain scratches, they excel at smoothing joints on cabinet face frames, doors, and other projects where boards meet at a right angle. If you have space and budget for only one hand sander, this is an excellent choice.

Detail and profile sanders have small triangular or rectangular sanding heads that allow them to get into tight spaces and corners. They work with a slight orbital motion. Some can accept different shapes of heads and pads for sanding curved and intricate surfaces.

Q I'd rather use Velcro-backed sandpaper than pressure-sensitive paper on my random orbital sander. Can I convert it?

A Yes. You can purchase a conversion kit (see Resources) that consists of a Velcro-faced pad you glue to your existing pressure-sensitive disc. You can also see if your tool was designed to accommodate both types of pads. If so, swapping out the old pad usually involves removing three small screws or one central screw (which may be reverse-threaded) from the bottom of the sander.

Q I've seen portable power planers at a nearby home center. What can they do that a belt sander or hand plane can't?

A A portable power planer is sort of a mutt: It's part belt sander, part hand plane, part router, and part jointer. It's designed like a small-scale, upside-down jointer with a rotating cutterhead flanked by short infeed and outfeed tables, or sole plates. You adjust the front plate to control the depth of the cut, while the stationary back plate serves as the outfeed table. It works faster than a hand plane and cuts a straighter line than a belt sander.

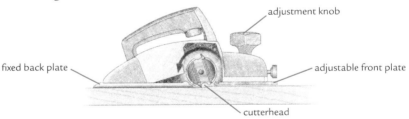

adjustment knob

fixed back plate

adjustable front plate

cutterhead

Q Do I need a portable power planer in my shop?

A A handheld power planer can be used as both a rough carpentry tool and a fine woodworking tool. It excels at:

- ⊙ **Chamfering.** Held at an angle, it can "soften" or bevel the edges of boards. Most machines have a groove in the bed or sole plate of the tool to keep them centered on the edges of a board.
- ⊙ **Fitting.** It's one of the best tools around for shaving the edges of doors to make them fit the jamb.
- ⊙ **Leveling.** A power planer quickly takes the bulge out of the bottom of a bowed joist or the face of a stud, if you need a level surface for hanging drywall or cabinets.

⊙ **Tapering.** With practice, you can become adept at following an angled line to create a tapered leg. Planers are also good for tasks such as creating tapered thresholds and transitions.

Jigsaws

Jigsaws are excellent for making curved cuts, but they also can be used to make straight, beveled, and angled cuts. With the right blade they can also be used for cutting metal, plastics, and other materials. Some first-time woodworkers find them less intimidating to use than circular saws, so if you're thinking about buying your first saw, take a look at a jigsaw.

Q When I use my jigsaw to cut a curve in walnut, I have trouble seeing the line. Any tricks?

A Apply masking tape to your workpiece, and draw the profile on that. Not only will you be able to see your line better, the tape will also prevent the base of your jigsaw from scratching the wood. And if you're cutting plywood, the masking tape will help minimize chipping.

Q Whenever I use my jigsaw to make a cutout in a countertop, the laminate chips. What's the cure?

A Jigsaw blades are designed to cut on the upstroke. The teeth push the workpiece up against the jigsaw's base plate for stability rather than pushing it away. Your laminate is splintering because the teeth are pushing it up and away from the substrate on the upstroke. To avoid splintering, either turn the countertop upside down or use a "reverse-tooth" or laminate blade with teeth designed to cut on the downstroke. The main drawback to reverse-tooth blades is they tend to make the saw jump around, so clamp down your workpiece and hang on tight. If your jigsaw has orbital action, turn it off. You can also make the cut with a fine-tooth metal-cutting blade. It will take longer, but chipping will be minimized.

Q I've made plunge cuts in the middle of a plywood panel with a circular saw before, but never with a jigsaw. How do I do it?

A With the jigsaw tilted up and the nose resting on the plywood, position the blade so it's directly over (but not touching) your cut line. Start the saw and slowly pivot the base downward — *slowly!* Be firm, but don't force the blade; you can easily wind up with a wrecked work-piece and a blade bent at 45 degrees. It may take 10 or 15 seconds for the blade to initially cut through the plywood, but once it has, position the shoe flat and finish your cut. Since shorter blades will flop around less than longer ones, use a short blade; "plunge tip" blades are also available.

If you've never made a plunge cut before, practice on a scrap, as it can take a while to get the hang of it. The alternative to a plunge cut is to drill a ½" starter hole through the plywood (on the waste side of your cut line), insert the blade into the hole, and cut away.

Q I'm looking at jigsaws to buy and note that some have orbital action. What is it and is it worth having?

A In orbital mode, the blade not only moves up and down, but also thrusts forward at a slight angle. The result is a faster cut. Most saws with orbital action have four settings. Set at 0, there's no orbital action, and the saw produces the cleanest, straightest cuts. As the numbers go higher, the orbital action is greater and cutting goes faster, which is especially handy in thicker material. The tradeoff is a slightly rougher and, sometimes, less vertical cut.

Q My home center sells "bimetal" blades. Are the teeth made of one material and the blade another?

A Standard jigsaw blades are made entirely of carbon steel or high-speed steel. Bimetal blades are composed of two types of metal bonded together in layers. The result is a blade that can last 5 to 10 times longer and won't break or shatter. In fact, if you accidentally bend a bimetal blade by bottoming it out, you can easily use a pliers to straighten it and go back to work. Expect to pay about 30 percent more for a bimetal blade.

Q What are some tips for making it easier to cut tight turns with my jigsaw?

A You can use a narrower blade, but making relief cuts will also help. Relief cuts run from the edge of the board (through the part that will become scrap) to the edge of your curve. They allow the waste to fall off in several small sections rather than one large unmanageable chunk. This creates more elbow room for your blade to make tight turns.

Circular Saws

Q I'm building an organizer out of ¾" plywood and need to make a few dozen really straight cuts. How do I do this without a table saw?

A Build a simple straightedge guide out of ½" plywood. Here's how:

1 Use your circular saw to cut a 4"-wide strip — one with a factory edge — from a piece of plywood about 16" wide and 4' to 8' long.

2 Use glue and ¾" drywall screws to secure the 4" strip on top of the remaining 12" piece, with the factory edge oriented as shown.

3 Place the wide part of your circular saw's baseplate against this factory edge and cut through the bottom piece. The cut edge is perfectly straight and is even with the inside edge of the saw blade.

You now have a straightedge guide. To use it, mark your workpiece on both ends, line up the straight-cut edge of your guide with your marks, and clamp or screw the guide in place. Set your saw deep enough to cut through your workpiece (remember to account for the ½" thickness of the guide), then run the wide edge of your circular saw's base plate against the factory edge of your 4" strip, as before. Your cut will be straight and true.

You can use your jig over and over, so label it "TOOL" and store it somewhere. Even woodworkers who own table saws often opt to use a straightedge guide rather than wrestle a heavy, cumbersome 4' × 8' sheet of plywood through their table saw.

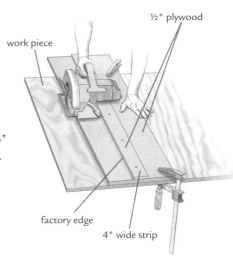

work piece

½" plywood

factory edge

4" wide strip

Q Is there any advantage to the straightedge guides I've seen for sale at woodworking stores?

A Some are actually less convenient than shop-made versions, because you need to measure from the edge of the jig to your cut marks to compensate for the width of your circular saw baseplate. However, some do have additional helpful features, such as built-in clamps and accessories to accommodate a router carriage or a hole-drilling guide.

ACCIDENTAL INVENTION

The history behind many handheld power tools is intriguing. The circular saw, for instance, was invented by Edmund Michel in 1921 while he was trying to develop a faster method to cut sugar cane. What started out as a 2" circular blade attached to the motor of a malted-milk mixer developed into the circular saw most of us have in our workshops today.

Q How do I clean the pitch and dark gunk from the surface of a circular saw blade? It seems to be creating drag as I cut.

A There are blade-cleaning products you can buy, but try this instead: remove the blade and spray it with a cleaner/degreaser, such as Formula 409. Let it sit for five minutes, then scrub it with an old toothbrush, and rinse. You can also try using good old WD–40. Some people use oven cleaner, but the fumes are nasty, and some manufacturers maintain that the caustic chemicals attack the material used to bind the carbide teeth to the blade.

Q There are lots of different sizes of circular saws. What's the smallest one that will cut through a 2×4?

A Circular saws are classified according to the maximum size of blade diameter they can accommodate. They range in size from 4½" trim saws to 16" saws used for landscaping and timber framing. At left is a list of saws and their maximum cutting depths. Note that when the saw is set at a 45-degree angle, the cut is substantially shallower, so plan and buy according to your project needs. The most popular size is the 7¼" version. It's large enough to cut through a 2×4 at a 45-degree angle, yet light enough (around 10 pounds) to operate without wearing you out.

CIRCULAR SAW CUTTING DEPTH		
BLADE DIAMETER	MAX 90-DEGREE CUT	MAX 45-DEGREE CUT
4½"	1¼"	1"
5½"	1¾"	1⁵⁄₁₆"
6½"	2⅛"	1⁹⁄₁₆"
7¼"	2⅜"	1¾"
8¼"	2⅞"	2¼"
10"	3¾"	2¾"
16"	6¼"	4¼"

Q I use the notch in the front of my circular saw's baseplate to follow the line when I cut, yet my cuts are often wavy. What am I doing wrong?

A The notch is a good way to line up the blade initially, but once the cutting starts, most carpenters and woodworkers guide the saw by watching the actual blade and line. Since right-handed people stand to the left of the saw, and the blade is usually on the right side of the saw, the view is blocked by the motor. This means leaning your head to the right so you can see the blade, or sighting through the little space near the front of the saw.

Q How do I make a cut in the center of a piece of ¾" plywood using a circular saw?

A The technique is known as "plunge cutting." Done correctly, you can create clean, crisp cuts. The key is to work decisively. Set the cutting depth to about ⅞". With the saw tilted and the nose of the baseplate pressed firmly against the plywood, retract the blade guard and hold it with your thumb, then visually align the blade with your line. Make sure the blade is well above the surface of the wood so it can spin freely. Pull the trigger and let the motor come up to full speed, then gradually — but with conviction and a firm grip on the saw — lower the spinning blade into the plywood and push forward.

If you approach this timidly, the blade can catch on the plywood, causing the saw to "run" back toward you. This can potentially damage both your workpiece and you, so stay clear of the "kickback" path. When you lower the blade, the initial plunge cut will be several inches long, so position your saw along the line so the initial plunge doesn't cut too far forward or aft. Practice on scrap plywood first.

Q How do I prevent hardwood plywood from splintering when I cut it with my circular saw?

A There are several steps that will help. The more of them you use, the crisper your cut will be:

⊙ Set your saw to the proper depth: about ⅛" deeper than the material is thick. The less amount of blade that runs through the wood, the less chance of burning, splintering, and kickback.

⊙ Use a fine-tooth blade designed for cutting plywood and melamine, or at least a 60- to 80-tooth blade.

⊙ Cut with the good side down. That way, the teeth are pushing the surface veneer (on the good side) up against the plywood core rather than away from it, which can cause chipping.

⊙ Mark your line by scoring it with a utility blade. A few passes will be enough to cut through the entire veneer layer. Then cut to the "scrap side" of the line. The scored mark will prevent splintering.

⊙ You can also try firmly pressing masking tape over the cut line to control splintering. When you remove it, pull it off in a perpendicular direction to the cut.

Routers

Though routers are most commonly used to cut profiles along the edges of boards, they can be used for dozens of other tasks: cutting grooves in the face of a board, crafting moldings, making cabinet doors, creating dovetails, and much more. They can really kick your woodworking skills up a notch. To get a general sense of their versatility and usefulness, just browse through the hundreds of router bits available in woodworking catalogs.

Q I've caught the woodworking bug and am itching to go router shopping. What should I look for?

A If you want a workhorse that can handle any task you throw at it now and in the future, buy one that has:

⊙ At least 12 amps or 2¼ horsepower. You can buy a larger one that will provide more oomph for a router table setup, but above a certain size they become unwieldy to control for handheld operations.

⊙ Variable speed so you can adjust the speed for different sizes of bits and different types of wood.

⊙ Collets for both ¼"- and ½"-shank bits. Switching collets usually takes less than a minute.

Also consider a router kit, which includes the router motor unit and two bases — a fixed base and a plunge base — that can be easily interchanged. Some woodworkers permanently mount the fixed base in their router table and use the plunge base for day-to-day routing.

Many woodworkers have more than one router in their tool arsenal, and those who do repetitive tasks, such as chamfering or rounding-over the edges of boards, often have routers dedicated to that specific task.

Q Why do some router bits have a roller or nub on the bottom?

A Almost every routing operation requires a guide — either the router bit, an edge guide, or a fence — to control the router or the workpiece (one exception is freehand carving, which involves no guide). The bits with a roller bearing or nub on the bottom are often referred to as *edge-guided* (or *bearing-guided*) bits. The roller or nub follows the edge of the board, while the cutter above cuts the profile. These bits are usually used in handheld routers and can follow a straight or curved edge. Due to their design, they can cut profiles only on the edges or ends of boards

EDGE-GUIDED BIT

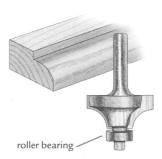

roller bearing

Those without a nub or roller are often referred to as *groove-forming* bits. These can cut grooves and profiles, as well as perform other tasks, anywhere on the face or edge of a board. They must be guided by a straightedge clamped to the workpiece, or by a template, or they are used in conjunction with a router table and fence. Most woodworkers keep both types in their arsenal of tools.

GROOVE-FORMING BIT

Q How do I prevent splintering, especially when I rout the end grain of a board?

A Picture your router bit as a spinning blade that bites into material, then "pushes" it out of the way as it moves along the board. There are three things you can do to ensure that it bites and pushes cleanly:

 1 Make sure the bit is sharp; dull, chipped or burned bits tend to tear the wood rather than cleanly cut it.
 2 If the profile you're cutting is deep and/or wide, make the cut in several progressively deeper passes.
 3 Rout the end grain first. That way, even if the end grain corner does chip or tear a little you can clean up the flaw when you rout the sides.

Q Does it matter which direction I move my router?

A Yes. You'll get a smoother, more controlled cut by moving the router so the cutters rotate into the wood. Router bits rotate clockwise (viewed from the top). Since you want the bits to bite into the wood (instead of "climbing" or "running" along it) move your router from left to right along the edge of a board that's facing you. On the inside of a cutout, move the router clockwise.

Q I often have trouble with splintered and choppy edges when I use large-diameter bits in my router. What am I doing wrong?

A Slow down. The larger the bit, the faster it moves at the outer rim. For instance, a ½"-diameter bit running at 25,000 rpm travels at about 35 mph at its perimeter, while a 3"-diameter bit spinning at the same 25,000 rpm is traveling over 200 mph at the perimeter. Perimeter speeds in excess of 100 mph increase vibration and also the likelihood of burning and tearout. High speeds can also shorten the life of your bit. These are all reasons why we recommend purchasing a variable-speed router. Here are the recommended approximate speeds for different sizes of router bits:

- ⊙ Less than 1" outer diameter — top speed
- ⊙ 1" to 2" outer diameter — 16,000 rpm
- ⊙ 2" to 3" outer diameter — 12,000 rpm
- ⊙ Over 3" outer diameter — 10,000 rpm

Q I have a friend who moves her router opposite to the recommended direction when routing highly figured and grainy wood. Isn't that dangerous?

A She's making a climb cut, and there are a few situations where it's a good idea. Picture this: You're routing the edge of a walnut board with your bit merrily biting and pushing the wood out of the way. You come to a beautifully figured part of the board where the grain swirls and changes directions. If you proceed in the normal direction, your bit could grab some of that wild and reversed grain and rip out a chunk of the grainy section it's approaching.

However, if you rout the "grainy" part of the board from the opposite direction, performing a climb cut, your bit is going to bite off just little bits of the grainy area in stages. After that, you go back and complete the unrouted portion in the normal left-to-right direction. When you reach the swirled section that's been climb-cut, the material that's most prone to catching and ripping has already been removed, yielding a smoother final cut. Always hold the router tightly during a climb cut, and move it with a steady hand; the router will want to pull itself into the cut. Always take light passes. If you've never done it before, practice on a scrap.

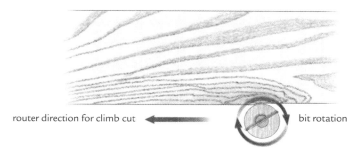

router direction for climb cut ◄———————— bit rotation

Q Even when I'm careful, I tend to burn some hardwoods when I rout them. What's the solution?

A Cherry, hard maple, and some other hardwoods can burn from being routed too quickly or too slowly. You want to find a happy medium: slow enough for a clean cut, yet fast enough to avoid burns. If you have a variable-speed router, try adjusting the speed. If that doesn't work, rout your edge just a whisker shy of your desired final depth, then adjust your router a whisker deeper and make one final, light — and ideally non-burning — pass.

Q I don't rout boards standing on edge very often, but when I do, I have trouble keeping the router balanced. I usually wind up with dips and gouges. Is there a trick?

A Clamp a 2×2 to your board so it's flush with the edge surface. The wider surface that's created will help keep your router from tipping. The ideal solution is to use a router table (see next chapter).

router

guide board

workpiece

Q I just wrecked a tabletop because the router bit slipped and cut deeper than I'd intended. What happened, and how can I prevent it in the future?

A If the collet holding the shank of the bit was tightened sufficiently, there are three things to check:

connected
to router
motor
shaft

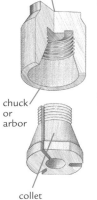

chuck
or
arbor

collet

1 Did you install the bit correctly? If you install the shank only partway into the collet, the jaws that close around the shank don't have as much to grip onto. To install a bit correctly, insert the shank until it bottoms out (or until the cutters contact the end of the collet), then pull it out about ⅛". Make sure to pull it out that small amount; a bit that's bottomed out may vibrate its way outward to increase the depth of cut. In addition, the heat transmitted can damage the motor.

2 Is the shank of your bit clean and smooth? Pitch, rust, oils, and other gunk can cause a bit to slip. Little nubs and spurs can prevent the collet from gripping the shank around its entire circumference. Remove gunk with WD-40, then use fine steel wool to polish the shank smooth and clean. Never use sandpaper; it can create grooves in the shank, giving the collet less "meat" to grip.

3 Is the collet doing its job? First, make sure it's clean. Use a fine-bristle brass brush (one that looks like a mini baby-bottle brush) to remove any pitch, grime, and rust from the hole inside the collet. Then, inspect the hole to see if it's worn more at the bottom and/or top than in the middle. This "bell-mouthing" means there's less contact area between the collet and the shank. If you see this or other forms of damage, replace the collet.

Q Can I sharpen a dull router bit?

A Yes, but sharpen only the flat sides of the cutters. For high-speed steel bits, use a regular oilstone or waterstone; for carbide bits, use a diamond hone. First, clean the bit with paint thinner or denatured alcohol. Run the flat side of one cutter across the stone for 5 to 10 strokes, then give the other cutter the same number of strokes. Repeat until the cutting edges are restored.

Never try to sharpen the beveled edge of a router bit; you'll change the cutting profile and could affect the balance of the bit. You can have bits reground and sharpened by a good sharpening shop, but it might cost more than buying a new one. **NOTE:** It's better to "touch up" the edges of a router bit occasionally, rather than waiting too long and trying to sharpen it when it's extremely dull.

Q What are the advantages of router bits with ½" shanks over those with ¼" shanks?

A Many routers, especially larger ones, can accommodate collets that can accept both shank sizes. Given the choice, buy bits with a ½" shank. The larger circumference gives the collet more surface area to grab onto, meaning less chance of slipping. They also run smoother and therefore cut cleaner. Home center tool aisles are dominated by bits with ¼" shanks. For the widest selection of ½"-shank bits, head to a specialty woodworking store or order online (see Resources).

Q Carbide bits cost three or four times as much as steel bits. Are they worth the money?

A Yes, carbide holds a sharp edge up to 25 times longer than steel. They cost more initially, but in the long run you'll be money ahead.

Q What are the advantages of spiral bits over straight bits?

A Straight bits have one or two cutting blades that "chop" the wood as they spin, while spiral bits have one long continuous cutter — with one part always in contact with the wood — that "shaves" the wood. This produces a cleaner, smoother cut. You can buy both "up-cutting" and "down-cutting" spiral bits, which offer another advantage: They'll press plywood veneers against, rather than away from, the plywood core to prevent splintering as they cut. Which type you use depends on whether the good side of the plywood is up or down and whether the bit is used in a handheld or table-mounted router.

Q I need to rout the edges of some 3"×3" corner blocks. They're too small to clamp down. How do I keep them from moving?

A Set your piece on a router pad, a thin mat made of natural rubber, or other nonslip material that clings to the workbench. When not in use, roll it up and store it out of the way. A cheap alternative is a scrap of carpet pad (although its stickiness diminishes over time, and the cushiness doesn't provide a rock-solid base). You can also place a strip of double-sided tape on your work surface to hold small pieces temporarily.

Q It seems like I need three hands to operate my plunge router for some tasks: two to hold the router in position and another to turn on the switch. Is there an easy solution?

A Consider purchasing a foot pedal switch. There are two kinds: The *standard* version turns it ON with one click and OFF with another. The *dead man* version directs power to the router only when you're pressing down on the pedal.

Q I've heard I can use my router as a jointer to create straight, square edges. Is that true?

A Yes. Build a straight-edge guide similar to the one shown in the section on circular saws (see page 97). To straighten the edge of a board, position your guide so the router bit will trim off about ⅛" of material. Insert a long straight-cutting bit in your router, then run the base of your router along the guide strip to trim and straighten the edge.

Tool Care and Maintenance

Q When I work on big woodworking projects in our backyard, the nearest outlet is over 40 feet away. What size of extension cord should I use so I don't overtax my tools?

A The farther you are from the outlet and the higher the amperage of the tool, the beefier the extension cord you need. In one of those weird numerical twists of fate, the smaller the gauge number, the more heavy-duty the cord is. For a 50' run, use the following size of extension cord based on the amperage rating of the tool. You can't go wrong using a heavier (lower gauge) extension cord than the recommended size.

- 1 to 10 amps: 18-gauge
- 11 to 14 amps: 16-gauge
- 15 to 18 amps: 14-gauge
- 19 to 20 amps: 12-gauge

Q My router seems to be losing its zip and emits a strange "burning electrical" smell. What's the problem?

A Chances are it's time to replace the brushes. Brushes are small chunks of carbon that press against the spinning commutator to deliver current to the motor. Small springs apply pressure to the brushes to keep them seated against the commutator, and eventually the brushes wear down and become shorter. After 50 to 100 hours of use, it's time to replace most brushes. Your first task is to find the correct replacement brushes. Purchase them from authorized tool dealers or from websites (see Resources).

To replace the brushes, unplug the tool and unscrew the small, round brush holder caps located on each side of the motor. Remove the worn brushes and springs. Install the new ones, making sure not to crimp the spring, then reinstall the caps. Run the router for five to ten minutes without any load so the brushes can seat themselves firmly against the commutator. If your tool's brushes aren't easily accessible, you might want to have a repair shop do the replacement.

Q I cut through the power cord of my circular saw. Is it okay to use wire nuts to splice the wires back together again?

A No, you should replace the entire cord. Bring the saw to a repair shop, or do the following:

1 Purchase an appropriate replacement cord with the correct amp rating for the tool (see Resources).

2 Unplug the saw. Remove the screws of the handle housing, and open up the housing.

3 Make a sketch or take a digital photo to show how the cord and its wires are routed and connected to the switch.

4 Free the old cord, as needed, without disconnecting the individual wires from the switch. You may need to remove a cord retainer to free the cord.

5 Place the new cord next to the old one and replace the wires one at a time, so you don't get them mixed up. Anchor the cord, as needed, then reassemble the handle housing.

tip: Blow 'em Away

If you have an air compressor, use a blower nozzle or gun to blow dust out of the motor vents of your power tools before storing them. It will help your tools run cooler and last longer.

Project: Router Perch

Every router needs a place to call home. This router perch provides a place to park your tool in an upright position, even when it's powered down and the bit is still coming to a stop. By cutting slots and drilling holes in the base, you can provide a convenient storage place for wrenches, collets, bushings, and bits. Router bases come in a variety of shapes and sizes; modify this plan to accommodate yours. A few key points:

◇ All the parts can be cut from ¾" plywood — a great opportunity to use up scraps.

◇ Build your perch so the "lips" of the angled sides stop your router over the V-shaped cutout with no chance of your largest bit contacting the surrounding wood.

◇ If you frequently use longer bits, make your platform taller to accommodate them.

◇ Use glue and wood screws to secure the router platform to the base.

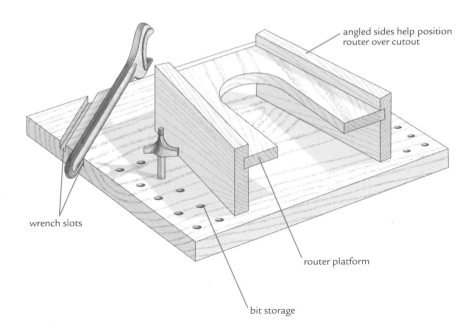

angled sides help position router over cutout

wrench slots

router platform

bit storage

Stationary Power Tools

5

*Man is a tool-using animal — without
tools he is nothing, with tools he is all.*
— THOMAS CARLYLE

As your woodworking skills grow, so will your desire to acquire large, sturdy, stationary power tools. The first logical purchase? A table saw. Second on the list? Most likely a miter saw, drill press, or bandsaw. If you yearn to turn rough lumber into finished lumber, sooner or later you'll need a jointer and surface planer, too. If you're cramped for space, check out benchtop tools. Manufacturers have come a long way in creating space-saving versions of the big boys that deliver excellent, accurate results. With power comes responsibility; your number one responsibility with these workhorses should be safety.

Table Saws and Radial Arm Saws

Table saws excel at ripping boards and plywood to width, and radial arm saws shine when it comes to cutting these materials to length. With the right jigs, skills, and know-how, they can each tackle one another's "specialty" with aplomb — and perform dozens of other tasks as well.

Q How high above the board's surface should the blade be when I'm making a cut with a table saw?

A Somewhere between ⅛" and ¼". This is high enough for sawdust and chips to be expelled from the cut, but low enough to minimize extra drag on the blade and potential hazards.

Q I've heard it's dangerous to run a table saw without a splitter. What is a splitter and what does it do?

A A splitter is a thin piece of material, usually metal, that is positioned directly behind and in line with the blade (see next question).

It helps prevent kickback in two ways. First, it helps keep the saw kerf open so the two sides of the cut don't pinch the back of the blade, causing it to throw the board back toward you.

Second, a less commonly understood function of the splitter is to help keep the board pressed solidly against the rip fence. If even a small gap opens up between the board and rip fence at the back of the blade, the piece can suddenly rotate (or try to rotate), become momentarily wedged between the fence and blade, then hurtle back toward you. To further minimize the risk of kickback, make certain your rip fence is evenly aligned with the blade, keep your blade guard in place, and use a push shoe (see Make Your Own Push Sticks and Shoes, on page 32) to keep the board flat against the table as you saw.

Q How do I create a straight edge on a board that has two crooked edges?

A Use screws to secure the board to a long, straight piece of plywood, with the part of the board you want to remove overhanging the edge of the plywood. Set the fence of your table saw to the width of your plywood and run the piece through to create a straight edge. If you want both edges straight, remove the board from the sled, adjust your fence, and run the board through your table saw with the newly straightened edge against the fence.

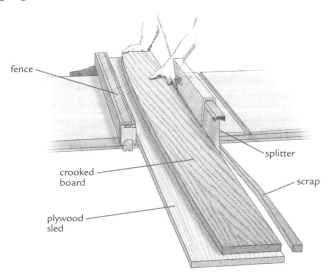

fence

splitter

crooked
board

scrap

plywood
sled

Q The miter gauge for my table saw wiggles in the slot. How do I eliminate that?

A If it only wiggles a little, move it to your workbench and use a center punch to create a series of dimples along one edge of the bar. The dimples should expand the bar enough to fill any gaps and eliminate any slop. Big wiggles require buying a new gauge or an adjustable version that you can adjust to fit snugly in the slot.

Q The arrow on my table saw's bevel gauge points to zero, but the edges of the boards I rip aren't square. How do I fix the problem?

A What the gauge reads and what the saw cuts aren't always one and the same. This is particularly true on smaller benchtop saws. To see if your blade is truly 90 degrees to the table, crank it all the way up and check the angle with a small engineer's square. Make sure the vertical leg is lying flat against the body of the blade, not touching the teeth, or you can get a false reading. To find out how to adjust the "stop" that positions your blade square to the table, consult your owner's manual. It usually involves adjusting a bolt and locknut.

Q Several times when ripping thin strips on my table saw, I've had them disappear in the gap between the blade and the throat plate. How do I avoid this accident-waiting-to-happen?

A Use a "zero-clearance" insert. As the name implies, it leaves no gap around the blade. You can purchase one through specialty woodworking stores (see Resources).

To make your own, remove the throat plate that came with your saw and trace the shape onto a piece of plywood or plastic that's the same thickness as the throat plate. Also mark any screw holes. Use a jigsaw or bandsaw to cut out the shape, then drill and countersink any mounting holes. Lower the blade of your saw, and test-fit the new insert for size and thickness. If it fits tight and flush, secure the new plate in place with screws or with the fence positioned over it but out of the way of the blade. Turn on the saw and slowly raise the blade up and through the insert to create your zero-clearance throat plate.

lower blade to proper height before use

zero-clearance throat plate

Q I'm making a set of play blocks and need to cut 100 the exact same size. I tried setting my rip fence "block width" away from the blade, then used my miter gauge to guide the board as I made the cut. The first block nearly launched itself through the wall. How do I do this safely?

A Pinching a small, unsupported cutoff piece between the rip fence and saw blade is a recipe for disaster. The safe way to cut multiple small pieces is to secure a stop block to your rip fence well in front of the blade. Use that to set the length of your cut, then hold the board tightly as you use your miter gauge to guide the block past the blade. You may need to attach an auxiliary fence to your miter gauge to give it enough length to guide your workpiece.

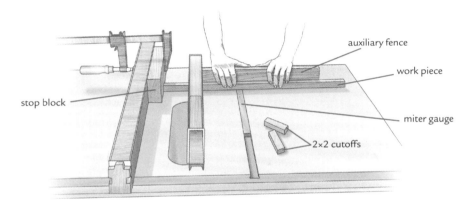

auxiliary fence

work piece

stop block

miter gauge

2×2 cutoffs

Q How can I tell when it's time to sharpen or toss my carbide-tipped blade?

A Replace or sharpen the blade if:
- The blade consistently creates burn marks on both sides of a cut
- Your saw bogs when you feed plywood through it at your normal rate
- It's generating "saw powder" rather than sawdust
- You feel like you're muscling your boards through the saw

Q Which makes more sense: to buy a new carbide-tipped blade or have an old one resharpened?

A If your blade gave you good service life when it was new, it's of a high enough quality to resharpen. You have three options:

1 Bring it to your neighborhood hardware store, although chances are they'll send it out, rather than sharpen it on-site.

2 Find your own local sharpener by looking online or in the phone book under "Saws: Sharpening & Repair."

3 Locate a sharpener via the Internet and send your blades out for sharpening. Most sharpeners charge by the number of teeth.

Q How do I make accurate miters on a table saw?

A You can make a semi-accurate miter using just the miter gauge, but for more serious woodworking, build a miter jig:

1 Cut two strips of wood to fit snugly in the miter slots in the table. Position these runners in the slots, then glue and screw a piece of ½" plywood to them, making sure the front edge of the plywood is centered and perpendicular to the slots.

2 Slide your "sled" into the blade to create a 6"-long kerf.

3 Use a framing square or triangle square to establish lines at a 45-degree angle to the kerf. Screw fences to the lines.

To use the jig, position your board on the jig, then slowly push the sled far enough into the blade to make the cut, then back the sled out again. If you remove your blade guard, work with the utmost caution.

To test your jig for accuracy, cut four 1×2s to 4" long with miters on each end. Assemble them into a frame, check for any gaps at the miters and adjust the fences accordingly. For wider stock, create a larger sled.

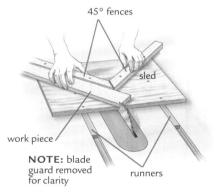

45° fences

sled

work piece

NOTE: blade guard removed for clarity

runners

Q How do I make accurate crosscuts on my table saw?

A You build a crosscut sled similar to the way you build a miter jig (see above), but instead of securing two fences at an angle, secure a solid fence perpendicular to the blade. You can use only one miter slot runner. Build your sled about 1" longer than needed, then raise the blade to the height of the fence, and trim the edge of the sled. When

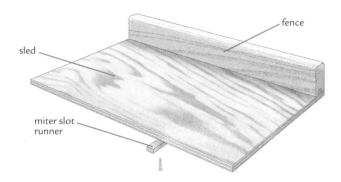

you make a crosscut, simply align your cut mark with the edge of the sled and cut away. It's easy to cut multiple pieces the exact same length by attaching stop blocks to the sled or by securing a clamp to the fence at the desired distance from the blade.

Q I'm going to make my own lattice panels and need dozens of thin, uniform strips of cedar. How do I cut these safely, without having to reset my fence with every cut?

A Since you need to support and push each strip all the way through, using a standard push stick is impossible. You'll need to make a special jig and push stick:

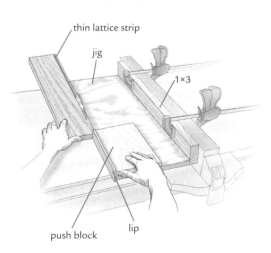

Note: Blade guard removed for clarity.

1 Secure a 1×3 to the edge of a piece of plywood to create an L. Clamp the L to your table saw fence, then adjust the fence so the distance between the edge of your jig and the blade is the width of your lattice strips.

2 Create a special low-profile push block by securing a 1¼"-wide strip to the edge of a ¾" scrap of plywood, so there's a lip on the bottom.

3 Feed your workpiece through the table saw using your jig as a temporary fence, and use the push block to push the cut strip safely past the blade.

Q I'm pondering whether to buy a table saw or a radial arm saw. What are the pros and cons of a radial arm saw?

A Radial arm saws have lost some of their popularity in recent years. Some cite safety as a cause: A large, partially exposed, whirling blade riding on a movable track created a recipe for disaster in the hands of some operators. The emergence of the sliding compound miter saw also made a dent in the radial arm saw market; like the radial arm saw, it excels in crosscutting wide boards and making compound angle cuts.

That said, radial arm saws have their strong points: With the right accessories, they can even be used for drum sanding and other tasks. They're ideal for cutting dadoes and rabbets, since you can line up your marks with the blade and see the actual grooves as they're being cut. Also, because of their design, they can be stationed against a wall (versus the middle of a shop) for most tasks.

On the downside, radial arm saws are problematic when it comes to ripping boards to width. Their ripping capacity is limited by the length of the arm. The board (and/or your push stick) must pass beneath the arm and motor housing during the cut. Radial arm saws also have more parts that require adjustment, and the cantilevered arm can flex or deflect under certain loads and conditions. Some call it a jack-of-all-trades but master of none.

A table saw, in combination with a sliding compound miter saw, will handle most tasks a radial arm saw can perform and do them more accurately. But if you have a small shop and a good head for safety, and you like the idea of a tool that can perform a multitude of tasks well but not perfectly, then look into a radial arm saw.

tip: Lock 'em Up

To prevent curious children and disaster-prone neighbors from playing with your table saw and other interesting power tools, feed a small luggage lock through the little hole in one of the plug prongs, and close the lock.

Q I need a new saw blade for my radial arm saw. Can I just use a standard table saw blade?

A No. A radial arm saw blade rotates away from you and cuts as it's pulled toward you. Because of this, the blade tends to want to "climb over" the wood as it cuts. This scenario creates a situation that's dangerous and can leave behind a rough cut. To minimize this tendency, use a saw blade with less aggressive teeth, one that has a very low (or even negative) hook angle. Most specialty woodworking stores sell them.

Q I have an old Sears radial arm saw. A woodworking buddy of mine told me that a free repair kit for a new blade guard was available for some older models. How do I find out if mine qualifies?

A In cooperation with the Consumer Product Safety Commission, Emerson Tool Company is recalling about 3.7 million Craftsman radial arm saws that were sold without a guard that completely covered the blade. The saws were sold between 1958 and 1992. For some saws that can't accept the new guard, Emerson is offering $100 for the return of the saw carriage and motor assembly. Visit www.rasrecall.com or call 800-511-2628 for more information.

Jointers

A jointer's main missions in life are to straighten edges, flatten faces, and square up stock. To do this, there is a fixed outfeed table set precisely to the height of the cutters and an infeed table that you adjust to control the depth of the cut. A fence holds your workpiece square to the table.

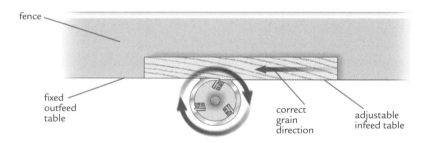

fence

fixed outfeed table

correct grain direction

adjustable infeed table

Q Does it matter which way I run a board through the jointer in regards to grain direction?

A You want to feed the board through the jointer with the grain running downhill, or from high to low as it approaches the cutterhead (see above). This will minimize tearout and give you a smoother cut.

Q How do I joint the edge of a board so it's ready for edge-gluing?

A Adjust the infeed table to take a cut about ¹⁄₃₂" deep. Place the board on the infeed table with one face pressed tightly against the fence. Apply pressure on the leading edge of the board as it passes over the cutting head, then gradually shift pressure to the outfeed table. Work slowly and keep your hands away from the cutterheads. This requires a special touch, so practice on scrap boards before working on the real thing.

Q When I use a jointer to flatten the face of a cupped board, do I put the concave or convex surface against the table?

A Put the concave side down so the board has two edges to rest on as you work. Make a number of shallow passes until the board is flat. Then run the board through your planer with the newly flattened side facedown. This will create a board of uniform thickness.

Q How do I prevent jointer accidents?

A Always leave the blade guard in place. Stand beside the jointer — not behind it — so you'll be out of harm's way if the wood kicks back. With shorter boards, position yourself so you can remain stationary through the entire process. Use push shoes and push sticks to maintain steady downward pressure, and keep your hands away from the cutterhead area. Avoid jointing boards less than 12" in length.

Q How do I joint a board when the grain direction changes or it has knots along the edge?

A Do the same thing you'd do if you were mowing tall grass: adjust the height of the mower so it cuts less per pass, slow down, and make sure your blade is sharp. More specifically:

⊙ To make several shallow cuts rather than one deep one, adjust the table so you remove only ¹⁄₆₄" per pass.

⊙ You can't adjust the speed of your jointer, but you can slow down the feed rate so your blades make more cuts per inch, reducing the chance of tearout.

⊙ Make sure your knives are sharp. Some woodworkers adjust their fence so there's a 1" section of the knives that they don't use for day-to-day jointing. That section of the cutterhead remains sharper and creates a smoother cut on troublesome boards.

Q I'm consistently winding up with concave edges after jointing. What am I doing wrong?

A It most likely has to do with how your infeed and/or outfeed tables are set. If they're not parallel to one another and are higher or peaked near the cutter, the result will be concave edges.

Thickness Planers and Sanders

Q I'm debating whether to buy a thickness planer, drum sander, or wide belt sander. I only have the space for one. Which should I buy?

A All three tools accomplish the final goal of creating boards of uniform thicknesses with smooth surfaces, but they go about it in different ways. Thickness planers use rotating knives to cut away surface material, while drum sanders and wide belt sanders use abrasive material to sand it away.

A *thickness planer* is probably your wisest choice if you surface lots of rough-sawn lumber. Most home workshop models have a 15" capacity, which is wide enough for most boards. It works quickly and can remove $1/16$" or more of material in a single pass. But there are trade-offs. The machined surface, though it might feel smooth, may still need to be smoothed or sanded to remove faint ridges or mill marks. Because planers cut the wood, they also have a tendency to tear the surface on boards where the grain changes direction or is highly figured.

A *drum sander* makes more sense if you do most of your work with wood that's already been surfaced. It can't remove material as quickly as a planer, but it can smooth boards and assemblies of any grain orientation, including wildly figured burls and face frames where the boards run at right angles to one another. Since drum sanders usually are open on one side, they can sand a board twice as wide as the drum capacity. It takes time to change the paper, which typically involves wrapping strips of sandpaper around the drum like a barber pole.

A *wide belt sander* works in a similar manner to the drum sander but uses wide continuous belts. It works quickly and accurately, and the price reflects this. Both ends are closed, so you're limited to the actual capacity, which can range from 18" to 50" or more.

Q How do I eliminate the snipe on the ends of boards when I run them through my planer?

A Make certain that the end of your board is well supported as it emerges from the planer. If that end drops, the opposite end will be "levered" up into the cutter as it emerges, creating a shallow gouge.

If that's not the problem, chances are your planer is out of adjustment. If the chip breaker directly in front of the cutter head, or the pressure bar directly after the cutter head, is set too high, gouges can occur. You can also get sniping if the lower infeed or outfeed rollers are set too high. Check your owner's manual for adjustment procedures.

Lighter-weight and less expensive machines sometimes are difficult or impossible to adjust, creating chronic sniping. If that's the case, you can compensate. Make sure your boards are long enough so you can cut off the sniped ends. And feed boards through the planer continuously, end against end, so the internal parts don't flex at the start and end as they would if the boards were fed through individually.

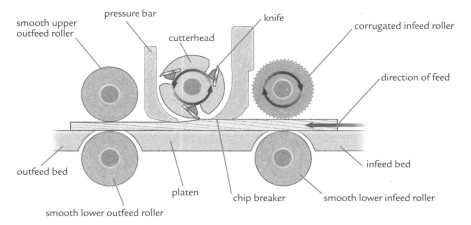

Q I can run a board through my benchtop planer a half a dozen times and it still doesn't remove the twist. What am I doing wrong?

A The only thing a planer will do to a warped or twisted board is to make it into a thinner warped or twisted board. You need to use a jointer or hand plane first to flatten one surface, then feed the board through the planer with that flat face down.

Q Is there any way I can use my planer to turn a twisted board into a flat one of uniform thickness?

A It's time-consuming, but it can be done. You need to create a cradle that solidly supports the twisted board "as is", so you can run it through your planer multiple times to gradually shave off the high spots and eventually create a flat upper surface:

1 Start with a flat ¾"-thick board, the same width and length as the twisted one, and secure 1×2s to all four sides to make a shallow box.

2 Set your twisted board inside the box and examine it. Your goal is to support the underside of the twisted board with blocks and shims (some people use stacks of playing cards for their easy adjustability) so it won't flex under the pressure of the rollers and cutterheads as it runs through the planer.

3 Insert your blocks and shims, set the board back in, and press down. If it rocks, remove the board and adjust the shims and blocks until the board is solidly supported.

4 Run the cradle and board through the planer repeatedly until the upper surface is flat. Remove the board from the cradle, and run it through your planer flat-side down in very small increments. Eventually you'll create a flat board of uniform thickness.

If the twisted board is thick enough, you can actually drive screws into it through the surrounding 1×2s of your shallow box, to lock the board in place. Needless to say, locate your screws so the cutterheads can't hit them.

Q There's a raised line running the length of my board after I run it through the planer. What's the problem?

A Chances are, something created a nick or chip in all of your knives. We say "all" because if there's a nick in just one knife, the other knives (or knife) will knock off the ridge when it passes by them. With some machines you can offset one of the knives just enough so the nicks in the knives don't all align. That way, the offset knife will remove the ridge the other one creates. Otherwise, the knives should be replaced or resharpened.

tip: Winding Sticks Detect Twists

Sometimes it's difficult to tell if a board has a twist in it by simply sighting along the surface. A more accurate way is to use a pair of winding sticks. Any sticks will do, as long as they're straight and uniform. Lay the sticks on each end of the board and sight along the top of one across to the other. If they're not parallel to each other, your board has a twist. Sighting *under* a winding stick will give you a clear sense of how much a board is cupped.

Q I can't adjust my planer to handle boards thinner than ½". Is there still a way to get the job done?

A Make a "planer board" to elevate your thin strips as they run through the planer. Use something flat and smooth, such as ¾" melamine-faced shelving material. Your planer board needs to remain stationary, so make it long enough to add a cleat that can hook over the edge of the infeed table to keep the planer board in place. Since any snipe will be especially apparent on thin material, use stock that's 6" to 8" longer than what you'll need, then cut off the damaged ends.

Miter Saws

Whether you're building a square picture frame or installing molding around the top of an octagonal table, you need a saw that can cut angles accurately and quickly. There's no better tool for the task than a power miter saw.

Q When I cut long moldings on my miter saw, I have trouble keeping the end I'm cutting flat on the table, and the free end flops around. What should I do?

A For safety, accuracy, speed, and your sanity, use some sort of support to hold the free end. That support must be at the same level as the miter saw's cutting surface (its table). You can use a miter saw stand designed specifically for that purpose, an adjustable outfeed roller, or scraps of wood to create the right height.

Consider building the simple stand shown on the next page. It's simply a 2×12 with support tables on each side that butt up to the miter saw table to prevent it from moving. You can build it in about an hour and store it on a wall or shelf when you're done.

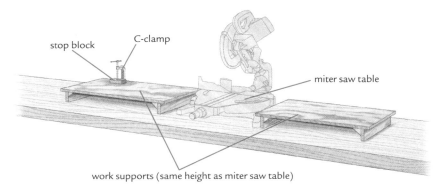

stop block
C-clamp
miter saw table
work supports (same height as miter saw table)

Q I need to cut 80 deck rail pickets the same length. What's a fast, accurate way to do this?

A Use a stop block as shown above, ideally with a miter saw stand like the one described in the preceding question. Measure and mark one picket, then position it on the miter saw so the mark is directly beneath the blade. Take a scrap block, butt it to the opposite end of the picket, and clamp the block to the support table. Make a test cut to make sure your stop block is positioned correctly, then cut away. Always hold onto the workpiece (the one that's between the saw blade and the stop block) to prevent the piece from kicking out.

Q My wood sometimes moves or creeps a little when I cut angles. How do I prevent this?

A If your saw is accurately adjusted and the blade is sharp, you need a better way to prevent the piece from moving as you cut. You can clamp your board to the table with the hold-downs that come with some saws, but using them is time-consuming, and they won't work with all shapes of workpieces. Try adhering strips of self-adhesive, grit-faced, anti-slip tape (grip tape) to the left and right sides of the back fence. This often provides enough grip to prevent your piece from moving.

Q Is there a simple way to check my miter saw to see if it's cutting squarely?

A Set your saw at 90 degrees and cut a scrap 1×2 in half. Place the two pieces on a flat surface, then flip one piece over and butt the two cut ends together. If the two halves create a straight line, your miter saw is adjusted correctly. If the two boards create a slight dogleg, your saw needs adjusting. You can adjust most saws by loosening the screws that secure the fence and pivoting the fence slightly; consult your owner's manual.

flipped over

Q How do I check to see if my miter saw is cutting true 45-degree angles?

A The simplest way is to set your saw at 45 degrees and cut four scrap pieces (all the exact same length, all on the same side of the blade) to create a small test frame. Assemble the pieces into a square and check for gaps at the joints. If there are gaps on the inside, reduce the angle. If there are gaps on the outside, increase the angle. In most cases, the adjustment will be less than 0.5 degrees.

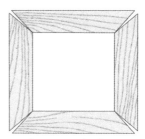

increase angle of cut

Q How do I cut a 50-degree angle with my miter saw?

A Set your miter saw at 5 degrees, and cut a long wedge from the end of a ¾" scrap of plywood. Reset your saw to 45 degrees, place the wedge against the fence, position your board against the wedge, clamp it down, and cut. Clamping is important: The greater the angle of the cut, the greater the tendency of the blade to grab and pull the workpiece.

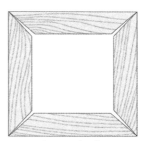

reduce angle of cut

Q My miter saw can't quite cut through a 1×8. Is there any way I can finish the cut without flipping the board over?

A You can often coax a little extra cutting capacity out of a blade. Prop up the board on a scrap block to raise it closer to the center of the blade, where it can cut using more of its diameter.

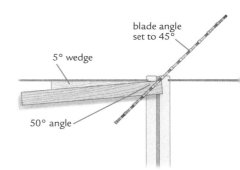

blade angle set to 45°

5° wedge

50° angle

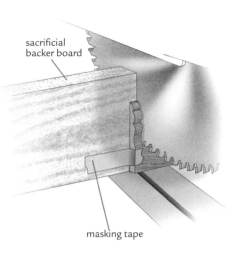

sacrificial
backer board

masking tape

Q When I use my miter saw to cut a small angeled piece or "return" from a molding, the part usually breaks or launches into the great unknown. What can I do to prevent this?

A Short cutoffs have a tendency to slip past the saw fence or get snagged and tossed by the blade once they're free. To prevent this, place a sacrificial backer board against the fence, then position your molding against the backer board, and make your cut. The backer board will support the piece so it stays put. Taping the small piece to the backer board will also help prevent it from being flung. After making your cut, leave the blade in the down position until the blade stops spinning. If you raise the blade while it's still spinning, it has another opportunity to fling your workpiece.

Scrollsaws

A scrollsaw is basically a coping saw blade installed in a sewing machine-like tool that rapidly moves the blade up and down. This allows you to effortlessly make intricate cutouts and turns.

Q How do I know exactly how tightly to install a blade?

A One scrollsaw aficionado tensions her blades so that when she plucks them, they "play" the note an octave above middle C. If you don't have perfect pitch, tension the blade until you hear a crisp melodic note or until the center of the blade deflects no more than ⅛" when gently poked. Your blades will make a thunking sound if installed without enough tension; they'll snap more frequently if installed with too much.

Q Any tips for getting more out of a dull scrollsaw blade?

A Make an auxiliary table for your scrollsaw out of smooth ¾" plywood or MDF. When your blade becomes dull, clamp this auxiliary table to the top of your scrollsaw table. This raises your work so the unused section of the blade higher up can do the cutting.

Q My woodworking store carries dozens of different kinds of blades. How do they differ from one another?

A Scrollsaw blades come in different widths, tooth configurations, and shapes. Blades are usually labeled on a numerical scale: The smaller the number, the narrower the blade and the greater the number of teeth per inch. The very thinnest are labeled with a number preceding the 0 (a #2/0 is narrower than a #2). For thin material or projects with tight turns, use a blade with a smaller number. Some common blades and their characteristics:

- **Standard blades** cut only on the downstroke, meaning they cut slowly but smoothly.
- **Reverse-tooth blades** have teeth at the bottom that cut on the upstroke, in addition to the upper teeth that cut on the downstroke. The result is a smooth cut on both surfaces. They do cause the blade to hop more, so you need to apply more downward pressure as you work.
- **Spiral blades** have cutting edges along their entire circumference so you can make cutouts by shifting the direction of the workpiece rather than rotating it — a handy feature when working with boards too large or unwieldy to turn. The tradeoff is that they create a wider, rougher kerf.
- **Skip-tooth blades** have fewer teeth but run cooler in hardwoods.
- **Crown-tooth blades** have pairs of teeth; one cuts on the upstroke, the other on the downstroke. When worn, these blades can be reversed for a fresh set of cutting teeth.

Q Besides carbon paper, what are some ways to transfer scrollsaw patterns onto wood?

A You have a couple of options:

Soft pencil tracing. For small projects, color the entire back of the pattern with a soft-lead pencil, then flip the pattern design-side-up and tape it to your wood. Use an ink pen to trace the lines and transfer the pattern onto the wood via the graphite you applied to the back.

Newspaper tracing. For larger projects, find a page with lots of printing (classified ads work well) and tape it facedown on the wood. Tape the pattern on top of the newspaper, then use firm pressure and a ballpoint pen to trace the pattern. The newspaper ink will transfer the pattern onto the wood. If you used the classifieds, your pattern will be a series of dashes, so use a pencil to connect the dots. This method works well on painted surfaces, since newspaper is less likely to leave smears and smudges the way graphite or carbon paper might.

Photocopy. You can also photocopy your pattern and, as quickly as possible, use an iron to transfer the ink onto the wood. This is quick and simple, but your image will be reversed.

Bandsaws

Q What's the tightest turning radius different bandsaw blades can cut?

A The narrower the blade, the tighter the radius it can cut. Approximate cutting limitations are:
- ¾" blade — 2½" radius
- ½" blade — 1¼" radius
- ¼" blade — ¾" radius
- ⅛" blade — ¼" radius

Q I need to make a number of 1"-radius turns but have a ½" blade in my bandsaw. Is there some way I can make these tight turns without changing to a thinner blade?

A Slightly rounding the back edges of the blade will allow it to make tighter turns. Set a sharpening stone on edge, hold it at a 45-degree angle to the back of the blade, turn on the saw, and gently press the stone against the blade. Repeat on the other side, then move the stone in a rounding motion to round the back of the blade. You can keep your fingers a safe distance from the blade by epoxy-gluing your sharpening stone to a scrap of wood to create a long-armed paddle. This rounding may also help your blade generally cut more smoothly.

Q Should I use the tensioning knob to loosen the tension on my bandsaw blade every evening?

A Maybe not every evening, but if your saw is going to sit unused for more than a few days, back off the tension a few turns. It will help prevent blades from prematurely breaking and keep the tires from prematurely flattening out. It may even prolong the life of your tension spring.

Q I want to resaw some 6/4" × 8" walnut boards into thinner panels. What's the best way to do this?

A Begin by installing a ¾"-wide blade designed for resawing. Increase the blade tension by a notch to help prevent the blade from bowing or wandering during the cut. You need some form of rip fence to hold the board vertically while resawing. There are two commonly used types of fence:

Tall resawing fence. A long vertical fence is supported and held rigid by right-angle blocks connected to a horizontal base. The base is clamped to your saw table, and the fence is used to guide the piece as you resaw. The drawback to a resaw fence is if your blade starts to drift or wander, you have few options for "steering" the board back on track. If your blade wanders or twists in a consistent manner, you can adjust the angle of the fence to compensate for the movement.

Single-point rip fence. This vertical fence, bullet-shaped in cross-section, is held rigid and upright by support blocks. While resawing with a single-point fence requires more guidance and focus on your part, it does allow you to adjust the course of the cut by steering the back of the board if your blade begins to drift.

Experiment with both types of fences to find the one that works best for you, your saw, your blade, and the type of wood you're resawing.

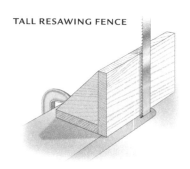

TALL RESAWING FENCE

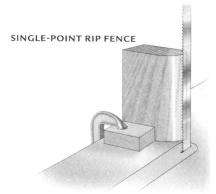

SINGLE-POINT RIP FENCE

Q I've had terrible luck trying to resaw boards wider than 6" on my bandsaw. The blade wanders, the motor bogs down, and I wind up with boards that are bowed and burned. What can I do?

A Sawing through 6" of material is no easy task, and your bandsaw simply may not have enough chutzpah for the job. To make it easier, do some of the preliminary work on your table saw. Raise your table saw blade, then run the board through to create deep kerfs on both edges.

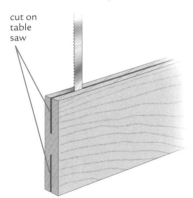

cut on table saw

This may leave you with only a couple of inches of wood left in the center for your bandsaw to cut through. Another advantage of these kerfs is they'll actually help guide your bandsaw blade as it makes the final cut.

The downside to this method is that you'll waste more material because of the wide kerf of the table saw blade. You'll also need to run your board through a planer or drum sander to flatten the uneven surface created by cutting with blades of two different thicknesses.

Q How far from the blade should the side guides and the thrust bearing be on the back?

A Adjust them so they're 0.002" to 0.003" away. This is about the thickness of a piece of notebook paper.

Q When I install a bandsaw blade, should I center it on the upper and lower tires?

A Center the deepest part of the tooth gullet, rather than the blade itself, on the wheel. That way, the wheels will support the part of the blade with the teeth as cuts are being made.

Q What are bandsaw Cool Blocks?

A Cool Blocks is a brand name for one of the many available after-market guide blocks. These are guides that prevent your blade from deflecting from side to side. They're made of a composite material consisting of graphite-impregnated phenolic resin and are intended to replace the original metal blocks on most bandsaws.

Because of their composition, the resin blocks run cooler than the metal-on-metal contact of steel guide blocks. This means you can adjust Cool Blocks so they actually touch the blade, which provides better support and stability. They'll also help extend the life of your blades. There are several other aftermarket guide systems, including some containing ball bearings and ceramic. Some enterprising woodworkers make their own guide blocks from dense, oily woods, such as teak or lignum vitae.

tip: Wax = Less Friction

Before cutting thick wood or curvy components, turn on your bandsaw, set a block of paraffin on the table, and press it along both sides of the blade while it's running. Your lubricated blade will cut cooler and faster. Sand the workpiece edges afterward so the wax doesn't taint your finish.

Lathes

The basic concept of turning is pretty straightforward: Put a piece of wood in a machine that makes it go round and round, and press a cutting tool against it until you've created something round. But once you get beyond the basics, things can get complex fast. Sharpening, bowl turning, segmented turning, and other activities are part art, part science. Learning the craft can be difficult, but the payoff can be fabulous. You'll be able to make everything from 8'-long porch posts to 1"-tall wine stoppers. Here we'll present some of the basics, but we encourage you to further your skills with help from some of the many excellent books and DVDs on the subject (see Resources).

Q What are the basic parts of a lathe, and what do they do?

A Standard lathes have four main components:

⊙ The *bed* is the base of the lathe. It's slotted so other components can slide along its length. The heavier and more rigid the bed, the better.

⊙ The *tailstock* assembly holds one end of the workpiece and can be positioned along the bed to accommodate stock of varying lengths. It contains the free-spinning center, which is normally connected to a piston that can be adjusted to lock the workpiece in place.

⊙ The *headstock* assembly is the motorized end of the lathe and holds the other end of the workpiece. It contains a hollow drive spindle that's tapered to accept a tapered spur center. The spur center is driven into the end of the workpiece before being inserted into the

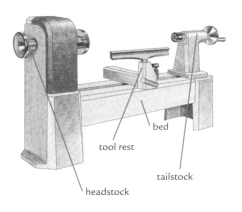

tool rest

bed

tailstock

headstock

drive spindle. Motor speed can be adjusted electronically or by rearranging drive belts on the pulleys.

⊙ The *tool rest* assembly is composed of two components: the sliding base and the tool rest. The base can be positioned anywhere along the bed and be moved in and out depending on the diameter of the workpiece. The tool rest supports your tool. It can be many shapes and sizes and has a shaft that allows it to be adjusted up and down.

Q What do lathe "swing" and "distance between centers" refer to?

A Swing refers to the largest-diameter cylinder that can be turned on a lathe. A lathe with a 16" swing has a little over 8" between the drive centers and bed, and it can accommodate a turning blank with a maximum diameter of 16". Distance between centers, or capacity, refers to the maximum length of a piece that can be accommodated. Most standard-size lathes have a capacity of 32" to 42" — long enough to turn a table leg, which is the longest thing most people turn.

Q Why do some woodturners keep sandbags stacked on the base of their lathe stand?

A Sandbags add mass and stability to the tool, which dampens vibrations and helps the lathe turn smoother and quieter.

Q I'm interested in getting started with turning, but when I walk into my local woodworking store and see dozens of different turning tools, I get overwhelmed. What tools do I really need to get started?

A There are two basic types of turning tools: *cutting tools,* which remove large amounts of material to create the basic shape, and *scraping tools,* which typically are used for removing smaller amounts of material and for smoothing. There are five basic tools that will allow you to get started and perform the most basic tasks:

- ⊙ 1¼" roughing gouge, for turning square stock into cylinders and creating basic shapes
- ⊙ ½" bowl gouge, for further refining the shape and cutting concave shapes
- ⊙ 1" flat skew chisel, for creating V-grooves and small beads
- ⊙ Round nose scraper, for creating and smoothing coves and hollows
- ⊙ ³⁄₁₆" parting tool, for establishing depth reference points before starting to shape the piece.

You'll be surprised at how much detailed work you can do with even a large roughing gouge. One turning expert uses his to make dinky ½"-tall spinning tops. Start with these five, then add tools as needed.

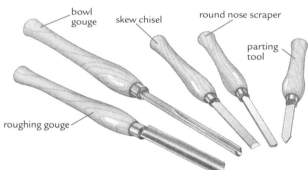

bowl gouge   skew chisel   round nose scraper   parting tool   roughing gouge

Q How can I tell when it's time to resharpen a turning tool?

A A well-sharpened tool will cut almost effortlessly. If you find yourself forcing the tool or generating sawdust instead of larger-size chips or shavings, it's time to resharpen. Torn grain is another sign that your tool is dull.

Q I know that sharpening turning tools is an art in and of itself, but what are some basics?

A Sharpening is a two-step process. First, you need to establish (or reestablish) the correct shape of the cutting edge (whether the tool is old or new) by grinding. Once it's the correct shape, you need to sharpen the cutting edge to the correct bevel angle. Most people use a 36-grit stone in their grinder for shaping and a 60- or 80-grit wheel for sharpening.

As you sharpen your cutting edge, watch the sparks as they fly. When they start trailing over the top of your tool, you'll know you've almost reached the right angle.

Q Lathes seem big, fast, and dangerous. What are some of the safety issues involved?

A Lathes are fairly safe because you control the cutting tool and push it away from you. You can also control the speed of the lathe. But some people are lulled into safety complacency because the tools don't make a lot of noise. There are three areas to watch:

Snags. Beware of loose clothing, jewelry, gloves, long hair, or other items that could get snagged by your spinning workpiece.

Dust. Several woods produce sawdust that can cause skin and respiratory reactions. You can minimize the dangers by using sharp tools that create shavings, not fine sawdust. You should also use some type of dust collection system and wear a good respiratory mask (see chapter 1).

Impact. On occasion, a workpiece can be thrown from the lathe. This happens most frequently when you first start working on the raw blank. Before starting the lathe, make sure all levers are tightened securely. Spin the piece by hand to make sure no part of the workpiece will hit the bed or tool rest. Check to make sure your motor is set to the correct speed for the size of the wood. If you're bowl or plate turning, make certain the blank is secured solidly to the faceplate. When you first switch on the lathe, stay to the side of the "red zone," the rainbow-shaped trajectory a piece would take if it flew off. Always wear a face shield and goggles.

Q Where do I position the tool rest for turning?

A For most turning operations, position the tool rest so the cutting edge of your tool is level with the centerline of your workpiece and about ⅛" away. This means you have to readjust it several times as you reduce the piece in size.

Q I'm building a four-poster bed with 6'-long legs. How do I turn them if my lathe capacity is only 36"?

A Turn your legs in two pieces, then join the pieces together. Create a round tenon 2" or 3" long on the end of one piece, and bore a mortise of the same diameter on the end of the other piece to create a solid joint.

Q What's outboard turning?

A When you want to turn large bowls or platters, the bed of the lathe gets in the way. Outboard turning solves the problem. Some lathes have heads that rotate, some are designed so you can mount your blank on the opposite side of the motor, some are designed specifically for outboard turning, and others won't allow it. Since the wood is mounted only to the headstock, you don't have a tailstock to help stabilize the workpiece, and special chucks and faceplates are required. Some screw to the wood, others bite onto it like a giant drill chuck. You also need a different tool rest setup.

Q What are some things to look for when buying a new or used lathe?

A First ask yourself, "What's the biggest thing I'll ever turn?" If your answer is "pens, wine stoppers, and small bowls," you can get by with a benchtop or mini-lathe. If your answer is "twenty-inch salad bowls" you'll need a massive, heavy-duty lathe that will allow you to do outboard turning.

Whether you're looking at new or used machines, check the locking mechanisms on the tailstock and tool rests to make sure they're solid. Slide the tailstock up to the headstock and make sure the points on the spindles line up exactly. Wiggle the spindles and make sure there's no play in the bearings. Visually inspect the tool for cracked castings. You can often get a great deal on an older lathe made of cast iron with heavy-duty components.

Q At a craft fair I saw some turned bowls that had a checkerboard pattern. How is that done?

A Segmented turning starts with a workpiece made up of multiple pieces of wood, usually of two or more species. The most common type is *ring construction*, which consists of several rings of wood that are glued and sandwiched atop one another like a stack of Lifesavers. Each ring is made of multiple pieces of wood with angled ends that have been glued together to create a circle.

The other common type is called *stave construction*, where longer pieces of wood have been glued together edge-to-edge, like the staves of a barrel. This creates a cylinder which is then turned on the lathe.

Drill Presses

SQUARING UP A DRILL PRESS TABLE

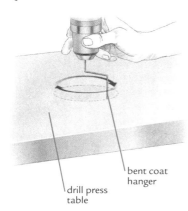

bent coat hanger

drill press table

Q How do I make sure the table of my drill press is square to the chuck?

A Snip off a straight, 8" section of wire coat hanger and make two 90-degree bends in it. Tighten one end in the chuck, then raise the table until the other end of the hanger barely touches the table. Slowly spin the chuck by hand and check for gaps between the end of the coat hanger and table. Adjust your table until the hanger remains at a consistent distance throughout the entire 360-degree rotation.

Q What are some useful accessories?

A A fence is a must. It will allow you to drill consistently aligned holes and, as a safety measure, prevent boards from "helicoptering" if a bit grabs them. Since the only adjustment you need to make to a fence is its distance from the bit, you can make one that pivots on one end and can be clamped on the other.

Q The table of my drill press is so small I have trouble using it for large parts. What's the solution?

A Most drill presses were designed as metal-working tools and haven't evolved much beyond that to make them convenient for woodworking. You can expand the size of the stock metal table by adding a plywood auxiliary table. You can clamp it on, screw it on, or add cleats to the

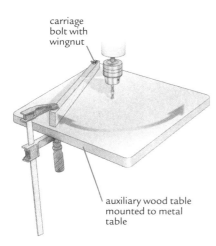

carriage bolt with wingnut

auxiliary wood table mounted to metal table

CREATING A SIMPLE FENCE

bottom so it slips over the existing table. This also provides a forgiving surface if you accidentally bore into it and makes it easy to add jigs and accessories.

Q How do I drill holes into the side of a large dowel or tube and make sure they're centered?

A Use your table saw to create the V-shaped jig shown. Put a small drill bit in the drill press chuck and use that to position the V so it's centered on the bit. Clamp the jig in place, and install the desired drill bit. Then, cradle your dowel in the jig, and drill your holes. If you need to make a series of holes, clamp a fence to the table of your drill press, then slide the jig and dowel along the fence as you bore holes.

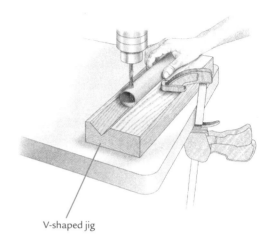

V-shaped jig

Q How does a hollow-chisel mortising attachment for a drill press work?

A These attachments allow you to fit a square peg into a round hole — or at least turn a round hole into a square one. These systems consist of a square, hollow chisel with sharp bevels on all four edges, an auger-type drill bit that fits inside the hollow chisel, and a chisel holder that attaches to your drill press (above the chuck) to position the hollow chisel and prevent it from turning. As the bit bores the hole, the hollow chisel follows directly behind and shears the wood to create the square corners. Shavings exit through the sides of the hollow chisel.

The drill press provides the power for boring the round hole, while your arm supplies the power for pushing the hollow chisel through the wood. Chisel holders can cost as little as $50, and bits run $20 and up, depending on quality and size.

Shapers and Router Tables

Think of a shaper as a router table on steroids. They both cut profiles along the edges and across the faces of boards, but shapers have heftier motors, fences, cutters, and everything else. While table-mounted routers accept standard router bits, a shaper has a stout ½", ¾", or larger spindle protruding through the top to which the cutter (or cutters) are mounted and held in place with a locknut. They're excellent for production work. Most woodworkers get by just fine with a router table. For the smoothest, cleanest results, use bits with ½" shanks, and adjust the speed downward as bit diameter increases (see Routers, in chapter 4).

Q I get the heebie-jeebies whenever I shape small parts on my router table. Is there a good way to hold on tight and maintain control while keeping my fingers safe?

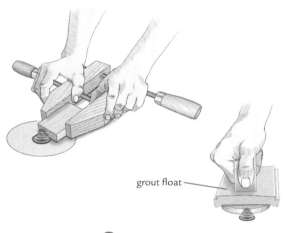

grout float

A You're wise to keep your fingers clear of a bit spinning at 25,000 rpm. You have two good options for holding the workpiece:

1 If the part is rectangular, you can tighten it into a wooden hand-screw clamp and use that to guide your piece past the bit.

2 For curved or irregularly shaped pieces, try holding the piece with a grout float. The rubber bottom grips tenaciously while creating a barrier between the bit and your hand.

Q While rounding the edges of a disc on my router table, the piece flew out of my hands when it first contacted the bit. How do I prevent this?

A You need a starter pin. Drill a hole in your router table 2" or 3" from the bit, and insert a temporary hardwood dowel. Brace the work-piece against the pin, then slowly pivot it into the bit. Move the work-piece so it's rotating into the cutters. For safety, never pinch the piece between the pin and the bit.

Simple Shop Cart

Stationary power tools are time-savers, and you can make them even more efficient with the addition of a shop cart. A wheeled 24" × 30" cart is large enough to help you convoy a full sheet of plywood through your shop, yet it's small enough to stash in a corner when not in use. It's great for production work, such as when you're running multiple boards through your planer or table saw multiple times. And it comes in handy for when you need an extra mini-workbench. If you build it the same height as your table saw, you'll have a ready-to-use outfeed table. Include a lower shelf for storage and locking casters for stability. Key construction details include:

◇ Buy your casters first, especially if you want your cart to be at the same height as your table saw. Swivel casters at least 3" in diameter will provide the smoothest ride.

◇ Dado out two sides of your 4×4s to accommodate the 2×4 framework of the top and lower shelves. Glue and screw the 2×4s in place for rigidity.

◇ Screw, but don't glue, the ¾" top shelf in place. This will make it easier to replace in the future.

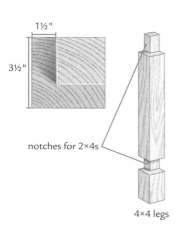

1½"

3½"

notches for 2×4s

4×4 legs

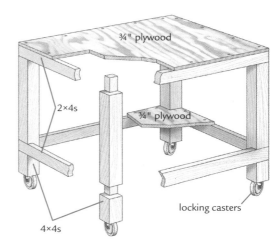

¾" plywood

2×4s

¾" plywood

locking casters

4×4s

6 Glues & Fasteners

Doing little things well is a step toward doing big things better.

— ANONYMOUS

Some say the main difference between a carpenter, a cabinetmaker, and a furniture builder lies in the methods they use to fasten boards to one another. Carpenters use nails and screws; cabinetmakers use glue, dowels, and biscuits; and furniture makers use interlocking joints crafted from the wood itself. It's an interesting way of pigeonholing woodworkers, but there are countless exceptions to the rule. Here we'll take a look at glues, mechanical fasteners, and their close relatives.

MAKING JOINT DECISIONS

The technique used to fasten two pieces of wood together can range from using a hammer to whap in a handful of 16d nails to using a fine-tooth saw to cut intricate dovetail joints. Many factors go into deciding which fastener or joint is best to use. The first question one must ask is: "Which _____ (screw, nail, dowel, glue, tenon, biscuit, or joint) is strong enough to do the job?" Once that question is answered (and there's always more than one right answer), the field is narrowed further by questions related to how long it will take, how much it will cost, and what it will look like.

One *can* use dovetail joints instead of 16d nails to frame the walls of a closet. One can also use imported sparkling water to wash their car. The question is, "Does the extra expense and effort make a difference?" Such is the decision-making process with fasteners.

Screws

Q Is there a rule of thumb for selecting the right length of screw?

A Use a screw three times as long as the thickness of the "top" piece (the piece being joined.) For a ¾" board, use a 2¼" screw. Make certain the screw is ¼" shorter than the combined thicknesses of the pieces being joined, or you may be in for a pointy surprise. Screw length is determined by the part of the screw that actually enters the wood.

Q The wood screws at my hardware store aren't labeled according to diameter but by gauge. How do you interpret those numbers?

A The traditional way of designating a screw's diameter is by gauge rather than fractional inch. The numbers go up in increments of approximately ¹⁄₆₄" per gauge number. Wood screws are measured at the shank, the smooth part just below the head. Common fractional and decimal equivalents are:

GAUGE	FRACTIONAL EQUIVILENT	DECIMAL EQUIVILENT	THREADS PER INCH
#0	¹⁄₁₆"	0.060	32
#4	⁷⁄₆₄"	0.112	22
#6	⁹⁄₆₄"	0.138	18
#8	⁵⁄₃₂"	0.164	14
#10	³⁄₁₆"	0.190	13
#14	¼"	0.250	10
#24	⅜"	0.375	7

tip: Quick Calculation for Screw Size

If you wish to dazzle your woodworking friends, share this tidbit with them. If you know only the screw gauge number and need to determine the diameter in fractions of an inch, multiply the gauge number by 13, then add 060 and add the decimal point. A #10 screw, for example, would be calculated:

10 × 13 = 130
130 + 060 = 190 (add decimal for 0.190)

4 SCREWS EVERY WOODWORKER SHOULD KEEP ON HAND

One company specializing in mail-order screws stocks over 120 "families" of screws, with each family containing up to 25 "members." Knowing that, one could easily become overwhelmed by the simple task of selecting the right screw. But once you clear away the clutter, you'll find four screws that will take care of most of your woodworking needs. Keep a variety of lengths of each type, and you'll avoid lots of trips to the hardware store.

wood screw

drywall screw

pan head screw

Confirmat-style screw

1 **Standard wood screws.** These are the traditional workhorses of the woodworking world. Available in a wide range of sizes (#0 to #24 gauge), lengths (¼" to 5"), and head styles (flat, round, and oval), there's one for every task. Most have slotted or Phillips-drive heads. They require stepped pilot holes of two or three diameters. "Production screws," which are rapidly becoming the standard, look similar but have deeper threads and, because of their design, require only a single pilot hole.

2 **Drywall screws.** While not suitable for most woodworking projects involving hardwoods due to their thread configuration and brittleness, these inexpensive screws are fabulous for assembling jigs, securing templates, and creating storage shelves and bins.

3 **Pan head screws.** These are ideal for mounting drawer glides, creating jigs, and other tasks where you need a flat surface on the bottom of a screw head for pinching materials together.

4 **Confirmat-style screws.** These screws have a specialty and they do it well: joining panels made of MDF and particleboard — including those that are melamine-coated — to one another. The unique threads and head combine to create a sort of steel dowel that resists pull-through. They're also good for plywood.

Q What do the numbers on screw packages mean?

A The first number indicates gauge, the second number indicates threads per inch, and the third number indicates length. A screw labeled 8–32×2 is an 8-gauge screw that has 32 threads per inch and is 2" long. However, most wood screws don't include the middle threads-per-inch number.

Q Why are you supposed to drill three different-size holes for a standard wood screw?

A Think of a screw as a mini-clamp. For the screw to clamp effectively, the head of the screw needs to be able to force the top board tightly against the bottom board. If that top board is being hindered from moving by the threads of the screw, you won't get a tight fit. To address this:

- The *pilot hole* is sized so the threads of the screw can bite into the lower piece of wood as it's driven.
- The *clearance hole* in the top board is sized so the smooth part of the shank is contained by, but not pinched by, the hole.
- The *countersink hole* provides room for the screw head to sit flush with, or beneath, the wood surface.

You can drill the hole with multiple bits or with a single countersink bit like the one shown.

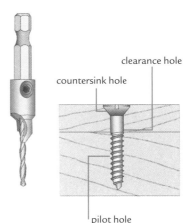

clearance hole

countersink hole

pilot hole

Q Why not use drywall screws for woodworking?

A For several reasons: They're threaded along their entire length, which means the threads in the top board can prevent the top board from making tight contact with the bottom board. They're also brittle and can easily snap when being driven. Finally, drywall screws have a bugle-shaped head that doesn't conform to the countersink profile of countersink bits.

tip: No Crying over Spilled Fasteners

Save time and frustration by using this tip to pick up a box load of spilled nails or screws. Place a magnet in an inside-out plastic sandwich bag. Run the magnet over the spilled fasteners, then turn the bag right side out and shake the magnet loose. Your spilled nails and screws will be "in the bag."

Q I have a friend who tossed all of his slotted screws and now uses only Robertson, or square-drive, screws. What makes them so good?

A The slot of a slotted screw is fairly shallow and provides only a small amount of surface area for a screwdriver to torque against. Because of this, they're susceptible to *camming out* (most of us would call this *stripping the head*). Robertson screws have a deep, tapered recess that allows the four sides of the bit to push against four sides of the "slot" for maximum force. They're also easy to use one-handed, since the tapered recess in the screw head fits snugly onto the tapered bit and is less likely to fall off.

Q When I install decorative hinges, I frequently strip the brass screw heads even though I drill pilot holes. How can I prevent this?

A The brass screws that come with hinges, clasps, and other types of decorative hardware are soft and have heads that are easily stripped. To prevent this, drill the correct size of pilot hole, drive in a steel screw with the same diameter as the brass one (to precut the threads), then remove the steel screw and drive in its brass cousin.

Nails

Q What does the "d" or "penny" part of a nail's name refer to?

A This is the most common explanation: The "d" dates back to the era when Romans occupied England and the monetary unit was the *denarius*, which had the same value as an English penny. It's conjectured that one hundred 3½" nails cost 16 pennies, making them "16d" nails, and so on. Though the designation is archaic, it seems the terminology is here to stay.

Q I'm building a pair of sawhorses and wondering how long the nails should be. Is there a rule of thumb on this?

A Always nail the thinner board to the thicker one, and use a nail that's three times as long as the top board is thick (without penetrating all the way through the bottom board). If you're using ¾"-thick material, your nails should be 2¼" long. It's the same rule of thumb you use for screws.

Q Why do some nails have grooves or spirals?

A Wood fibers wedge themselves into the grooves as the nail is driven, increasing the gripping power of the nail. Spiral nails rotate as they're pounded in, increasing their holding power even further. Flooring, drywall, and boat nails are nearly always "ring-shank," or ribbed, to counteract the inevitable movement, expanding, and shrinking of the wood in those environments.

Q If I need to predrill before installing finish nails, what size should the hole be?

A Make the hole 75 to 85 percent of the nail's diameter and about two-thirds of its length.

Q How can I avoid the telltale pecker mark made by my hammerhead when driving a nail?

A Keep the hammerhead square to the wood surface, and drive the nail in until it protrudes about ¼". Then, use a nail set to finish driving it in. If you're applying putty to the hole, sink the head about ⅛" below the surface.

If your aim is off, make a protective shroud from a sample piece of plastic laminate (free at home centers). Create a V-shaped slot in the sample and slip it around the nail to protect the wood while you hammer. You can also make a little slot at the crotch of the V for holding small brads while you start them.

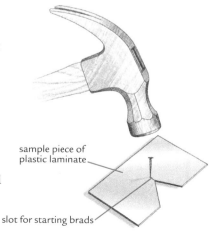

sample piece of plastic laminate

slot for starting brads

tip: A Penny for Your Length

There is a mathematical formula for nails 2d to 10d that allows you to translate the "penny" designation of a nail into a length. Divide the "d" number by four, then add ½" to get the length. For instance, to determine the length of an 8d nail, divide 8 by 4 to get 2; add ½" to that to get 2½". After 10d, the formula falls apart.

Q I've heard that if I stand a finish nail on its head and blunt the tip with my hammer, it's less likely to split the wood. Is that true?

A Sometimes. The theory is that by blunting the tip it "crushes" its way through the wood, rather than acting like a wedge, which splits the wood. It only works in softwoods, such as pine and cedar, and even then you should predrill holes if they're close to an edge or end of a board.

Q I'd like to purchase a finish nailer and compressor for my workshop. How large should the compressor be?

A If you foresee using it only for small finish guns and brad nailers, you can get by with something small: around 1 hp with a 2- to 3-gallon tank. If you'd also like to use the compressor for spraying finishes or operating pneumatic sanders, you'll need something with a larger tank that can generate more cubic feet per minute (CFM). In that case, check the CFM requirements of the tools and make your compressor purchase based on those.

Q What's the difference between an oil-less and an oil-lubricated compressor?

A An *oil-lubricated compressor*, like your car, has a crankcase that holds oil to lubricate the crankshaft and bearings. They're generally quieter than oil-less compressors and, until recently, had an edge over oil-less compressors in their ability to run for an extended amount of time without overheating.

An *oil-less compressor* has sealed bearings and Teflon-coated piston rings to reduce friction. They cost less, require less maintenance, and don't need to sit on a level surface like their oil-lubricated counterparts. As quality has increased, so has longevity. Because of these advantages, the majority of home workshop compressors sold today are oil-less.

Glues and Adhesives

Q Which is better: yellow glue or white glue?

A White glues are adequate for many situations, but yellow glues are the safest bet. Here's why: There are many varieties of white glue, and they vary greatly in composition. Some are "school glues" with weak bonds and low melting points, which makes them more susceptible to gumming up under power sanding. Other white glues have additives that make them perform more like yellow glues, but it's difficult for the consumer to know which is which by the label alone.

Yellow glues are dyed to differentiate themselves from the pack. They have additives that make them superior for woodworking, have higher heat resistance for sanding, and are less prone to "glue creep" — the tendency of boards to slightly move or creep over time. If you need the thinner viscosity of white glue for a project, you can thin yellow glues by diluting them with ordinary tap water by up to 5 percent. There are many specialized glues on the market, including ones that offer extended working time and greater water resistance. Read the labels to find the one best for your project.

Q How much glue should I use when gluing two boards together?

A Fortunately, the answer is simple: Use just enough. Unfortunately, knowing how much is "just enough" comes only through experience. Your goal should be to have a thin line of small glue beads or "squeeze-out" evenly distributed along the joint after clamping; something about the diameter of a piece of string is ideal. Using too much glue can create problems: In addition to wasting glue, cleanup is more difficult, and pieces tend to slip and slide more during the glue-up process.

Q I always wipe off excess glue with a damp rag as I glue up my projects, yet when I apply stain I often wind up with light, blotchy spots in those areas. What am I doing wrong?

A A quick swipe with a damp rag can be the worst way to remove wet glue. The rag becomes saturated with dissolved glue and smears it around. That glue seals the wood pores, preventing the stain from absorbing into the wood evenly. If you do choose to wipe away glue with a damp rag, do it several times, using a clean cloth (or a clean side of the cloth) each time you wipe. Better yet, use a dampened low-abrasive scrub sponge (such as Scotch-Brite) to clean away the glue, then wipe with a clean, dry rag.

Many woodworkers prefer waiting about an hour until the glue skims over, then using a chisel or stiff putty knife to scrape off the thin line of glue beads. You can wait until the glue fully hardens, then remove it with a sharp chisel, but you risk gouging the wood or pulling out fibers along with the glue as you remove it.

There's another option that virtually ensures no staining problems: Finish the wood first. This method also allows you to apply the finish evenly, even in awkward and tight places. Avoid getting the finish on the parts that will be glued by covering them with masking tape. If you don't, the wood fibers become sealed, making it impossible for your glue to do its job.

Q I've had trouble creating strong glue joints when working with rosewood and other oily woods. What's the solution?

A The oils and resins in many tropical woods can prevent the glue from creating a good bond. To minimize the problem, clean the surfaces with a light sanding, or pass them through the jointer. Then, glue them up before oil has a chance to migrate to the surface again. You can also lightly wipe the surfaces to be joined with naphtha, which will quickly evaporate, carrying away surface oils. Again, glue up the parts as quickly as possible before more oil seeps to the surface. Using epoxy or urethane glues will also help create a stronger bond.

tip: Glue at the Ready

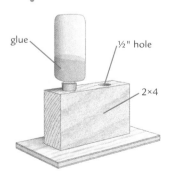

glue

½" hole

2×4

You probably have a ketchup bottle "standing on its head" in the refrigerator so the contents come out faster. Do the same with your glue bottles. Drill ½" holes in a 2×4 and insert your sealed bottles "nozzle down" after each use. You'll be surprised at how much time you save.

Q What are sunken joints, and how do I avoid them?

A Sunken joints are small dips that can form along the joints of boards that have been edge-glued. The process begins when glue swells the joint, leaving a temporary ridge. If this ridge is sanded or planed flat while the wood is still moist and swollen, it will create a sunken area when the wood dries and regains its normal shape. To avoid this, wait a day or two before sanding your edge-glued boards.

Q When working with yellow and white glue, what's the difference between open time, clamping time, and curing time?

A **Open time** is how much working time you have between spreading the glue and getting the pieces positioned and clamped. For most carpenter glues, this is 5 to 10 minutes. The problem with leaving glue "open" for too long is that it skins over, resulting in a weaker bond.

Clamping time is how long you should leave the clamps in place. For most woodworking glues, this is about an hour.

Curing time is how long it takes for a glue to reach full strength. For wood glues, this is about 24 hours.

Q What creates the black marks along glue lines when I edge-glue and clamp boards?

A When an iron clamp comes in contact with wet glue, a black stain often forms. Since the stain is the result of a chemical reaction that occurs within the wood, not just on the glue, you need to sand, scrape, or plane the wood to remove the stain. Minimizing the amount of glue squeeze-out is the first step. You may also want to create a buffer between the wood and the bars of the clamp: Apply strips of masking tape to the bars, or cut wax paper into 2" strips, crease them, and lay them over the bar of the clamp before gluing up.

tip: Wipe, Baby, Wipe

Keep a plastic container of baby wipes in your shop for removing wet glue from your clamps, tools, hands, and projects. They're always moist, just the right size, and have more cleaning power than a damp rag.

Q I left some yellow carpenter's glue in my garage all last winter. I'm sure it froze and thawed several times. Can I still use it?

A Manufacturers formulate yellow glues to withstand a freeze or two that might occur during shipping, but for the most part, they're not designed to withstand repeated freezes. If the glue is lumpy and "cottage-cheesy," throw it out. It's just not worth the risk. To ensure you're using fresh glue, mark the purchase date on the bottle, and toss any glues that have been around over a year. And keep them inside.

tip: Hot-Melt Glue to the Rescue

You may think of hot melt glue guns as "craft" tools, but they come in handy for woodworking, too. They're perfect for building small project mock-ups, temporarily holding parts in place, and clamping things where a clamp won't fit. To disassemble a piece that has been hot-melt-glued, it's easiest (and least damaging) to twist it rather than to pry or pull it.

Q I've heard some furniture makers and musical instrument makers use hide glue because it's "reversible." What does that mean?

A Traditional hide glues get their adhesive qualities from the proteins found in animal skins, tissues, and bone. They're "reversible" in the sense they can be re-softened by the application of heat or moisture. This is an attractive feature if someone down the road needs to replace a broken chair leg or install a new violin neck without damaging the rest of the piece.

Traditional hide glues come in granular form and must be heated in a pot and applied while warm. Ready-to-use liquid hide glues, which don't require heating or mixing, are also available. Like their traditional cousins, ready-to-use glues offer a long open time and allow for easy disassembly later down the road. One of their downsides is a short shelf life. Because of their vulnerability to moisture, never use hide glue for outdoor projects or in areas subject to moisture.

Q The directions for polyurethane glue state that the wood needs to have a moisture content of 8 percent or more for the glue to work. How am I supposed to determine that without a moisture meter?

A Polyurethane glues need moisture to cure properly. To be on the safe side, wipe one or both of the surfaces to be joined with a damp rag (if the wood darkens slightly, it's damp enough), then apply the glue and join the pieces to one another. Do the same thing if you're using polyurethane glue on MDF or plywood, which most likely will have inadequate moisture content.

Q I made mortise-and-tenon joints for some cabinet doors, but I cut the tenons too small. Since polyurethane is gap-filling, wouldn't that be the best glue to use for tightening up the joints?

A No. Polyurethane glue may fill gaps as it expands, but that gap-filling material is weak. For polyurethane glue to really bond, your gaps shouldn't be any greater than they would be if you were using yellow glue (no more than the thickness of a sheet of notebook paper). Your best bet is to use epoxy glue; it will bond across gaps as large as 1/16".

GLUE SPREADING SIMPLIFIED

Applying glue is an integral part of woodworking, and anything you can do to make the job easier, neater, and faster is a good thing. Here are a few tips for glue application:

◇ **Narrow surfaces.** Use an old toothbrush. It's just the right size, spreads glue evenly, and cleans up easily. Keep it dust-free by storing it in a traveling toothbrush holder.

◇ **Wide surfaces.** Use a 3" foam paint roller saturated with glue. You can also use a pinking shears to cut a sawtooth edge on an expired credit card to spread glue evenly.

◇ **Inside corners.** Apply masking tape to both sides of a joint before assembly to catch oozing glue. Do the final cleanup by scooping up excess with the pinched tip of a drinking straw.

◇ **Cracks and crevices.** Place glue along the crack, then use a drinking straw to blow it deeper into the crevice. As an alternative, try using your shop vacuum to suck the glue down into the joint.

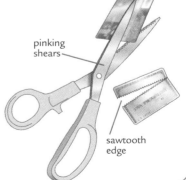

pinking shears

sawtooth edge

Dowels

Despite the recent emergence of many "newfangled" fasteners, dowels remain an effective way of joining two pieces of wood to each other. Creating a dowel joint requires only a few simple tools, skills, and steps. There are a variety of jigs and methods for getting the job done. The simplest jigs may be little more than a hardened sleeve that helps center and guide your drill bit as you drill the dowel holes. More complex versions include adjustable features for offsetting holes and indexing pins to ensure proper hole spacing.

DOWELING BASICS

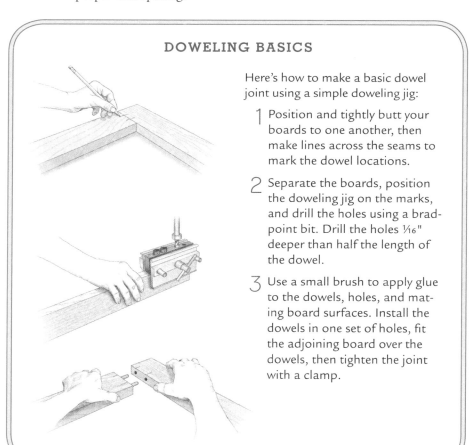

Here's how to make a basic dowel joint using a simple doweling jig:

1 Position and tightly butt your boards to one another, then make lines across the seams to mark the dowel locations.

2 Separate the boards, position the doweling jig on the marks, and drill the holes using a brad-point bit. Drill the holes 1/16" deeper than half the length of the dowel.

3 Use a small brush to apply glue to the dowels, holes, and mating board surfaces. Install the dowels in one set of holes, fit the adjoining board over the dowels, then tighten the joint with a clamp.

tip: Do-It-Yourself Dowels

To make your own fluted dowels from a standard dowel rod, clamp the dowel upright in a vise. Adjust and close the jaws of a locking pliers around the dowel, then use a hammer to tap the pliers downward. The jaw serrations will cut small flutes. To get flutes on all sides of the dowel, rotate the pliers and repeat. Another method is to tap the dowel through a 12-point box wrench that's slightly smaller than the dowel. Each point of the wrench will create a small groove.

Q How many dowels should I use when building a frame, and how far apart should I space them?

A To prevent a joint from twisting, always use at least two dowels. Space them no more than 3" apart when joining boards at right angles. Use three dowels for workpieces wider than 4". Inset the dowels at least ⅛" from the narrow edge of a board (¼" is even better).

Q What size dowel should I use when joining ¾"-thick boards?

A The rule of thumb is that the dowel diameter should be no more than half the thickness of the pieces being joined. The length should be about five times the diameter of the dowel. For ¾" boards, use a ⅜"×2" dowel.

Q Why do dowels have spirals and flutes?

A Grooves and spirals help evenly distribute glue along the length of the hole as they go in, provide an escape route for excess glue and air, and allow room for the dowel to expand slightly without splitting the wood. Solid dowels cut from dowel rods tend to scrape the sides of the holes and plow the glue towards the bottom of the hole as they go in.

Q After positioning the dowels in one board, I often have trouble lining them up with the holes in the second board. Is there a trick for making this easier?

A You can slightly bevel the dowel ends with a utility knife, sandpaper, or pencil sharpener. If that's not enough, use a countersink bit to create a chamfer about 1/16" deep around the actual holes. This last step will also remove any small splinters from the edges of the hole and provide a mini-reservoir for excess glue.

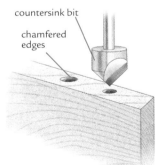

countersink bit

chamfered edges

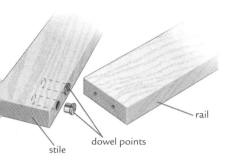

rail

dowel points

stile

Q How do you use dowel points?

A Mark the dowel positions on the end or side of one of the mating boards, then use a drill press, jig, or steady hand to drill the holes. Insert the dowel points into the holes, align the two boards, and tap one of the boards to transfer the center marks onto the mating board. Drill the holes in the mating board.

tip: In-a-Pinch Dowel Points

If you left your dowel points in your other pants pockets, try this: Mark the centers of the dowel holes on the end of one board, then use a nail set to make small indentations. With the marked surface positioned horizontally, place a small BB in each indentation, carefully position the adjoining board, then tap it with a wood or rubber mallet to transfer the center marks from one board to the other.

Q The dowels at my home center are often larger than the label indicates. How do I bring them down to a uniform diameter?

A Find a sturdy piece of metal, such as an L-bracket or a leftover hinge, and drill (or re-drill) a hole to the final size you'd like your dowels to be. Clamp the metal to a solid surface with the enlarged hole hanging over the edge, then chuck the dowel in your drill, pull the trigger, and push the spinning dowel down through the hole. The metal edges of the hole will shave your dowel down to size. If the dowel is significantly oversized, you may need to drill two progressively smaller holes and run your dowels through both of them.

Biscuit Joinery

Biscuit and dowel joinery are close cousins. Both use a small piece of wood glued into a small opening to connect boards to each other, but that's where the similarities end. A biscuit joint uses football-shaped pieces of compressed beech (the biscuits) that are glued and inserted into specially cut slots in each of the mating pieces. The biscuits swell slightly from the moisture in the glue, adding strength to the joint.

BISCUIT JOINER BASICS

Cutting the "half-moon" slots in the boards requires a special tool called a biscuit joiner, which houses a small, thick, retractable blade for performing the task. The tool has adjustable fences and a faceplate that allow you to drill slots for various sizes of biscuits in a variety of configurations. The slots are slightly wider than the biscuits, allowing for some side-to-side adjustment of the pieces before clamping — a benefit you don't get with dowels and other types of joints and fasteners. Using the common task of edge-joining boards as an example, the procedure goes as follows:

1 Cut the boards to length, then lay them side-by-side in their final configuration.

2 Make small tick marks every 6" across the joint, then separate the pieces.

3 Position the center mark of the biscuit joiner on each tick mark, making sure the top fence is riding on top of the board, then pull the trigger and press the tool forward to cut the slot.

4 Once all the slots are cut, apply glue to the slots and mating surfaces, insert the biscuits, line up the boards, and clamp them together.

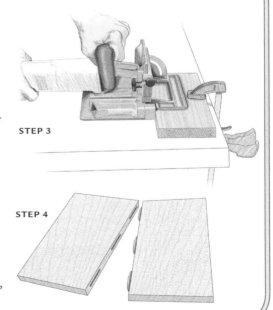

STEP 3

STEP 4

Q I'm building a rocking chair and considering using biscuits for joining the legs, seat frame, rockers, and arms. Are they strong enough?

A Biscuits are great for building cabinets, bookcases, small tables, and other pieces of "static" furniture, but some woodworkers are wary of using them for chairs and other pieces of furniture subject to lots of stress and movement. Tests show that mortise-and-tenon joints are five times stronger than biscuits, while doweled joints are about three times stronger. Play it safe and use one of the stronger joints for your rocker.

Q Why does my woodworking store sell three different biscuit sizes? Do I need to adjust my joiner or change blades when I switch sizes?

A The three standard biscuit sizes are #0, #10, and #20. The #0 biscuits measure 1¾" long and ⁹⁄₁₆" wide, while the #20 biscuits measure 2⅜" in length and almost 1" in width. Regardless of size, all are the same thickness. Plate joiners are easily adjusted to cut slots of the proper depth for each; it usually takes just a twist of a dial.

Why the different sizes? The bigger the biscuit, the stronger the joint. Yet there are times you need to use smaller biscuits so the slots or biscuits don't extend beyond the edges of the boards. For instance, the slot required to accommodate a #20 biscuit is nearly 3" wide. If your rail is only 2" wide, part of the slot and biscuit would show.

Q Is there a rule of thumb for how to space biscuits when building something like a plywood cabinet case?

A Use one biscuit for every 6" of joint length. Keep the outermost biscuits at least 2" away from the edges.

Q What's the best glue to use, and what's the best way to apply it?

A White and yellow glues are the best; the moisture in them swells the biscuit to create an even tighter joint. You can apply glue to either the biscuit or the slot, though most woodworkers apply it to the slot. This is because a glue-soaked biscuit can start swelling, making it more difficult (and messier) to fit it into the slot. Special glue applicators with a wide, oval tip help distribute the glue evenly and neatly into the slot. Make sure to apply glue to the mating wood surfaces, too.

Q I used my biscuit joiner to build a face frame, but the surfaces aren't flush. What happened?

A There are a several possibilities. You could be "rocking" the joiner while cutting the slots, there may be wood chips holding the joiner's face plate off the surface of the wood, or you could be inadvertently flipping one piece over during assembly so the slots are slightly different distances from the surfaces.

Q I'm building a large box with mitered corners. Is there a simple technique I can use for joining the corners with biscuits?

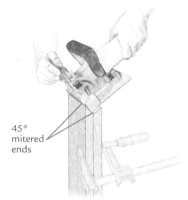

45°
mitered
ends

A Cut your pieces to the desired length, then clamp the 45-degree mitered ends together to create a V. Use the surface of one miter as a platform for your joiner to cut the slots in the other board, then do the same for the uncut board. Practice ahead of time with scrap lumber so you get the position and size of the biscuits correct.

Q I used my biscuit joiner for edge-gluing boards for a tabletop. Now I'm noticing football-shaped dents in the surface. What happened?

A Though biscuits aren't usually necessary for strength when edge-gluing, they do come in handy for aligning the boards and keeping their surfaces flush. Chances are your problem arose from sanding or planing the top too soon after gluing. The biscuits initially expand, creating slight football-shaped humps on the surface. If you sand your top while the biscuits and wood are swollen, you'll wind up with football-shaped dents when the wood contracts to normal size.

Pocket Screw Joints

If you're looking for a fast, secure way to build cabinet face frames, attach table legs to aprons, or install fixed shelves, you'd be hard pressed to find a better way than the pocket hole, or pocket screw, system. The system is easy to use and is often sold in kit form with all the necessary jigs, bits, screws, and accessories in one package (see Resources for more information).

POCKET SCREW JIG BASICS

Here are the basic steps involved in using the pocket screw system:

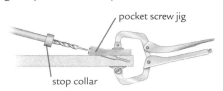

1 Use the special jig to drill a pair of steeply slanted (15-degree) holes in one piece of wood. The bit doesn't penetrate all the way but rather leaves a "pocket" that the head of the screw uses to pull this board against the other.

pocket screw jig

stop collar

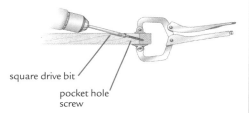

2 Apply glue to the joint, and clamp the two pieces together.

3 Use a long bit to drive the special screw through the pocket and into the other board.

square drive bit

pocket hole screw

The result is a joint that's surprisingly strong. You can join different thicknesses of wood by adjusting the depth of the stop collar on the drill bit and using an appropriate length of screw to join the pieces together. Perhaps the biggest downside to the system is the large, oval-shaped hole that's created. But for cabinet face frames and parts of other projects that are rarely seen, this usually isn't a problem.

Q How do I secure the fixed shelves of a bookcase to the sides and make sure they're positioned exactly where I want them?

A Begin by drilling pocket holes every 3" or 4" at the ends of the shelves. Lightly mark the location of the tops of your shelves onto the sides of your bookcase, then clamp a 1×2 to that line. Butt the shelf to the 1×2 and install the pocket screws. The 1×2 will hold the shelf in the correct position so it won't shift.

Q You can purchase both fine-thread and coarse-thread screws for pocket screw connections. When do you use which?

A Use the coarse-threaded screws for softwoods, plywood, and MDF; use the fine-threaded screws for hardwoods. The deep, wide threads of the coarse screws "bite" better into soft materials.

Q How do I hide or fill the large oval holes when they're visible?

A The easiest way is to use special plugs. You can purchase wood plugs that you glue and tap in place, or plastic plugs that snap into place. The wood ones are available in pine, oak, cherry, and other commonly used woods. The plastic ones are available in a variety of colors. When installing wood plugs, you'll get the best — and least visible — results by leaving them slightly proud of the surface, then sanding or planing them smooth.

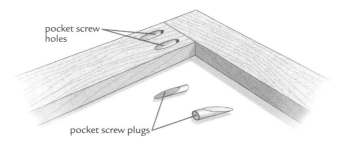

pocket screw holes

pocket screw plugs

Q What other tasks are pocket screw joints used for?

A They excel at joining pieces of wood that meet at right angles, but other common uses include:

⊙ Installing solid-wood nosing on plywood shelves

⊙ Securing face frames and corner blocks to cabinet boxes

⊙ Joining oddly shaped items, such as octagonal mirror frames that are difficult to clamp or otherwise join

⊙ Securing side and top door moldings to one another before installation (for both mitered and square-butted corners)

⊙ Securing hardwood treads and risers to stair jacks (when accessible from below)

Loose Tenon Systems

Q I've noticed tools that promote themselves as "loose tenon" systems. Just what are they, and are they any good?

A The loose tenon systems you're referring to create mortises in two pieces of wood, then use a separate tenon inserted in both mortises to connect the two.

BeadLOCK uses a simple jig as a guide for drilling a slot consisting of three or five overlapping holes. A loose tenon with three or five corresponding humps (with glue applied) is used to make the connection. The jig is relatively inexpensive, and you can buy router bits for creating your own loose tenons.

The Festool Domino system uses a special (and expensive) tool to bore oblong mortises. The connection is made by gluing in a similarly shaped loose tenon.

Both systems create strong, long-lasting joints. The loose tenons provide a substantial amount of surface area for glue to adhere to, prevent joints from twisting, and help distribute pressure more equally across joints.

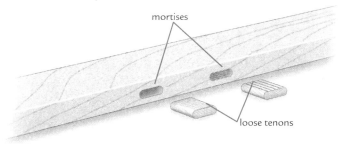

mortises

loose tenons

Q How strong are these loose tenon joints?

A Tests have shown them to be stronger than biscuit joints, weaker than true mortise-and-tenon joints, and equal in strength to high-quality dowel systems. They're durable enough to be used for any kind of furniture.

Joints & Special Techniques

Arguments with furniture are rarely productive.

— KEHLOG ALBRAN

A cabinet or piece of furniture is only as strong as the joints used to hold it together. Some joints, such as dovetail and box joints, are not only functional, they can be an attractive part of the design as well. Others, such as the biscuits, dowels, and metal fasteners discussed in chapter 6, are more the "strong, silent type."

One rule of thumb is to use the simplest joint for the job, but there's more to consider than that. Appearance is important, and crafting a well-made joint can be deeply satisfying. It can also be very time-consuming. Figuring out the best joint for your project is time well spent. In this chapter, we'll also look at the basics of some techniques that can make your project truly unique: bending wood, veneering, and carving.

Edge-Gluing Boards

Put ten woodworkers in a room, ask them the best way to glue up a table-top, and you'll get ten different answers. And all ten answers will be correct! If a certain technique produces the results you want, then that's the best technique for you. Here are some commonly pondered questions about edge-gluing.

Q One article I read said to alternate the direction of growth rings when gluing up boards for a tabletop. Another article said it didn't matter. Which should I believe?

A Those who favor alternating the rings maintain that it results in a flatter panel. The theory goes that because alternating boards will cup in alternating directions, you'll wind up with several small, easily flattened, and less noticeable undulations instead of one big arc.

But there are other factors to consider, appearance being one. You could wind up with mismatched grain patterns by alternating annual rings, or wind up with the "good side down" on some boards. Others will argue that the alternate-ring technique applies more to softwoods or woods that haven't been thoroughly dried and are more likely to cup than kiln-dried hardwoods. A third argument asserts that since the panel will most likely be confined by a frame or secured to a table apron, there's less chance of it bowing anyway. If all factors are equal, alternate the growth rings. Otherwise, take the other considerations into account.

Q It seems like I never have enough time to get the glue applied, clamps on, and boards lined up when I edge-glue. Are there some shortcuts?

A There aren't many shortcuts, but there are some "smartcuts." Dry-fit your boards to check for edge gaps and appearance, then draw a large chalk triangle across the faces of the boards (see opposite page) so you can remember which side goes up and in what order. Position the bar clamps on your work surface so the outer clamps are about 8" from each end of the panel and the others are evenly spaced in between. Adjust the distance between the jaws of your clamps so you can give the handles just a few twists to make contact. Finally, use an "extended-time glue" to buy a little extra working time.

Q What are the basic steps for gluing up and clamping a large panel?

A Once you've completed your prep work and dry-fitting, the basic steps are:

⊙ Apply a light coat of wood glue to both edges of all the boards (except the two outer edges, of course).

⊙ Lay the boards on top of evenly spaced bar clamps. To prevent an upward or downward bow, you want the pressure points of the jaws to align with the centers of the boards, so use strips of wood to prop up the boards to "center of jaw" level.

⊙ Lightly tighten one clamp, then move down the line and lightly tighten the others. Use your fingertips to feel the joints and push or tap boards up or down until they're flush. Once all the boards are flush, tighten each clamp. Install alternating top clamps for better clamping power.

⊙ Allow the panel to sit flat on your workbench, or stand it vertically, until the glue has dried.

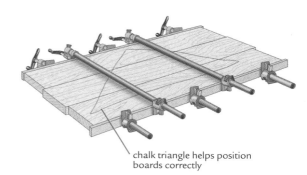

chalk triangle helps position boards correctly

Q When I glue up panels, the boards slip and slide around as I clamp them together. What am I doing wrong?

A You could be using too much glue. Try applying a light coat of glue to each surface, then rub the boards back and forth against each other a few times. You'll feel the glue become a little tacky, which will help the boards stay put while you apply the clamps. Doing this will also help remove excess glue, distribute it evenly, and create a thin, strong glue line.

Q How many clamps do I need if I'm gluing up a 6'-long tabletop? And do I need to put them on both sides of the panel?

A One rule of thumb is to use one clamp per foot. If you're applying clamps to both sides of the panel, round up to the next odd number in order to keep the clamp spacing uniform. For your 6' table, use seven clamps: four below the panel and three above.

Q I glued up a tabletop, but when I removed the clamps, a gap opened up between two boards. What caused this, and how can I prevent this in the future?

A You were short on something: glue, clamping pressure, patience, or proper stock preparation. Always dry-fit your boards before applying the glue. That way, you can make sure the edges meet squarely and that there are no bows, twists, or gaps. Remember, clamps are intended to hold boards together during glue-up, not to force edges together that are bowed or uneven.

DRILL AND CHISEL

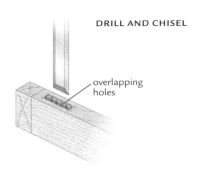

overlapping holes

PLUNGE ROUTER

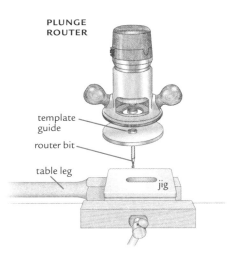

template guide

router bit

table leg

jig

HOLLOW CHISEL

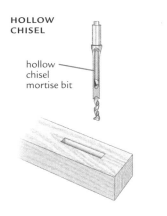

hollow chisel mortise bit

Mortise-and-Tenon Joints

The mortise-and-tenon joint is a staple of the woodworking world, used for centuries for constructing everything from timber frame houses to coffee tables. No wonder there are so many ways to create them!

Q So, how do I cut a mortise?

A Here are three ways to create a mortise:

Drill and chisel. Mark the edges of the mortise, then install a Forstner drill bit the same diameter as your mortise (or a hair smaller) in your drill. Use a drill guide or doweling jig to drill both end holes, then make a series of overlapping holes in between. Use a narrow chisel to square up the ends of the mortise and a wide chisel to square up the sides.

Plunge router. This requires installing a template guide (collar) on your router base and creating a simple jig to guide it. Create a slot in your jig that's the same width as the template guide and use a router bit that's the same diameter as the width of your mortise. Clamp the jig to your stock, and cut the mortise with a series of gradually deeper passes.

Hollow chisel mortising attachment. This is a special bit that consists of a square collar the width of the mortise that houses a close-fitting drill bit. The leading edge of the square collar has sharpened edges. As the drill bit removes the bulk of the material, the square collar cuts the sides of the hole clean and square. Repeat this for the length of the mortise. This requires either a dedicated mortising machine or a special mortising attachment for your drill press. The drill press version will work in most hardwoods, but will cut slower than the dedicated mortiser.

Q How do I cut a tenon?

A Again, there are three common ways to approach it:

Tenon saw. Mark the outline of the tenon on the ends and edges of the board. Position the board at a 45-degree angle in the vise, and use a tenon saw to cut along the waste side of each line. Reposition the stock and repeat on the other side. Position the board perpendicularly, and complete the cuts level with the shoulder. Finally, saw along the shoulder line to remove the waste.

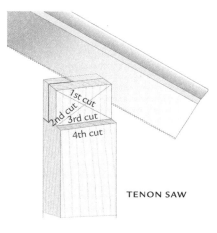

TENON SAW

Table saw. Cut the cheeks by using a tenoning jig to hold the stock vertically as you move it past the blade (set for the length of the cheek). Then cut the shoulders of the tenon using a miter gauge to guide the stock past the blade that's been set to the depth of the cheek.

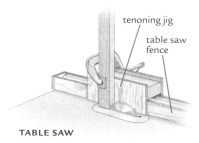

tenoning jig

table saw fence

TABLE SAW

Router table. Set the fence of the router table so it's the same distance from the outer edge of the bit as the cheek is deep. Adjust the bit to the depth of the cheek. Use a miter gauge to guide the stock past the bit. It will take at least two passes for each cut.

Q How do I widen a tenon that's too thin?

A Glue a thin shim, a piece of veneer, or a plane shaving to each face of the cheek. (You do both sides so the tenon stays centered.) When the glue dries, use a rabbeting plane or sanding block to reduce the thickness as needed. Be careful not to round the edges of the shoulders or your assembled joint won't look as crisp.

ROUTER TABLE

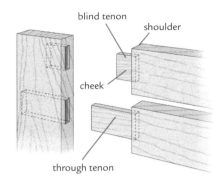

blind tenon

shoulder

cheek

through tenon

Q What's the difference between a through mortise-and-tenon joint and a blind one?

A A *blind* mortise-and-tenon joint is cut only partway into the workpiece. Make the mortise ¹⁄₁₆" deeper than the tenon length to allow room for glue.

A *through* mortise-and-tenon joint has a mortise that's been cut entirely through the workpiece, so the end of the tenon can be seen on the opposite side. This isn't normally required for strength but is often used as a decorative detail. Make a through tenon about ¹⁄₁₆" longer than the mortise so it can be sanded flush after assembly.

Q Does it matter whether you cut the tenon or the mortise first?

A In a perfect world, it wouldn't matter. But in the world of woodworking you're better off cutting the mortise first. It's easier to adjust the width of the tenon if you make a mistake.

Q What's a mortise gauge?

A A mortise gauge is a small tool with two adjustable "fangs" that mark the edges of the mortises and tenons. An adjustable stop block helps you position it correctly on the workpiece.

Q Is there a rule of thumb on how wide to make a mortise?

A The norm is to make it one-third the thickness of the workpiece. This creates a tenon of suitable strength and a mortise with suitably thick sidewalls. If you're working with ¾" stock, your mortise should be ¼" wide.

tenon

MORTISE GAUGE

Q How tightly should a tenon fit into a mortise before gluing?

A If the fit is too tight, the tenon will plow the glue into the bottom of the mortise as it's inserted, resulting in a starved joint. If it's too loose, the glue can't bridge the gap to create a good bond. So how do you know what's right? In terms of touch and feel, if you can easily push the joint together by hand — and not have it fall apart when you let go — your fit is about right.

Q A friend of mine leaves a few extra inches of material on the end of his stock where he's cutting a mortise, then removes it later. Why?

A The extra material (see the Drill and Chisel illustration on page 162) helps prevent the end of the stock from splitting while the mortise is being made. This is especially important if you're working with hand tools and chisels.

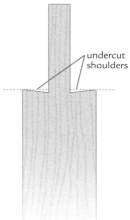

undercut shoulders

Q I've heard you can get a tighter fit by undercutting the shoulders of a tenon. What does that involve?

A Undercutting involves removing a bit of material so only the outer edges of the shoulders make contact with the mortised piece. This creates a tighter-looking joint without weakening the connection.

Dadoes and Rabbets

Q What's the difference between a dado and a rabbet?

A A dado is a rectangular recess or groove made across the face of a board. A rabbet is a recess made on an edge or end of a board.

Q Whoops! I cut a dozen dadoes for the shelves of a bookcase all too wide. Can I correct the problem or do I need to start over?

A You need to either thicken the shelves or narrow the dadoes. There are ways of doing both, as described below. Whichever method you use, experiment first to make sure you get the results you want.

If the gap is smaller than 1/16", you may want to "thicken" each shelf. Cut 1/2"-deep slots in the ends of the shelves with a table saw or a

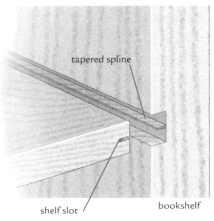

tapered spline

shelf slot

bookshelf

router with a slotting cutter. Cut long wedge-shaped splines with 5-degree bevels on each side, making the narrow part of the wedge the same thickness as the slot. Tap the splines partway into the slots, then tap the shelves into the dadoes. The splines will expand the shelf ends to create a tight fit.

For wider gaps, you'll want to narrow the dadoes. Cut strips of wood or veneer to match the thickness of the gap. Then, with the shelves in place, apply glue and insert the strips under each shelf. When the glue has set, use a sharp utility knife to trim the edges and ends.

Q I need to make a dado only occasionally and can't justify the expense of buying a dado blade. Can I make dadoes using a standard blade in a table saw?

A Yes. It's more time-consuming and relies more on a keen eye, but with a simple jig and some practice, you can make accurate dadoes:

⊙ To make your jig, secure a straight 1×3 fence to your miter gauge, adjust the height of your saw blade so it's ¼" taller than your workpiece, then push your jig past the blade to create a saw kerf in the 1×3. From the outside of this kerf, make a mark on your fence a "dado width" away.

⊙ Lower your blade to "dado depth" and make a test cut through a scrap piece to make sure it's correct.

⊙ Lay out the positions and thickness of your dadoes on the side of the board opposite of where the dadoes will be cut.

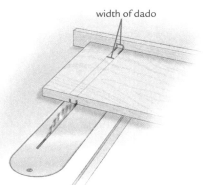

width of dado

⊙ Line up one edge of the layout mark on your workpiece with the kerf in the fence, and make your first pass. Shift the workpiece so the layout mark for the other side of the dado aligns with the other mark on the fence, then make your second pass.

⊙ Once you have both edges of the dado cut, make a series of passes to remove the material in between.

Q Can I make dadoes and rabbets using only a circular saw?

A Yes. Start by marking the position and width of your dado or rabbet on your workpiece. Set your circular saw to the desired dado depth, then use a triangle square or straightedge guide to guide the base of your saw while making a series of cuts (the closer together the better) between your marks. Use a sharp chisel the same width as the dado or rabbet to remove the waste.

Dovetail and Box Joints

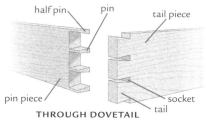

THROUGH DOVETAIL

Q What's the difference between a through dovetail and a half-blind dovetail?

A *Through* dovetails are the wider and stronger of the two. They're an excellent choice where you need strength or wish to expose the beauty of the joint from both sides.

Half-blind dovetails are constructed so only half of the joint is visible. They're a good choice for drawer fronts and other projects where part of the joint will be concealed.

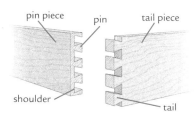

HALF-BLIND DOVETAIL

Q I want to build a chest of drawers, but don't feel prepared — tool-wise or skills-wise — to make the dozens of dovetail joints the plans call for. Are they necessary?

A No other woodworking joint carries the same mystique as the dovetail. It's beautiful to look at, it's as strong as oak, and it's the signature by which fine craftspeople are known. But it helps to look at this joint in its proper historical context.

Dovetail joints have been around for hundreds of years. They were concocted during an era when nails were expensive and screws were as rare as hens' teeth. They were used to construct drawers that, without the aid of slides and glides, were subject to all manner of swelling, tugging, and abuse. And they were a sturdy, foolproof joint ideal for building a hope chest that might spend weeks in the cargo hold of a sailing ship crashing across the Atlantic. Today, nails and screws cost pennies, ball-bearing glides allow us to open a drawer with the touch of a pinky finger, and most of us roll our luggage around on wheels when we journey overseas.

None of this makes the dovetail joint any less attractive or strong, it just makes it less essential. If you just need a functional joint that can survive in today's world, there are simpler alternatives. But if you wish to make a classic dovetail joint, use one of the many jigs available.

Q What's the basic premise behind a dovetail jig?

A Dovetail jigs are adjustable templates that contain a series of grooves that guide special router bits and bushings to accurately cut both sides of a dovetail joint. Once the jig is set to the correct spacing, width, and depth, the two members are aligned and routed. All jigs come with good instructions, and some even with DVDs. Proper setup is the key, so follow the directions. A few general keys to success include:

⊙ Remember that your jig is a well-planned system. Make certain to use the router bits, router guides, and templates supplied in the kit.

⊙ Make sure all of your boards are flat, square, and correctly dimensioned. Mill all of your components at the same time; if the parts are consistent, your results will be consistent.

⊙ Label all of your parts to avoid mass mistakes.

⊙ Make test cuts in scraps of wood that have the same dimensions as your workpieces.

⊙ Adjust your router speed downward. Burned pins and tails don't look good, glue well, or fit as tightly.

Q I saw some drawer corners that had heart-shaped dovetail joints. How are those created?

A Some dovetail jig makers have brought the craft to a whole new level. With the proper templates, bits, and bushings, you can make "dovetail joints" in the shapes of dog bones, arrowheads, and even teddy bears. They're made using the same basic steps as true dovetails.

BOX JOINT BASICS

Box joints, or finger joints, like their close cousin the dovetail joint, are both attractive and functional. Their multiple fingers interlock to create numerous gluing surfaces for a sturdy joint. And you can create box joints with only a dado blade and a simple shop-made jig. The key to simplicity is to make the fingers and the slots the exact same size by making the cuts with a dado blade the exact same width. To make the jig:

1 Attach a wood pin that's the exact width of a finger to a 1×3 fence.

2 Secure the fence to your miter gauge so that this finger is "finger width" away from the dado blade.

3 Make your first cut, then position that cutout onto the pin, and make the second cut. Continue leapfrogging your board along the pin until all of the slots are cut.

It may take some trial and error and adjustment of the blade width and pin position to get the fingers to interlock exactly, but once you have things aligned properly, cutting the joints is simple.

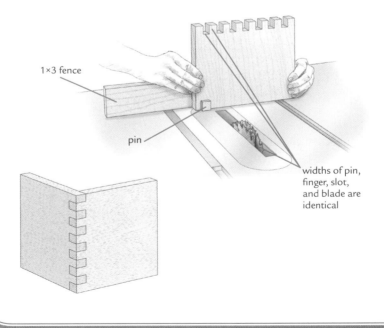

1×3 fence

pin

widths of pin, finger, slot, and blade are identical

Bending and Curving Wood

Whether it's making rockers for a chair, curved slats for a seat back, or gunnels for a wood boat, sooner or later you'll need wood that's something other than straight. You can get your curved pieces by cutting them from solid wood or by forming and bending wood that's been steamed, laminated, or kerfed. Learning these techniques is a milestone on your journey to becoming a better woodworker. Here are some basics.

Q What are some woods that bend easily — and not so easily?

A Some woods behave better than others because of their cell and grain structure. The best bending woods are long-grained woods, such as white and red oak, ash, and hickory. Elm, maple, walnut, and cherry can be bent, but with more difficulty. Woods you should avoid include softwoods, such as fir, pine, spruce, and dense or oily tropical woods, such as lignum vitae and African mahogany. Whatever wood you select, make sure it's straight-grained and knot-free.

Q How long do you need to steam the wood for it to become pliable enough to bend?

A The rule of thumb is to steam it one hour per inch of thickness. With too little time you'll have trouble shaping it; with too much time the wood can become trickier to work with.

Q What happens to wood during the steam-bending process?

A Wood fibers are bound together with lignin, a gluelike substance that surrounds the cells. When wood is steam-heated to a temperature of between 190 and 225°F, the lignin softens, allowing fibers to stretch or compress during the bending process. When the wood cools, the lignin rehardens and the fibers are locked back together in their new shape.

Q Is freshly cut "green" wood easier to steam-bend than wood that's been dried?

A Yes. Green wood will be more pliable, and the fresher the cut, the better. Next in line of workability is air-dried wood, followed by kiln-dried wood.

Q I want to curve some back slats for a rocking chair. Is there a way to build a small, simple steam-bending contraption?

A Contraption is a good term, since most steam-bending boxes are just that: a collection of odds and ends. All you need are a source of steam and a box. The simplest source of heat is an electric teapot, while a wallpaper steamer is a close second. The easiest steaming chamber to build is a box made from ¾" plywood. Here are a few basics:

⊙ Make the box only as large as necessary, since the steam needs to heat the entire chamber to be effective.

⊙ Run dowels though the chamber to create a shelf for holding the wood, so it will be steamed evenly on all sides.

⊙ Rig up a simple device for directing the steam from the source to the box. This can usually be done with PVC pipe and a few fittings.

⊙ Don't make the chamber airtight. Drill a few ¼" holes to allow steam and water to escape and for checking the temperature with a meat thermometer.

⊙ Slant the box slightly so excess water can escape.

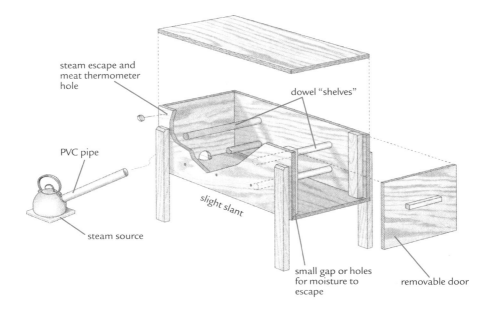

steam escape and meat thermometer hole

dowel "shelves"

PVC pipe

slight slant

steam source

small gap or holes for moisture to escape

removable door

Q How do I build and use a bending form for steamed wood?

A Build the basic form out of multiple layers of ¾" plywood or wood glued side-by-side. Put angled blocks on the bottom of the form near the ends so the clamps have a solid surface to grab onto.

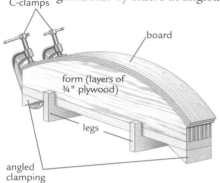

C-clamps

board

form (layers of ¾" plywood)

legs

angled clamping blocks

Wearing gloves, remove your piece from the steam box. Position it onto the form, and clamp one end down, using a scrap block to distribute pressure evenly across the width of the board. Press the other end down and clamp it in the same manner. It's best to get the piece onto the form immediately after removing it from the box.

Q I'm building a set of hoop-back dining room chairs, but would rather glue up several thin strips than steam-bend one thick strip. How thin do the laminations need to be for making the hoops, and how do I prepare the wood before gluing?

A Most woods become pliable when cut to a thickness of ⅛" or less. For cutting your laminations, start with a board that's thick enough to account for the combined thickness of your laminate strips, plus the saw kerfs. You'll also want to start with stock that's longer than what you need so you can cut the hoop to final length after it's been formed.

Cut one laminate strip on a table saw equipped with a smooth cutting blade, and set it aside (see page 114). Run the edge of the remaining board through the jointer to smooth it, cut the next strip, and repeat. By jointing the board before ripping the next piece, one face of each laminate will have a smooth gluing face. Keep the strips stacked in the same order they were cut.

Q How do I build and use a laminating form?

A Begin building your form by cutting plywood or MDF to the shape of the inside of the curve you want (actually a little smaller to account for spring-back). You'll need to secure two or three layers together for wide laminations. Use a spade bit to create holes a couple of inches back from the edge for clamps to grab onto. Secure this to a sheet of plywood.

Cut a series of arched pressure blocks to help distribute clamping pressure on the outside of the laminate pieces. Apply glue to the laminate strips, sandwich them together, and clamp one end to the form. Continue to add clamps and blocks while forcing the strips against the inner form. Tap down the edges of the strips from time to time to help keep them flush to one another. Let the clamps sit overnight before removing them.

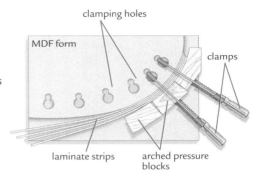

Q What's the best type of glue to use on the laminate strips?

A You want to use a glue that sets hard; epoxy, polyurethane, resorcinol, and plastic resin glues are all good candidates. Resorcinol glue is fine for darker woods but presents a noticeable dark glue line when used on lighter woods. On lighter woods, consider using a special light-colored resin glue available at woodworking specialty stores.

Q I know most bent woods will spring back slightly once you remove them from the form. How do I compensate for that?

A There's no exact formula, since temperature, time left on the form, type and thickness of wood, degree of bend, and other factors come into play. It's better to overbend than underbend the wood. Wood with too much curve can be slightly straightened by heating it with a hair dryer or placing a wet towel on the concave part after removing it from the form. But trying to add more bend to a piece once it's cooled is difficult. Your best bet is to experiment before building the actual piece.

tip: Just an Old Softy

If you're bending a thin strip or two in a gentle curve, try soaking the wood in your bathtub containing warm water with a dash of fabric softener. The mixture will help relax the fibers.

Q How do you kerf-bend wood?

A Kerf bending, as the name implies, involves cutting a series of kerfs across the width of the board to make it flexible enough to bend. Usually the kerfs are spaced ½" to 1" apart (depending on how tight a curve you need) and deep enough to leave about ⅛" of solid wood on the face. There are drawbacks to this method: The kerfs show along the edges of the board and must be covered somehow. Also, unless the kerfs are perfectly spaced and at the right depth, the wood can kink.

Q I'm not crazy about building a steam box or a bending jig just to create two rockers. Can't I just saw them from solid wood?

A Yes. Begin by making a template of the rockers from thick card stock. Select straight-grained, defect-free hardwood, and place the pattern on it. Examine the curve and its relationship to the grain. The more perpendicular the grain runs to the curve of the rocker (i.e. near the ends), the more vulnerable these parts are to splitting. If the curve is moderate, this may not be an issue. Once the pattern is optimally positioned, trace it onto the wood. For more dramatic curves, you may want to thicken these areas with "ball ends." These add more meat for strength and also create round ends that are less likely to bruise little shins.

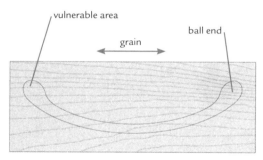

vulnerable area

grain

ball end

Veneering, Banding, and Inlays

Q I love the "butterfly" symmetry of book-matched veneer. Is this something I can do?

A Yes. Your first task is to locate two sheets of veneer that were consecutively cut from the same log. The more figured the veneers, the more interesting the pattern they will create. Stack them with the edges to be joined as closely aligned as possible. Use a straightedge and razor knife to make a perfectly straight cut through the edges of both pieces, removing as little material as possible.

Turn the top piece over (like you'd turn the page of a book) and butt the two straight edges against each other. Align the two to create the most pleasing pattern, check that there are no gaps at the seam, then draw the seam tightly together by stretching short pieces of masking tape (the type designed for delicate surfaces is best) across it every 3" or 4". Run a continuous piece of masking tape down the full length of the seam, and your book-matched veneer is ready to be glued down.

add masking tape the full length of the seam

consecutively cut veneers

straight edges butted together

Q I've heard mixed opinions about using contact cement for applying veneers. What's the scoop?

A It's safe to use contact cement for installing paper-backed veneers or veneers that are already backed with a cross-grain veneer, but many woodworkers won't use contact cement for raw wood veneers. Contact cement doesn't dry hard, which means when veneers expand and contract (yep, they're wood, so they behave like wood), they can pull away from the substrate, then crack and ripple. And once contact is made between the two pieces, repositioning is difficult to impossible. Many woodworkers use yellow glue, but this has problems, too. It allows the veneer to creep and, because of the glue's thin consistency, it can bleed through and discolor the wood. For raw wood veneers, it's safest to use a special "cold-press veneer glue" (see Resources).

Q I was given a 6/4 walnut board containing a beautifully figured crotch pattern. I'd love to "stretch" this board across the face of a credenza I'm building. Can I cut my own veneers?

A Yes, woodworkers have been cutting veneers to make the most of figured wood since the Egyptians used them to decorate sarcophagi thousands of years ago. Most store-bought veneers are $1/32$" to $1/40$" thick. While you'd have trouble producing veneer that thin, you can create veneers that are in the $1/16$" to $1/8$" range, using a bandsaw. As a bonus, your "homemade" veneers will be easier to handle and more durable.

Begin by smoothing one face of your board on a stationary drum sander. You can use a planer or jointer, but the sander will create less tearout on highly figured wood like yours.

Set the fence on your bandsaw a "veneer thickness" away from the blade. Then, using a blade designed for resawing (a sharp one!), carefully cut one veneer panel and set it aside (see page 127 for help with ripping wide stock). Run your board through your drum sander to smooth the face you just cut your veneer panel from, then repeat.

Stack the veneers in the order that you cut them. Since each veneer panel will have one rough and one smooth face, and the thickness will vary, use your drum sander to smooth the cut face and even out the thickness. To do this, use a couple of short pieces of double-sided tape to stick the very ends of your veneer to a piece of MDF (with the veneer rough-side-up), and use it as a sled to run your wood through your sander. If all goes well, your 1½"-thick board should yield 10 to 12 beautiful veneer panels.

Q What precautions should I take when using veneer to create a large tabletop?

A Use a stable substrate such as MDF or particleboard, or a high-quality plywood such as Baltic birch. Unlike solid wood, these materials are less prone to warping, expansion, and contraction, which can wreak havoc on large expanses of veneer. For stability, use an inexpensive veneer such as poplar on the underside of the tabletop to create a "sandwich" that has uniform properties above and below.

Carving

Q I want to try my hand at woodcarving. What are some good woods to use?

A Your best bet is to use a straight-grained hardwood, such as butternut, basswood, or walnut. Softwoods, such as pine, are physically easier to carve, but because of their coarse grain, they tend to splinter when carved with the grain and tear when they're carved across the grain. Finer textured woods, such as basswood, also have a less distinct grain pattern, which is often preferred so the grain doesn't detract from the workpiece.

Select a wood that complements the subject matter of your carving. Basswood might be the wood of choice when carving seagulls, while walnut may be a better choice for bears.

Q What's a good starting set of tools for someone getting into carving?

A There are so many different types of carving — chip carving, low-relief carving, carving in the round, sign making — that it's impossible to give one right answer. For small, delicate carvings you might want to use palm tools; for larger projects you'll want substantial gouges and chisels. The best advice is to find an object or pattern similar to the one you intend to carve, bring it to a specialty woodworking store, and have someone there show you what tools you'll need to create the shapes involved. For carving common decorative elements such as shells or finials, check into the beginner's sets sold by some specialty retailers; they contain all the tools needed to handle the task.

Q I'm having trouble finding the right clamp to hold my workpiece while I carve. Any suggestions?

A If you're carving "in the round," try using a carver's bench screw. It's basically a long rod with coarse threads on one end that you screw into the base of the wood. The other end, which is finely threaded, is inserted in a hole in your workbench and secured with a large wingnut.

One variation of this is called a pivoting clamp. It works in a similar manner but has a ball-and-socket mechanism that allows you to tilt and secure the piece at any angle.

Q Why should I buy a carver's mallet when I have plenty of other hammers I can use?

A Wood mallets are easier on the wood handles of chisels and gouges than metal hammerheads are. Plus they're lighter, with shorter handles, making them easier to use for extended periods of time. The round head of the mallet is well balanced and allows you to strike your tools from any angle without having to re-grip the handle. And though many carver's mallets today are made of high-density polyurethane, traditional beech and lignum vitae mallets are small works of art in and of themselves.

8 Building Furniture

Trees have a yearning to live again,
perhaps to provide the beauty, strength,
and utility to serve man, even to become
an object of great artistic worth.

— GEORGE NAKASHIMA

To some people, the terms *woodworking* and *furniture making* are synonymous. And surely when you build a fine piece of furniture, you'll use your sharpest tools, your finest woods, and your most exacting standards. Many of the general questions you might have about furniture making are dealt with in other sections; use the index and table of contents to track down the information you need. Here we'll look at some questions regarding specific pieces of furniture.

Planning

Q I precut all the pieces for a wooden jewelry box based on the cutting list in a magazine, but when I went to assemble the lid, it didn't fit. What good is a cutting list if things don't turn out right?

A The cutting plans for projects you find in books and magazines are usually based on dimensions taken from the actual finished piece. But no two projects, boards, tools, or woodworkers are exactly the same. Your wood may have been a hair thicker, your dadoes may have been a bit deeper, and the strips you ripped on your table saw may have been a bit wider. By the time all the little differences are compounded, it's easy to end up with discrepancies, especially as you near the end. It's best to use the given dimensions as good, but not exact, guidelines. Cut and fit as you build, and you'll have better-fitting parts (and less aggravation).

Q I saw plans for a bookcase I like, but want to modify the size so it will fit in the corner of our family room. How can I make sure the proportions are right?

A Invest a few hours building a simple prototype out of cardboard, MDF, or even sheets of rigid foam board. Your mockup will help give you a sense of the right proportions for the piece, as well as how it will fit in the room. It may even give you clues as to how best to construct the piece and the amount of material you'll need. You'll find it time well spent.

---

5 RULES FOR MISTAKE-FREE FURNITURE BUILDING

The techniques used for building a bent-willow rocker and a Craftsman-style bookcase are different indeed. Still, the two projects share some basic fundamentals, especially in regard to minimizing mistakes and maximizing longevity. As you head into any project keep these tips in mind:

1 Start right, stay right. Make sure your lumber is uniform and your joints tight every step of the way, so you don't wind up fighting your mistake near the end.

2 Measure twice, mark twice, cut once. Make one mark to indicate your cut line; the other to indicate the waste side of your cut. You'll avoid miscut pieces and mismatched lengths.

3 Test your tool settings on a scrap piece of wood. A dado that's ⅛" too deep or a tenon ¼" too narrow can mean starting over. If you're building a table, consider crafting five legs — one test leg and four usable legs. By foreseeing and avoiding multiple mistakes, you may actually save time and materials.

4 Think and plan two steps ahead. Dry-fit and label your pieces before final assembly. Multiple minor mistakes add up to major problems.

5 Strive to remove the least amount of wood while creating the strongest joint. Longevity is all about sturdy joints; craft them with care.

Tables and Desks

Q What are some key dimensions for building a dining room table?

A The size and design of a table can make dining a delightful experience or one that produces indigestion and banged shins. Here are a few basic guidelines:

- ⊙ Standard height: 28" to 30"
- ⊙ Minimum amount of elbow room per person: 24"
- ⊙ Minimum amount of legroom (between tabletop support rails and floor): 24"
- ⊙ Horizontal knee clearance (measured from edge of tabletop to table leg or other obstruction): 10"
- ⊙ Minimum size of rectangular table seating six people: 40" × 60"
- ⊙ Circular table capacities: 40"-diameter table will seat four comfortably; 48"-diameter will seat six; 60"-diameter will seat eight

You should also take into account the size of the room. There should be at least 28" from the edge of the tabletop to the walls or other pieces of furniture, so people have adequate room to push their chairs back to stand up. If you want room for people to get past seated diners, you need a minimum of 36".

Q A woodworker friend of mine was talking about putting breadboard ends on a table. What are they, and what function do they serve?

A Breadboard ends are strips of wood that run perpendicular to the boards oriented "the long way" in a tabletop. They do two things: cover and protect the end grain and help keep the tabletop flat.

You can't just glue or screw a breadboard end in place. Wood shrinks and expands much more *across* the grain than *along* the grain, so the tabletop will crack if you glue the breadboard ends directly to

BREADBOARD ENDS

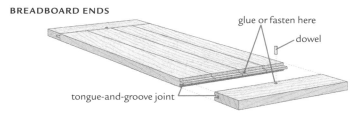

glue or fasten here

dowel

tongue-and-groove joint

it. The challenge is to create a method whereby the breadboard ends can do their job while allowing the top to shrink and expand independently. There are several effective options for this, and most involve securing the breadboard end in the middle while allowing the ends to move. This can be done with dowels, slotted holes, tongue-and-groove joints, and/or mortise-and-tenon joints.

Q I edge-glued five 8'-long oak boards to create a 30"-wide desktop. Looks like it might take days with a belt sander to get it absolutely smooth. Any tricks for saving time, my arm, and my belt sander?

A Sometimes the best trick is to let someone else do the work. Call some local cabinet shops to see if they have a stationary drum or belt sander wide enough for your top. It may cost you $40 to $50 (you might spend that much in sander belts anyway), but in a few passes they'll be able to flatten and smooth your top better than you can. Make sure to scrape off all beads of glue on both sides before bringing it in.

Q How do I attach a solid wood top to the table apron to allow it to move independently when it expands and contracts?

A Since the tabletop will expand and contract a different amount than the apron or base it's adhered to, you're right about needing to use the correct fastening system. Here are two common methods:

The **tongue-and-groove system** involves cutting a groove near the upper edge of the apron, then making blocks with a small tongue on one side. Mount the blocks to the underside of the tabletop so the tongue fits into the groove.

The **bracket system** involves securing L-shaped metal tabletop fasteners to the apron and tabletop. The elongated slot in the top of the L-bracket allows the tabletop to expand and contract without cracking.

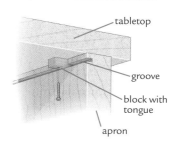

TONGUE-AND-GROOVE SYSTEM

tabletop

groove

block with tongue

apron

BRACKET SYSTEM

tabletop

slot

bracket

apron

¾" thick

**HOLLOW COLUMN
OF SOLID WOOD**

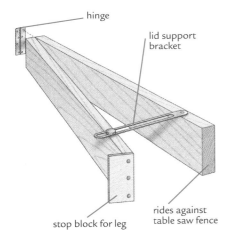

hinge

lid support
bracket

stop block for leg

rides against
table saw fence

Q I'm building a table with massive legs. Can I use solid 6×6s?

A You can, but unless your wood is cut and dried properly, chances are excellent that those large chunks of solid wood will twist and split. One good alternative is to create hollow columns using ¾"-thick boards (see page 235 for assembly tips). The legs will be more stable, the grain will be more uniform, and you won't need a crane to move your table.

Q I want to build a desk with tapered legs. How do I cut them so the taper is consistent?

A Use a taper jig and your table saw. You can purchase a jig or make your own by hinging two 1×4s together. Include lid support hardware so you can adjust the angle, and add a stop block for pushing the leg through the saw.

To use your jig, adjust it to the desired taper (you'd be wise to make some test cuts), then run one arm of the jig against your table saw fence while using the other arm to guide the leg past the blade. If you're tapering opposite sides of the leg, you'll need to adjust the angle of the jig to get a consistent taper on opposing sides.

Q I want to build an oval-top coffee table. I've seen some complicated methods for drawing an oval, but I'm wondering if there are any methods we non-Einsteins can use.

A Yes, here's how:

1 Draw intersecting vertical and horizontal lines on your tabletop blank. Measure out the length of your oval on the horizontal axis and mark those two points A. Measure out the width of your oval on the vertical axis and mark those two points B.

2 On the edge of a stick, make a mark near one end and label it X. Measure from the point where the layout lines intersect (the center point) to A on your layout, then make a mark on the stick representing that distance from X and mark it A on the stick. Do the same for B.

3 Position your stick so the A mark falls anywhere on the vertical line and the B falls on the horizontal line. Make a dot next to the X. Reposition your stick slightly, keeping the A on the vertical axis and the B on the horizontal axis; make another dot at the X. Keep doing this until you've created a dashed oval, then connect the dots.

Q I'm building a pair of 24"-diameter side tables from oak. How do I cut perfect circles for the tops?

A Cut them with a beam jig and a router:

1 Begin with a scrap piece of plywood that's at least ½" × 10" × 20". Set your router on one end (a plunge router will make the entire process easier), then solidly box it in with 1×2s on all four sides. An alternative is to remove the router baseplate and screw the router directly to the plywood. Bore a hole through the plywood for the router bit to extend through.

2 Insert a straight-cutting bit, and adjust the bit depth so the bit will extend ¼" below your plywood jig. Next establish the correct radius for your jig. For a 24"-diameter top, measure 12" over from the inside edge of your bit and drill a small pivot hole in the plywood. Mark the centerpoint of your glued-up boards, then drive a screw through the pivot hole and into this centerpoint.

3 Lift your router so the bit isn't in contact with the top; if you're using a plunge router, simply retract the bit. Turn on the router, lower it into

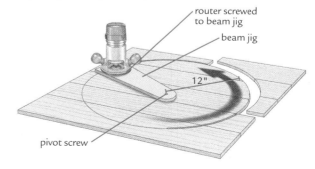

router screwed to beam jig

beam jig

12"

pivot screw

the wood, and cut a ¼"-deep circular groove on your first rotation. Continue lowering your bit in increments of ¼" or less, making additional passes until you've completely cut through the wood. Either cut your top good-side-down or add a dab of wood putty to fill the pivot hole when you're done.

Q I have a wonderful 2"-thick slab of rough-sawn crotch walnut with natural edges that I'd like to use for a tabletop. Are there any special techniques I should use to prepare the slab?

A Begin by flooding the surface with mineral spirits to accentuate the grain. This will allow you to get a feel for the overall grain pattern, which is especially important if you'll be crosscutting or removing parts of the slab. Here are some general guidelines to follow:

⊙ Decide whether you want to preserve or remove the bark. If you want to remove it, pry off the loose stuff, then use a grinder to remove the well-adhered stuff. Keep an eye on the grain and contours of the wood so your natural edge continues to look natural. If you want to keep the bark intact, you can stabilize any marginally adhered material by saturating it with epoxy or cyanoacrylate glue. Follow the manufacturer's safety precautions, since these glues dry quickly, grip tenaciously, and have a strong odor.

⊙ Since your slab comes from an area of the tree where the grain changes direction frequently, you'll have less grain tearout if you run the slab through a wide belt sander, instead of a planer, while smoothing the top. If it's too large for either, break out the belt sander and finish up with a random orbital sander with 220-grit paper.

⊙ When finishing the tabletop, apply just as many coats to the bottom and edges as you do to the top surface.

⊙ As with any wide wood tabletop, secure it to its base with a fastening system that allows the top to expand and contract without hindrance.

If you want to purchase a natural-edge slab, contact one of the hardwood companies listed under chapter 2 in Resources. Many stock fabulous woods from around the world.

Q I love the look of bowtie- or butterfly-shaped splines on tabletops. How hard is it to make them?

A You can make them the old-fashioned way by cutting the recess with a chisel, and the bowtie-shaped key with a handsaw. But you can also get fast, accurate results using one of the router template systems on the market. (Search the Internet using the keywords "butterfly template.") These systems consist of a butterfly-shaped template, a router guide bushing that follows the template, and a fluted router bit that does the cutting. Most systems allow you to cut both the recess and the key.

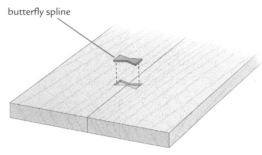

butterfly spline

Make your inlay at least ¼" thick so it has enough strength to hold the joint or crack tightly together, but keep it under 3" in length so the expansion and contraction of the butterfly itself don't become an issue.

Q I want to build a drop-leaf table. Are hinges alone strong enough to support the leaf where it meets the tabletop?

A For the sturdiest connection, consider joining the leaf to the tabletop using a *rule joint*. In the raised position, the convex edge of the tabletop supports the concave edge of the leaf, minimizing the strain on the hinges. The convex tabletop edges can be created with a router and a roundover bit; the concave edge of the leaf is made with a matching cove bit.

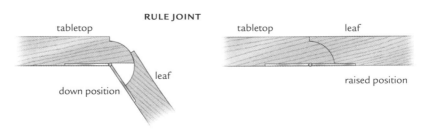

RULE JOINT

tabletop

leaf

down position

tabletop

leaf

raised position

Chairs and Stools

Q I'd like to build a set of dining room chairs. What are some guidelines for comfort and usability?

A A well-built dining room chair is a thing of beauty. It's sturdy enough to hold a 300-pound person yet light enough to be moved by a child. It can accommodate a wide range of heights and widths while feeling just as good as it looks. Basic guidelines include:

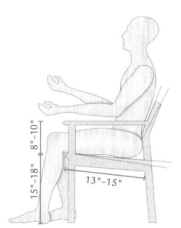

- ⊙ Standard seat height: 15" to 18" (at front edge)
- ⊙ Standard seat width: 17" to 18" (at front, narrowing at back for elbow comfort)
- ⊙ Standard seat angle: 5 to 8 degrees (sloped toward back)
- ⊙ Armrest height: 8" to 10" above seat
- ⊙ Angle of backrest: 20 to 25 degrees from vertical
- ⊙ Height of backrest: varies greatly, but supporting the lumbar or lower spine region (8" to 12" above the seat) is critical for comfort

You may want to mock up a chair out of plywood and experiment with heights and angles to find the perfect design for you and your family.

Q How do I determine the position of the legs for a three-legged stool with a round top?

A Use a compass to draw two circles: one for the seat itself, the other to indicate the radius of the legs. Without changing the compass setting for the smaller inner circle, start anywhere on the inner circle, and step off six small arcs. Your last arc should intersect exactly with your starting point. Every other tick mark will indicate the position of a leg.

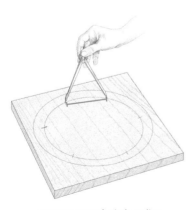

compass spread=circle radius

Q Is there a simple way to create a round tenon on the end of a square leg spindle?

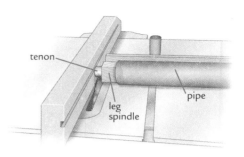

A Locate a piece of pipe with an inside diameter that will snugly hold the square leg spindle. Set the fence of your table saw so it's the same distance from the outer edge of the blade as the tenon is long, and adjust the blade height. You'll have to experiment with blade height to get the right diameter for your tenon. Use your miter gauge to hold the pipe square to the blade as you push the leg end across the saw blade multiple times — both rotating and shifting it back and forth — until you've created a round tenon.

If you can't find the right size of pipe, bore a hole in the end of the spindle and glue in a section of dowel to create your tenon.

Q The cabriolet legs I want to create for my chairs curve in both directions. How do I cut them out on my bandsaw?

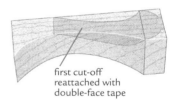

first cut-off reattached with double-face tape

A Create a pattern out of MDF or cardboard, and transfer the shape onto two adjacent sides of the leg blank. Cut out the pattern on one side of your leg blank, keeping your cutoffs whole.

Secure the cutoffs back in their original positions with double-sided tape, then cut out the shapes on the other face. Your work has just begun; there's tons of hand-shaping involved in finishing the legs.

Q I built a set of stools, but some of them rock slightly. How do I correct this?

A Use your table saw — not as a way of cutting the legs shorter but as a flat platform for fine-tuning your work. Lower the blade, remove the rip fence, and set one of your rocking stools on the table. Determine which leg needs to be shortened to eliminate the rocking. Tape a piece of coarse sandpaper to the table and move the long leg back and forth across it to remove material, then recheck for rocking without the sandpaper beneath the leg. This is also a good way to establish the correct angle on the bottoms of the legs.

Q Why are most Windsor chairs — especially old ones — painted black?

A Traditional Windsor chairs are crafted from several different types of wood, each with its own special attribute. The paint covers up the mishmash of grains and colors that would show if the chairs were left unfinished. Poplar, a wood that's stable and available in thick slabs, is used for the scooped-out seat. Maple, with its fine, straight grain, is used for the legs. Hickory, with its legendary strength, is traditionally used for the spindles. And ash, because of its strength and "bend-ability," is used for the curved back frame and other curved parts.

Bookcases and Entertainment Centers

Q I'm building a bookcase. I'd like to make it as wide as possible without the shelves sagging. How far can a typical shelf span?

A It depends on the type of material, the thickness of the material, and how the shelf is constructed. Figure that your shelves need to support 20 to 25 pounds per running foot. For appearances, you want those shelves to sag less than ⅛". Adding a ¾" × 1¼" apron to the front or front and back of a ¾" shelf increases the strength, and thus the recommended span, appreciably. Your aprons can be straight strips of wood or have a rabbet on one edge. The chart on the facing page shows the recommended maximum span for 10"-deep shelves of various materials.

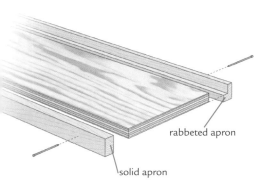

rabbeted apron

solid apron

Q The bookcase I'm building will use pins to support the shelves. How do I make sure all the holes are positioned and spaced correctly?

A You need rows of evenly spaced ¼" holes. Pegboard just happens to be made of rows of evenly spaced ¼" holes. It's a marriage made in heaven. Cut a piece of pegboard to match the bookcase sides. On the pegboard template, clearly mark the top, then mark the two vertical rows and the horizontal

MAXIMUM SHELF SPANS				
		RECOMMENDED SPAN		
MATERIAL	THICKNESS	SHELF ONLY	W/FRONT APRON	W/FRONT & BACK APRONS
Particleboard	¾"	24"	30"	36"
Melamine	¾"	30"	n/a	n/a
Hardwood plywood	¾"	30"	42"	48"
Pine	¾"	32"	45"	52"
Pine	1½"	60"	n/a	n/a
Red oak	¾"	40"	52"	60"
Red oak	1½"	72"	n/a	n/a

rows (which will establish the shelf spacing). Clamp your template to the bookshelf sides and drill away.

Q How can I make sure all the shelf-pin holes I need to drill in the sides of my bookcase are at the same depth?

A You can use the old trick of wrapping masking tape around the bit to indicate the right depth. However, after a few dozen holes the tape tends to creep and tatter. You can also buy metal stop collars that tighten onto your bit, but even those can slip.

The surefire way is to make your own stop collar from a small block of wood. If you need ½"-deep holes and your bit extends 3" past the tip of the chuck, bore a hole through a 2½"-long block, leave the block on the bit, then drill away. If you're using pegboard or some other material as a guide, take into account the thickness of the material when crafting your stop block.

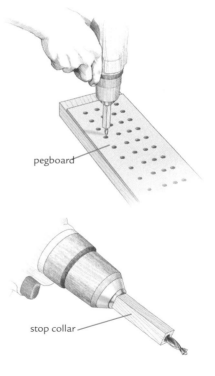

pegboard

stop collar

FROM KITCHEN CABINET
TO ENTERTAINMENT CENTER

If you look at custom-built and store-bought entertainment centers, you'll find they consist mostly of base cabinets, upper cabinets, shelves, and drawers — hmmm, the same components you'll find in the "kitchen cabinet" department of your home center. If you're hesitant to tackle cabinetmaking, you can save yourself a lot of work and use stock cabinets, some plywood, and a little creativity to build all (or part) of your own entertainment center. Study the components available in the manufacturers' catalogs. Everything you need might be right there for the ordering.

Q I'm creating a built-in entertainment center and want to include doors to conceal the sound equipment. How do I build it so the doors aren't in the way when they're open?

A Install flipper door slides and hinges. These mechanisms allow you to swing the doors open like normal doors, then slide them inside the cabinet (along the side) and out of the way. Plan ahead to make sure your cabinet is deep enough to accommodate the door width and wide enough to accommodate the thickness of the doors and mechanisms. Buy your hardware before you start planning and building to make sure you have room for everything.

tip: Break Out the Board Stretcher!

Ever cut a mitered piece of furniture trim a little too short — and it was the last piece you had? Never fear, sometimes you can stretch that board to make it work. Use a hand plane or table saw to carefully remove a thin slice of material — less than 1/16" — from the inside edge of the too-short piece. This will effectively make that edge longer. You'll have to sand the corners of the adjoining pieces a little after this piece is installed to make them match up.

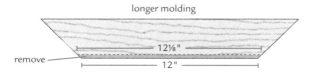

longer molding

12⅛"

remove —

12"

Q What's the easiest and most accurate way to cut dadoes in the sides of a bookcase with a router?

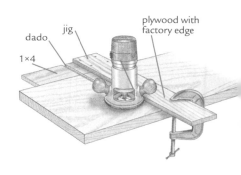

A You'll get consistent results with a dado jig. Here's how to build one:

1 Secure the factory edge of a ½" piece of plywood to a 1×4 crosspiece. Your dados will only be as accurate as your jig, so square up the two pieces carefully, and glue and screw them together.

2 Run the base of your router along the factory edge of the plywood to create a groove in your crosspiece.

3 When it's time to cut your dadoes, line up the groove in the crosspiece with each shelf location on your bookcase side. Firmly clamp the jig to the side piece, then rout your dado.

For the straightest dado, don't rotate the base of your router during the cut; the base may not be perfectly concentric to the bit.

Q How can I make sure the dadoes I cut on both sides of the bookcase line up exactly?

A Your best bet is to start with material that's twice as wide as a finished side piece, rout all of your dadoes, then rip the material in half to create the two sides. You'll save time and your dadoes will be dead even.

Other Types of Furniture

Q I want to build a bed for my granddaughter. What's the simplest kind of hardware to install so it can be taken apart and set up easily?

A One sturdy, hidden system is the bed-rail fastener. The part of the bracket with female slots is set into a shallow mortise in the headboard, and a metal plate with male fingers is mortised into the end of the rail. When assembling the bed, the fingers fit into the slots. As you add weight, the two parts wedge themselves even more tightly together.

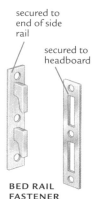

BED RAIL
FASTENER

Q What's the best type of finish to use inside a chest of drawers?

A Some finishes, such as Danish oil and oil varnishes, can smell for months if they're trapped in a drawer. Rather than risk the chance of a finish or odor transferring to the clothing, most finishers leave the insides of drawers unfinished. If you insist on using some kind of finish, try shellac or a water-based coating.

Q I'm building a dresser with drawers almost 12" tall. Should I install the drawer slides at the bottom, middle, or top? What about the pulls?

A Your drawer will have the best feel and smoothest action if your slides and pull are on approximately the same plane. If you want your pulls centered height-wise on your drawer, position the slides in line with them.

Q I'm building a desk and using 1/16"-thick walnut veneer, sawed on my bandsaw, for the top. Some of the pieces have hairline cracks in them. Is there a simple way of patching the cracks without destroying the looks?

A Use 220-grit sandpaper to lightly sand the surface. Don't blow or brush off the dust; let it settle into the cracks. Apply a small bead of cyanoacrylate glue to the cracks using a syringe or the small tip of the glue bottle. Let the glue dry, then sand again. Your homemade filler should blend in well with the veneer. You can do this either before or after applying the veneer to the desktop.

Q I'm making the base for a floor lamp out of a 4×4 and need to drill a hole through the middle of a 52"-long piece for the cord. How do I do that?

A You could drill through each end using long-shank spade bits and shank extenders, but guiding them and having them meet in the center is an iffy proposition. The easiest way may actually be with your table saw. Rip the 4×4 in half with two passes on your table saw. Lower your blade, adjust it to 45 degrees, set the fence about 1½" away from the blade, and make two more passes on one or both halves to create a V-groove down the center. Then glue it back together again. If you're careful, the cut line will disappear.

Continuous-Grain Box

At first glance it seems impossible: From a single board, build a box where the grain runs continuously — around the corners, never-ending, without disruption. A board has two ends, so that's impossible, right? Not if you do it this way:

1 Start with a board that's twice as thick as the sides of your proposed box and the exact same length as one side, plus one end joined together end-to-end.

2 Resaw the board lengthwise on your table saw or bandsaw. These resawn faces will become the outer surfaces of the box.

3 Lay out the 45-degree cuts as shown.

4 Cut the miters. If you use a radial arm saw or table saw with a cross-cut sled (see page 114), you can make your cuts without removing hardly any of the material at the outside corners.

5 Glue the four sides back together as shown.

There's your box with the unbroken grain. The more pronounced the grain (think spalted or crotch wood), the more "impossible" your box will be.

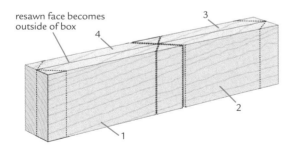

resawn face becomes
outside of box

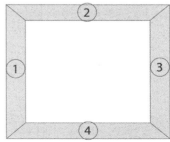

9 Cabinets & Countertops

Ah, to build, to build! That is the noblest
of all the arts.
— HENRY WADSWORTH LONGFELLOW

Cabinetmaking is an enormously popular activity among woodworkers, most likely because cabinets themselves are enormously popular. We use them in kitchens, bathrooms, family rooms, workshops, laundry rooms, and almost every other room in the house. If you take into account all the variables a cabinet can have — style, size, configuration, door and drawer design, hardware, and wood species, to name a few — you wind up with thousands of possibilities. This is a blessing and a curse. It's a blessing in that it allows you to build cabinets that meet your needs and aesthetic tastes. It's a curse in that it's hard to know where to begin. This chapter is designed to help you begin.

Design Considerations

Q We're gutting our kitchen and starting over from scratch. What are some guidelines and rules of thumb for cabinet layout and construction?

A The National Kitchen and Bath Association (NKBA) website holds a wealth of information that will help you with your design decisions, including its "Thirty-One Ways to a Better Kitchen" guidelines (see Resources). Here are a few basics:

⊙ Standard base cabinets are 34½" tall. This puts the countertop at a comfortable working height of 35½" to 36" for most people. Standard base cabinet depth is 24". Both dimensions can be adjusted for taller or shorter users.

- Standard upper cabinets are 12" deep (though 13" or 14" is common for cabinets with inset doors.) Provide at least 18" of space between the top of your counter and the bottoms of the upper cabinets.

- Arrange cabinets, dishwashers, ovens, and refrigerators so doors don't interfere with one another when open. Pay special attention to corners. Sometimes two narrow doors can replace a single wide door to alleviate congestion.

- Provide at least a 24"-wide landing area on one side of the sink and 18" on the other. Include at least 15" of countertop next to, or directly across from, the refrigerator. Provide at least 12" of countertop on one side of the cooking surface and 15" on the other. Provide at least a 15" landing area above, below, or next to the microwave.

Q A friend of mine maintains you don't have to build a kitchen cabinet as solidly as a china cabinet. They're both cabinets — why wouldn't you build them with the same care?

A Your friend may be referring to the notion that a china cabinet needs to be built to withstand being tilted on its side, dragged across the floor and/or loaded onto a truck, and transported hundreds of miles. It just takes one weak spot or "oops" to ruin it. A kitchen cabinet mainly just sits there. It's fastened to a wall, topped with something durable, and often is supported on either side by other cabinets. But while the case of the cabinet may not sustain much wear and tear, other components will. For kitchen cabinets, you may want to pour more time and energy into building solid, smooth-operating doors and drawers to withstand daily use and abuse.

tip: How Are You Going to Use That Cabinet?

A standard base cabinet has a 6"-high drawer opening and a 20"-high door opening. But before you build any cabinet, figure out what's going inside. You may want all drawers for storing cosmetics in a bathroom vanity, vertical dividers for cookie sheets in a kitchen cabinet, or rollout shelves spaced 7" apart for a workshop cabinet storing pints of paint. It's wise to customize.

4 BASIC DOOR AND DRAWER TYPES

There are four basic ways that cabinet doors and drawers can interact with the cabinet case (box). They can cover the cabinet face frame, sit in the opening, or do a little bit of each. The type and style of the door and drawer, and how it's installed, impact how the cabinet looks and operates and how it is built. Selecting door and drawer type is one of the first decisions you need to make when embarking on a cabinet project. The four basic door and drawer configurations are:

1 *Partial overlay* doors and drawers overlap the face frame of the cabinet by ⅜" to ½". Hinges can be exposed or concealed. They have a traditional look and are the most common type of cabinet found on the shelves at home centers.

2 *Full overlay*, or *European style*, doors and drawers completely overlap the framework of the openings. The front of the cabinet case is usually, but not always, frameless (only ¾" thick) and is created by the four sides of the cabinet box. Hinges are always concealed. When unadorned laminate doors are used, the look is sleek and contemporary.

3 *Inset* doors and drawers actually sit in the opening, flush with the face frame of the cabinet. This style offers a very traditional — even vintage — look, especially when exposed hinges are used. Since any unevenness in the gap around the doors and drawers is there for all to see, components must fit precisely. This is arguably the most difficult type of cabinet to construct.

4 *Lipped* doors and drawers have a ⅜" rabbet around the edges so they "nest" into the face frame, and are sort of a cross between the overlay and inset styles. They require special offset hinges, which are widely available. The look is clean and usually leans toward the traditional. Many 1950s and '60s cabinets were made in this style.

PARTIAL OVERLAY DOOR

FULL OVERLAY DOOR

INSET DOOR

⅜" LIPPED DOOR

Cabinets: Doors and Hardware

Q What thickness of material should I use for constructing cabinet cases?

A You can get by with ½"-thick material for the sides and bottom, but ¾" material will allow you to cut deeper dadoes and rabbets, use biscuit and pocket screw joinery, and install longer screws for mounting hardware. In terms of selection, you often have more choices and more readily available materials with ¾" sheet goods. And although ¾" material is 50 percent thicker than ½", you won't pay 50 percent more for it.

Q Should I use ¾"-thick material for the cabinet back, too?

A That's overkill. Cabinet backs don't sustain much wear and tear, and, with a hanging strip (see next question), they don't need to support much weight. Backs are there to enclose the case and hold the cabinet square. Use ¼" or ⅜" material instead. Thinner material is lighter and cheaper and requires smaller rabbets to hold it in place.

Q What's a hanging strip?

A Since the backs of most upper cabinets are thin and can't support the weight of fully loaded shelves, hanging strips are built into the cabinet backs to do the job. They're normally ¾" wood strips firmly secured to the cabinet sides near the top and bottom; they may be notched, dadoed, or screwed in place. The upper strip is usually snug to the inside top of the cabinet. The lower one may be inside the cabinet or in the little recess underneath the cabinet.

Base cabinets usually have just one strip near the top that does double duty in supporting the back of the countertop. When mounting a cabinet to the wall studs, always drive your fasteners through the hanging strips.

Q How do I cover the exposed edges of the plywood I'm using to build the cases of frameless kitchen cabinets?

A You have several options in regard to what material to use and how and when to apply it. The simplest solution is to use veneer tape or *edge banding* that has hot-melt glue on one side and wood veneer or laminate on the other (see page 56). Apply it by rolling it out with one hand, while using the other hand to guide a household iron (set at medium) to activate the glue and adhere the banding to the edge.

Next in terms of simplicity are ⅛"-thick wood strips glued to the edge. Often you can clamp these in place simply with strips of masking tape stretched tightly over the edge every few inches. Wider solid-wood nosing can be applied using glue, fasteners, or biscuits.

You can add the edging after the cabinets are built, but you might find it easier to rip your components to width, apply the edging in 8' lengths, cut the parts to their final length, then assemble the cabinet.

Q It seems like I need three hands to keep all the parts balanced and aligned when I'm building cabinet boxes. Any tips for making the job easier?

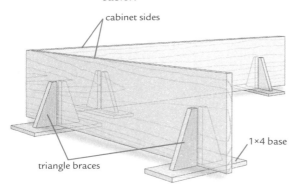

cabinet sides

triangle braces

1×4 base

A Build these simple panel holders out of scrap wood. Each consists of a 1×4 base with two right triangles secured to it ¾" apart. The triangles can be made of plywood, 1×6s, or 2×6s. It takes only a few minutes to make each holder, and you'll be able to work faster and more accurately with these helping hands.

Q Why are frame-and-panel doors used so often in kitchens? Because they look good or because they perform well?

A Frame-and-panel doors are attractive, but the real reason doors are constructed this way is to deal with our old friend, wood movement. A typical cabinet door is 20" to 30" tall and 16" to 20" wide. There are several problems with building a door that size with a solid panel. First, the end grain is exposed along the top and bottom edges; a not-so-attractive look and an invitation for moisture and water. But a bigger problem has to do with the way wood moves. A solid piece of wood the size of a cabinet door will expand and contract a noticeable amount and, if left uncontained, may warp and twist.

Frame-and-panel construction solves these problems. The rigid frame prevents the panel from warping and also minimizes the amount of end grain exposed along the edges. Since the edges of the panel can expand and contract freely within the grooves of the frame, cracking is minimized. That's why frame-and-panel construction is used for everything from wood garage doors to wainscoting to jewelry boxes.

¼"- to ½"-deep groove holds panel in frame

raised panel with tapered edges

panel expands and contracts in this direction

stile

rail

Q Most cabinet doors I've seen have the vertical stile running from top to bottom with the horizontal rails sandwiched in between. Can I build them the opposite way?

A No. For starters, the continuous stile creates a solid "spine" from which the door hangs, and it allows the hinges to be mounted away from the ends of the stiles to minimize splitting. Finally, if the stile should shrink a bit, the ends of the rails won't protrude, which would look awkward and even prevent the hinges from operating correctly.

Q What material is normally used for the panels?

A You can use either plywood or solid wood. If you use plywood, make sure it's the right thickness to fit in the groove; the standard is ¼". If you use solid wood, you need to reduce the edge of the panel down to ¼" so it will fit in the groove. This is normally done with a raised-panel router bit. But you can also bevel the edges by running the four edges of the panel vertically through your table saw with the blade set at a 15-degree angle.

Q Is there a way to keep the panel of a raised-panel door centered in the frame and rattle-free?

A The oversized groove of the frame, which allows your panel to expand and contract, can sometimes allow the panel to move too freely. To keep the panel centered, insert little ¼" rubber balls (one brand is called Space Balls) in the groove of the frame before assembling the door. They'll compress and expand along with the panel and

COPE AND STICK SYSTEM

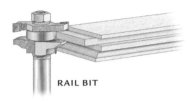

RAIL BIT

STILE BIT

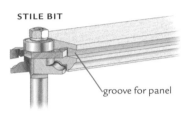

groove for panel

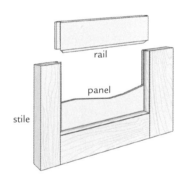

rail

panel

stile

BRIDLE JOINT   BISCUIT JOINT

solve both problems. Two on each side of the panel are usually all you need. Foam beads, rubber bands and other improvised materials can also be used.

Q I've heard you can make your own cabinet doors with a router table and a rail and stile bit set. How does it all work?

A It's actually an ingenious system. Also called "cope and stick," it's used by cabinet-makers to construct the frame part of frame-and-panel doors. You need two bits and a router table or shaper. The *stile bit* cuts a groove along the inner edge of all four members of the door frame; this bit usually also cuts a small bead, bevel or other decorative profile on the front. The *rail bit* cuts the ends of the rails to create a tongue that fits into the groove made by the stile bit as well as any matching profiles; these nest tightly into the profile created by the stile bit. The frame is assembled around the panel, the four components are glued and clamped together, and voilà — a frame-and-panel door. Setting the router bits at the precisely correct height is critical for the frames to turn out flat and sturdy.

Q What other kinds of corner joints are there for frame-and-panel doors?

A Oh, let us count the ways. You can use mortise-and-tenon joints, dowels, reinforced miters, and even pocket screws (if you don't mind the backs of your doors having plugs or holes in them). The stronger the joint, the better — and this is usually dictated by the amount of gluing surface. But even weak joints can gain strength by gluing plywood panels into the grooves.

Two simple joints are *bridle* and *biscuit* joints. With a bridle joint, both the open mortise and the tenon can be cut on the table saw (see page 164). The biscuit joint should be made as strong as possible by using large biscuits (double biscuits, if possible) and by gluing plywood panels into the grooves for added strength.

Q I need four raised-panel doors for a bathroom vanity, but I don't want to invest in the tools to build them. Can I buy them somewhere?

A Contact a local cabinetmaker, or search the Internet or Yellow Pages using the words "Kitchen Refacing" or "Replacement Doors." There are several companies specializing in doors and supplies for kitchen refacing projects that will also custom-make cabinet doors. Some specialty woodworking stores also have custom door programs (see Resources).

Q I'm building cabinets for our basement amusement room and want doors that are simple, cheap, and quick to build. What are some options?

A Here are three options: simple, simpler, and simplest.

The *simplest* version is just a plywood panel. For a cleaner look, cover the edges with thin strips of wood. To add a little pizzazz, use small base cap or chair rail molding to create a decorative frame on the face of each door.

The *simpler* version is tongue-and-groove (T & G) boards secured with battens. For a rustic look, put the battens on the front; for a more refined look, use T & G beadboard and put the battens on the back. To prevent sagging, include a cross batten running from the lower hinge corner to the opposite upper corner.

The *simple* version is to create a 1×3 frame using pocket screws. Use a rabbeting bit to cut a rabbet around the back inside edge, then install a plywood panel and hold it in with glue and stops. It's a quick way to create a mock Shaker-style door.

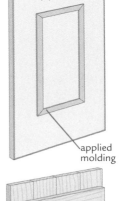

SIMPLEST

edging

plywood

applied molding

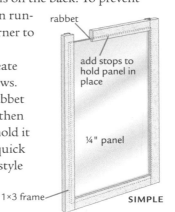

rabbet

add stops to hold panel in place

¼" panel

1×3 frame

SIMPLE

batten

cross batten

tongue and groove boards

SIMPLER

Q What's the right amount of space to leave between an inset door and the surrounding face frame?

A Break out your coin purse. Size your doors so there's a gap the thickness of a nickel on all four sides. This will allow enough room for seasonal changes in humidity.

Q What's the easiest way to make a glass-front door?

A After constructing the door frame, use a router to cut a rabbet, about ⅜" deep and ½" wide, around the inner perimeter of the frame on the back of the door. Use a chisel to square up the corners. Order glass, undersized about ⅛" in both directions, lay it in the rabbet, then secure it in place with clear silicone, brads, and small wood stops. You can use textured, seeded, or translucent glass if you wish to obscure the cabinet's contents. For safety, use tempered glass.

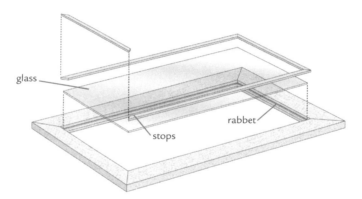

tip: Add Glass to Existing Doors

You can remove the panel from an existing door and add glass, but it requires a few extra steps. Remove the old panel by using a circular saw (set for a very shallow cut) and sharp chisel to remove just the back of the dado holding the panel in place. Once the panel is removed, use a chisel to clean up the newly created rabbet. Install the glass just as you would with a new door.

Q I'd like to use concealed hinges. What are the advantages, and just how hard are they to install?

A Concealed hinges, also called cup or Euro hinges, may seem mysterious at first, but once you understand them you'll discover their beauty. They can adjust the door in three directions: up and down, in and out, and side to side. You need to invest in a 35mm Forstner bit and have access to a drill press (or a special handheld drill jig) for boring the "cup hole," but beyond that, you can install them with a standard drill and screwdriver.

In a nutshell, you install the cup part of the hinge into the hole in the door and secure the base plate to the side of the cabinet. The two parts snap or screw together once installed. All adjustments can be made with a screwdriver.

Q I have cabinet pulls with mounting holes 3" apart. How do I position and drill the holes accurately so the handles of the doors line up in a row?

A Build a simple hole-drilling jig. Determine the position of your handles, and mark the mounting hole locations onto one of the doors. Handles are usually centered vertically on the stile, 2" to 3" from the lower or upper edge of the door. Nail 1×2s to two sides of a scrap 1×4, creating a slight lip on each side. Transfer your marks from the cabinet door to the 1×4, and drill two guide holes for the two mounting-screw holes. Flip or somersault the jig as needed to drill the mounting holes in the upper, lower, left-hand, and right-hand doors.

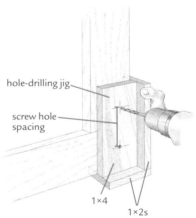

hole-drilling jig

screw hole spacing

1×4

1×2s

Q How do I drill holes accurately for those same pulls so they're centered on the drawers, both side-to-side and top-to-bottom?

A If you have just a few drawers, run a few strips of masking tape across the face of each drawer, then use your tape measure to find the

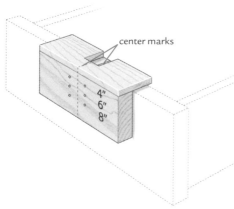

center marks

4″
6″
8″

centers and mark the holes. If you have lots of drawers, you can either purchase a "drawer-pull jig" from a specialty woodworking store or make your own as follows:

1 Mark a centerline on a 1×6, and, for pulls with 3″ screw spacing, draw parallel lines 1½″ to either side of the centerline.

2 Measure the height of your drawers, divide those numbers in half, then make crosshair marks across the parallel lines based on those measurements.

3 Drill the pairs of guide holes based on the screw hole spacing of your pulls.

4 Nail a piece of ¼″ plywood with a notch in the center to the top of your jig.

To use your jig, mark the center of the drawer along the top edge, hook your jig over the drawer and align the center marks, then drill the holes using the correct set of holes for the height of the drawer. For the 8″ tall drawer in the example, use the bottom set of holes as drill guides.

Drawers

Q: I've noticed that some drawers are made so the front of the box is what you see, and others have false fronts applied to them. Is one better than the other? And when do you use each type?

A You're referring to *integral front* and *applied front* drawers. Integral front drawers, because of their traditional look and light weight, often are used for furniture. They're frequently installed without a mechanical slide and, since there's no slide to adjust, careful fitting of the drawer into the opening is critical. Having no false front also means there's nothing to hide joints or fasteners, so more care must be taken in crafting them. Joinery can range from a simple rabbeted joint to a dovetail.

Applied front drawers allow you to build the drawer box and drawer front independently. The applied fronts, nearly always larger than the drawer box, effectively hide the slide mechanism from view when the drawer is closed. You can align the drawer with adjacent doors and drawers by adjusting the slide. And you have another chance to align them when you secure the drawer face to the box. They allow you to replace a damaged front without having to build a whole new drawer. The false front also hides the box construction, so more functional types of joints, such as biscuits, can be used.

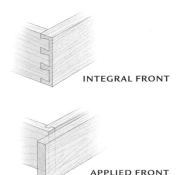

INTEGRAL FRONT

APPLIED FRONT

Q How much space do I need to leave between the drawer sides and the sides of a cabinet for standard drawer slides to fit?

A The industry standard for drawer sides is ½" per side, so make your drawer 1" narrower than the inside dimension of the cabinet case. It's best to err on the side of leaving a hair too much clearance than not enough. You can always put shims between the slide and the mounting surface to fill a gap that's too big, but a gap that's too small will either produce binding drawers or force you to modify one of the parts to create the space needed for the slide to operate smoothly.

Q I'm building a vintage-style center island for our kitchen and don't want to use visible hardware. What can I use besides metal slides or glides to help the drawers operate more smoothly?

A Try using low-friction nylon tape available at specialty woodworking stores. You apply this self-adhering tape to the bottom of the drawer opening where the drawer sides ride. You can also use it on the sides of the opening to help larger drawers open more smoothly. The tape is normally around 10 mils thick and available in ½" and ¾" widths.

Q Our current kitchen drawers open only about two-thirds of the way, making it difficult to get at the stuff in the back. How can I eliminate this wasted space in the new cabinets I'm building?

A Use full-extension drawer slides that telescope out so you can access your drawer from front to back. You can even purchase "overtravel" slides that extend your drawers even further beyond the lip of the countertop. These slides are usually wider (but not thicker) to accommodate the extending mechanism. They're also more expensive.

BUILDING A SIMPLE DRAWER

There are dozens of ways to build a drawer. This method calls for a table saw equipped with a dado blade and a few basic tools:

1 Cut a ¼" × ¼" dado or groove about ¼" in from one edge of your rough drawer stock. (TIP: A good material for drawers that's both stable and attractive is ½" Baltic birch plywood.)

2 Cut your drawer sides to length, then cut a ¼" × ½" rabbet on each end. Cut the front and back drawer parts to length, and rip ½" off the bottom of the drawer back to remove the dado.

3 Assemble the drawer box, gluing and nailing the corners. Slide the ¼"-thick drawer bottom into the groove (that's why you removed the dado from the back), square up the drawer, then nail the bottom to the drawer back. You can glue the bottom into the dado for added strength, or skip the glue so it can easily be replaced later down the road.

4 Secure the drawer face to the drawer box with four screws driven in from the back. Drill oversize holes in the drawer box front and don't use glue, so you can adjust the face later on, if needed.

5 Mount the drawer pull. Buy 1½" mounting screws, since most supplied screws are too short to go through both the drawer box and face.

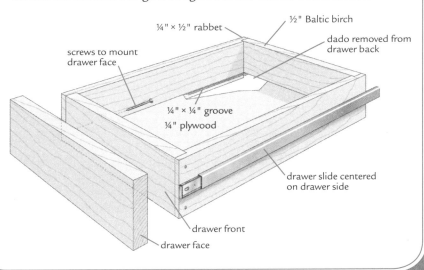

¼" × ½" rabbet

½" Baltic birch

dado removed from drawer back

screws to mount drawer face

¼" × ¼" groove

¼" plywood

drawer slide centered on drawer side

drawer front

drawer face

Q Why do some drawer slides cost so much more than others?

A You pretty much get what you pay for. Four things determine the price of a slide: quality, weight capacity, extension, and length. You can purchase a simple bottom-mount slide for a standard kitchen cabinet for around $10, but the weight capacity will be 35 pounds, it won't operate as smoothly as better slides, and it will only extend two-thirds of the way out. Its heavier-duty counterpart may cost three or four times as much but its capacity will be 150 pounds, it will extend all the way out, and it may even have a self-closing or soft-close feature. Base your slide selection on how (and how often) the drawer will be used.

Installing Cabinets

Q Which cabinets should I install first: the tops or bottoms?

A If you have a tall pantry unit or other tall cabinet that both lower and upper cabinets butt into, you have to start with that cabinet or the base cabinets. Otherwise, you can do it either way; each has its pros and cons.

Those in the "bottom cabinets first" camp argue that getting the base cabinets in and leveled provides a good reference point for installing the uppers. You can set 2×4s on the base cabinets to prop up the uppers while you install them, and, by laying scraps of plywood across the lower cabinets, you create a great workbench for setting your drill, clamps, coffee, and other tools on while installing the uppers.

Those preferring to install the uppers first maintain that the lower cabinets get in the way, forcing you to perform all manner of back-breaking maneuvers to reach over the lowers. Installed lower cabinets also are at risk of being scratched or dinged during the installation of the uppers.

Q When I'm installing cabinets, should I screw them to one another or to the wall first?

A Whenever possible, screw them to one another first. That way, you can easily adjust the cabinet face frames in or out and up or down until they meet flush and even. If you have to screw them to the wall first, like you might if you're installing upper cabinets alone, don't drive the screws all the way into the wall initially. This allows you to adjust the cabinets to line up the face frames before screwing them together.

Q What's the best way to secure cabinets to one another?

A Remove doors or drawers that are in the way, then even up the fronts of the two cabinets you're joining, and use a pair of squeeze-type bar clamps or something similar to hold them tightly to each other. Drill a pilot hole through both cabinet stiles, then bore a larger counterbore hole through the first one. Drive in the screw. The counterbore hole will allow the screw head to suck the first cabinet tightly against the second. Three screws per cabinet are usually adequate. Since the screws are rarely seen, some people use large-head "cabinet hanger" screws, which apply plenty of pressure. If looks are an issue, drill a countersink hole and use a standard wood screw, driving the screw so the head is just below the wood surface.

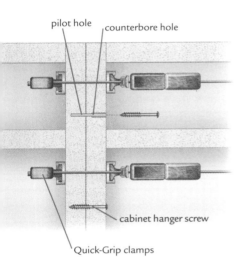

pilot hole   counterbore hole

cabinet hanger screw

Quick-Grip clamps

Q I have several cabinets in a row where the openings are so narrow I can't get a drill inside to bore holes or drive screws. What's the solution?

A Rent, borrow, or buy a right-angle drill or right-angle drill attachment for your drill. The heads on some are under 3" long, which should allow you to get a drill bit and driver bit into the space. You can buy special short "stubby" drill bits that will allow you to get into even narrower spaces.

Q I'm going to install new kitchen cabinets in our 1920s house. The floor dips and slants so much that there's over an inch of difference between the high and low spots. How do I install my base cabinets so hardboiled eggs won't roll off the counter?

A Install your kitchen cabinets level, regardless of what the floor does. Your eggs will stay put and you'll save time and hassle when it comes to installing countertops and tackling other tasks. Here's the general procedure:

1 Use a level to find the highest point of the floor along the cabinet walls, make a mark 34½" up (or whatever your cabinet height is), and draw level lines on the walls out from that point.

2 Set your first cabinet in place and insert shims until the back is level to the line, and the cabinet itself is level in all directions.

3 Level and screw the next cabinet to the first, then secure them both to the wall. Or, screw the cabinet to the wall, set the next cabinet in place, and keep going down the line.

4 After all the base cabinets are set, use construction adhesive to glue the visible shims in place so they don't get kicked out or dislodged. The uneven gap at the bottom will be covered by the continuous strip (the toe kick) of wood or plywood you'll install after all the cabinets are in.

Q I have 75" worth of base cabinets and 77" of wall space to fill. How do I handle the missing 2"?

A You need to add a filler strip (or two.) Filler strips are pieces of wood the same height as the cabinet face frame that you install to fill in extra space. You can position them between cabinets, at an inside corner, or at the very end of a row to fill the gap between the last cabinet and the wall.

Sometimes it's most strategic to position filler strips at inside corners to create more clearance for drawers to open and doors to swing. But more often they're positioned at the end of the row where they can inconspicuously fill the void. In this position, they can also be scribed and cut to conform to out-of-plumb walls. Some custom-made cabinets will come with a filler strip already attached. Otherwise, the strips are secured to the edges of adjacent cabinets with glue and screws.

tip: Easier Driving

Before driving in screws to secure cabinets to the wall or each other, drag the threads across an old bar of soap or a candle. The soap or wax will lubricate the screw, making it easier to drive in and less likely to snap. It will also silence the ear-piercing screech that often accompanies the task.

Countertops

Q I want to make my own wood-edged countertops. Do I apply the wood nosing before or after installing the laminate?

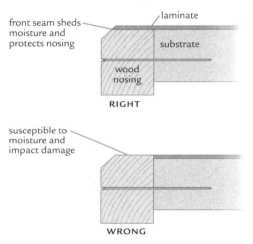

front seam sheds moisture and protects nosing

laminate

substrate

wood nosing

RIGHT

susceptible to moisture and impact damage

WRONG

A Your countertop will last longer and perform better if you install the wood edging first, then apply the laminate over it. Once this is done, you can use a router to round over or chamfer the front edge. With the seam on the front, rather than the top, the substrate will be less susceptible to moisture damage and "crumb infiltration." The laminate will also help protect the top of the wood nosing from impact and water damage.

Q What are the basic steps in building a wood-edged laminate top?

A It's much, much easier building the top in your workshop or garage before installing it, versus trying to build it in place. Here's what you do:

1 Secure the wood edging to the substrate with biscuits or glue and nails, keeping the edging just a hair above the substrate surface. Use a belt sander to flatten the edging even with the substrate, then clean the surfaces.

2 Use a sponge roller to apply contact adhesive to the countertop and back of the laminate (which you've cut at least an inch or two oversize.) Let the glue dry, then add a second band of contact adhesive around the perimeter of both surfaces for good measure. Once the adhesive dries, install the laminate, with overhang on all four edges.

3 Use a laminate roller (J-roller) or rolling pin to press the laminate firmly in place. Trim the front edge flush with a router and a bearing-guided straight bit, then go back and chamfer the front edge. You can also use a round-over, beading, or other bit to create a front edge with a more decorative look.

Q When I positioned the laminate on the countertop substrate, I lined it up wrong and the contact adhesive grabbed so tight I couldn't reposition it. I wrecked everything. How can I prevent this?

A For future reference, working mineral spirits into the "stuck" area can loosen small areas of contact cement and give you a second chance. But to avoid this scenario entirely, try this: Lay spacers, such as old Venetian blind slats, over the substrate once the glue is dry, spacing them every few inches. Position the laminate over the slats, then remove the slats one by one as you press the laminate onto the substrate. You can also use dowels or pieces of rope for spacers. Make sure your spacers are absolutely clean; a lump created by a speck of sawdust, a rope thread, or dirt will forever be a part of your countertop.

Q I had a disastrous (and expensive) experience cutting a piece of laminate to size on my table saw. The thin edge slid under the fence so my cut was crooked, and the blade chipped the laminate. How do I avoid this in the future?

A The chipping part you can solve by installing a special laminate-cutting blade, setting it to cut so the teeth are only a hair above the laminate. Make sure you cut the laminate good-side-up.

To prevent the thin laminate from sliding under your fence or riding up, build a simple auxiliary fence. Rip a 5-degree angle on a straight board and position it against the table saw fence with the angled edge pressed firmly against the table. Add a second offset fence slightly above the table, and clamp the two temporary fences to the table saw fence. The auxiliary fence will create a stable edge for your

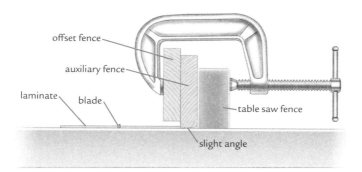

offset fence
auxiliary fence
laminate
blade
table saw fence
slight angle

laminate to follow, and the offset fence will help keep the laminate lying flat against the table.

Q I had a post-formed countertop custom-made, but when I went to install it, I found gaps, some almost ½" wide, between it and the wall. Should I just apply caulk?

A One rule of thumb for kitchens (or any type of woodworking or carpentry) is to use as little caulk as possible; it's a weak and temporary fix. You have three ways of dealing with the problem (unfortunately, you're too late for the first one):

- **Start with a straight wall.** Your wavy wall is the result of studs bowing in and out. When framing walls where cabinets, vanities, and built-in bookcases will go, select straight studs (or at least make sure they all bow in the same direction), and try to keep the drywall mud buildup in the corners to a minimum. If it's a remodel, secure shims and strips of wood to the studs to create a flat surface. Before installing drywall, use a long, straight board to make sure the wall surface is flat at countertop level.

- **Scribe the back of your countertop.** The backsplash has a built-in ¾" lip at the top for this purpose. Run a strip of masking tape along the top of the backsplash, then position the countertop. Find the widest gap, set a compass to that distance, then run the pointed leg of the compass against the wall while you mark the masking tape with the pencil. Use a belt sander to remove material up to the line. Angle your belt sander a few degrees so the upper edge of the lip is slightly proud; this makes it easier to "fine-tune" your scribe if necessary.

- **Slam-dunk it.** If you still have gaps even after scribing, position the countertop and run a sharp utility knife along the top edge of the backsplash in the trouble spots. Pull the top out, then use a hammer and a block of wood to indent the drywall in those areas to create a shallow cavity that the backsplash can actually slip into. This is a last resort and an inelegant solution, but it does the trick. Apply a thin bead of caulk to the back of the backsplash before permanently installing it, and add another bead afterward.

Q What are the pros and cons of installing a wood countertop on our kitchen island? And what about the finish?

A On the plus side, wood countertops create a warm, dining-table-like surface, great for when you eat meals around your island. They're visually appealing and less likely to break tipped glasses and dropped plates. They're also relatively easy to make and/or install yourself.

On the negative side, they'll scratch and dent more easily than other types of tops, they're more susceptible to water damage (especially if moisture works its way into the end grain), and they require some maintenance.

There are tradeoffs on the finishes, too. Polyurethane creates a durable, water-resistant finish, but scratches and gouges are more difficult to repair if someone uses your island top as a cutting board. Walnut oil is food-safe, easy to apply, dries hard, and is easy to renew, but it won't protect your top against standing moisture. Tung oil falls somewhere in between these two, in terms of durability and maintenance.

Q If I make my own wood top, which way should I orient the grain?

A You've got three options; base your decision on the look and function you want:

- ⊙ **Face grain up**, where the widest face of the board shows. This presents interesting grain patterns but is the least dent-resistant of the three surfaces. Since this top will expand and contract the most, the top must be mounted to the cabinet in a way that will allow it to move (see page 181).
- ⊙ **Edge grain up** is a more common and traditional look. You'll have to use 33 to 34 strips of ¾" material to get the 25" width you need, but you'll have a denser surface that will expand and contract less.
- ⊙ **End grain up** (with squares of wood arranged and glued together like a checkerboard) creates a true working surface like you'd find in a traditional butcher's chopping block. It's durable and easy to cut on, since the wood fibers are separated rather than cut. It's also substantially more work to build.

10 Windows, Doors & Moldings

Take pride in your work. Quality, craftsmanship, and tradition are the threads that secure excellence.

— ANONYMOUS

A handcrafted bookcase or dining room table can have a huge impact on the look of your house, but so can the trim around your windows, the wainscot that surrounds your dining room walls, and the other millwork that adorns your interior spaces. Crown molding can bring a ho-hum living room a touch of class, paneling can turn a drab dining room into a showpiece, and new door trim can give a sterile house the warm look and feel of a Craftsman bungalow.

Windows and Doors

You'll use many of the same skills, materials, and tools for installing moldings as you do for other woodworking tasks. So don't limit yourself to furniture and cabinets — take on the whole house! Truth be told, many beginners have caught the "woodworking bug" while innocently cutting and fitting a miter for a window or door molding. They experience that "Aha!" moment: "I can make a tight joint," "I can use that tool." Installing trim is a skill builder and a confidence booster and, as a bonus, it adds value to your house.

Q We purchased a badly remodeled house. I want to replace the plain-Jane 2"-wide window and door moldings with something more substantial and authentic. What are some options?

A The ranch-style moldings that were installed were inexpensive and easy to install, but that's about it. For something with a more distinct style try one of these:

⊙ **Corner and plinth blocks.** This system not only looks great but is simple to install, since your cuts are square, not mitered. You can purchase corner and base plinth blocks at most home centers or order them over the Internet, or you can make your own.

⊙ **Multiple-piece mitered casings.** You can create trim with a more substantial look by building up moldings in two or three layers. You can either prebuild your moldings in long lengths, then cut them to size, or cut and miter each individual piece as you go. Window bottoms can be mitered but look more authentic if they terminate at an apron.

⊙ **Backbanded casings.** Casings consist of flat boards butted squarely at the corners and edged in an L shape with strips that are mitered. Head casing boards are usually wider than side casings.

⊙ **Crosshead and apron.** Doors and windows are capped with a multiple-piece "crosshead" consisting of a wide frieze board, small crown molding, top cap, and bottom strip. Side casings can be plain or decorative, terminating with an apron.

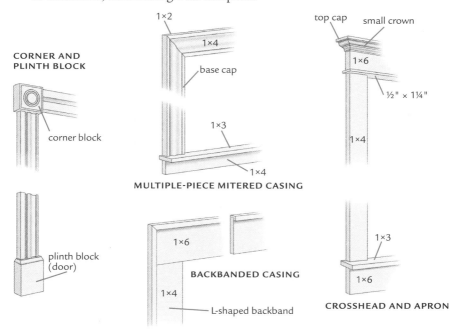

CORNER AND
PLINTH BLOCK

corner block

plinth block
(door)

1×2
1×4
base cap
1×3
1×4
MULTIPLE-PIECE MITERED CASING

1×6
BACKBANDED CASING
1×4
L-shaped backband

top cap   small crown
1×6
½" × 1¼"
1×4

1×3
1×6
CROSSHEAD AND APRON

Q What size of nail should I use for installing door and window trim?

A Use two sizes. If you're hand-nailing the trim, use 6d or 8d finish nails for securing the edge of the molding to the wall. The nail needs be long enough to penetrate the molding and drywall and at least 1½" into the underlying wall stud. Use 3d finish nails for securing the inner edge of thin moldings to the window or door jamb; use longer nails for thicker trim. If you're using pneumatic nailers, use 15- or 16-gauge nails at least 2" long for the outer edge, and 18-gauge brads at least 3 times as long as the trim piece is thick for the inner edge.

Q How do I make the space between the edge of my door jambs and the edge of my trim consistent?

A The space you're referring to is called the *reveal*. It's usually about ¼" wide and provides a transitional step-back from the face of the frame to the edge of the molding. In the case of doors, it also provides "elbow room" for the hinges. To get a consistent reveal, use a ¼"-thick block of wood (a thick paint stick or the fat end of a wood shim works well) as a marking guide for your pencil (your *sharp* pencil). Initially, you may want to mark lines around the entire jamb, but as your eye improves you'll be able to get by with just marking the corners and a few other places along the jamb to get a consistent reveal.

Q Why is there a wide shallow groove running along the backs of most moldings?

A The groove allows the molding to flex a little so it can conform to irregularities in the wall or jamb and still lie flat. It also helps the molding to bridge gaps (even if the jamb protrudes beyond the wall surface, or vice versa) without rocking.

Q A few of the windows in our house have jambs that protrude past the drywall by ⅛". I've been installing moldings, and there are gaps at all the corners. How do I correct this?

A The protruding window jambs are making it so your moldings can't lie flat against the wall. The result? The backs of the moldings are touching, but the fronts aren't; thus the gap. If you have a good hand plane, you can shave down the protruding jamb. (Watch out for metal fasteners!) But this is time-consuming and requires a special touch.

The simplest way to solve this problem is to remove material from the back edge of the miter so the front edges can touch. You could use a sanding block to remove a little of the material from the back of the miter, but that's also time-consuming. Try doing what many professional carpenters do: Improvise! Use your miter saw to cut a normal 45-degree angle, then place a thin shim under the angled end, and cut again. This will remove enough material from the back of the miter so your corners will fit tightly in front. You may also need to adjust the angle of the cut slightly for a good fit.

tip: Mark, Don't Measure

You'll save time and make fewer mistakes by marking door and window moldings in place rather than transferring lots of measurements. Hold your trim against the doorjamb, and make a tick mark where you need to make your cut. It's foolproof.

Q When I install my window and door trim, will my miters stay tighter if I apply glue to them?

A Wood end grain — the stuff of which miters are made — is only moderately "glueable." The open pores and end grain absorb glue and also provide less "meat" for the glue to adhere to. That said, you should still apply glue to the joint and also cross-pin the corners (drive in a brad or nail from each direction) to help hold the joint tight.

You may want to apply glue for yet another reason: If your miter doesn't fit perfectly, you can lightly sand it with fine sandpaper, creating a fine dust that will mix with the wet glue to form a sort of natural putty to fill the gap. It's cheating a little, but if you do it right and make sure to remove all the glue from the surface, it's difficult to spot. It works best with wood that hasn't been pre-stained or painted.

Q I split the mitered end of a piece of window trim as I was installing the last nail. Is there a way to fix the split without removing the entire piece?

A Use a nail set to punch the nail all the way through, then leave the nail set in place so it's wedging the split open. Force a small amount of glue into the split; you can push it in with the edge of a piece of sandpaper or blow it in with a straw. Remove the nail set, wipe off excess glue, then use masking tape to clamp the split back together.

tip: Just a Hair

Sometimes you need to shorten up a molding "just a hair" (literally, about a hair's width) to make it fit perfectly. How do you position it on your miter saw to do just that? Lower the blade all the way down, then press the end of the molding against the body (not the teeth) of the blade. Without moving the molding, raise the blade back up, then make your cut. The thickness or "set" of the teeth will shave off just that hair you needed.

Q When installing door trim, is it best to install the sides or the head-piece first?

A There are two schools of thought. Some prefer installing the head-piece first. That way, you only need to fine-tune one miter at a time as you install each side jamb. But if you're working in a room with a wood floor, where any gap between the trim and floor would be notice-able, install the side casings first, butting them tightly to the floor. This means you'll have to fine-tune both ends of the headpiece before installing it, but you won't have gaps where the trim meets the floor.

Q We installed newer, thicker carpeting in our bedroom and now we can't close the door. How do I cut off the bottom of a hollow-core door without damaging it?

A You have two challenges: The first is making a clean, crisp cut so the veneer doesn't chip. The second is filling in the bottom of the hollow-core door (if it winds up being hollow).

With the door removed, measure from the bottom surface of the top doorjamb to the top of the carpet, then subtract ¼" to ½", depend-ing on how tight you want the door to fit. Mark the bottom of the door (make sure it's the bottom, not the top!), then use a straightedge and sharp utility knife to score this cut line along the entire width of the door. Place your door on a pair of sawhorses and use a circular saw with a fine-tooth blade to cut just to the outside of this line. The veneer on the scrap side of your cut may splinter, but the door should wind up with a clean edge. (The veneer on the other side of the door is less likely to splinter because the saw's teeth will be pushing it into the door, rather than away from it.)

If you had to remove more than ¾" from the bottom of the door, you also wound up removing the solid piece of wood from the bottom edge. Cut a replacement piece and glue it in place between the door's veneers. If you're careful, you may be able to salvage the old bottom piece by using a sharp chisel to remove the veneer on each side.

Q The new door I hung last winter is binding and scraping against the jamb, but I can't figure out where. How do I locate the trouble spot?

A A change in seasons often brings about a change in humidity, which can easily make doors swell and stick. Take a piece of good, old-fashioned carbon paper and place it (carbon side toward the door) between the jamb and the door, then shut the door. Repeat this all along the edge and top, then check the edge of the door. The areas showing carbon marks need to be planed or sanded down. Remove just a small amount of material at a time; it usually doesn't take much to stop the binding. Bevel the cut slightly so the leading edge of the door is less likely to hit the doorjamb as it closes. Make sure to apply finish to the areas you shaved down so they don't absorb moisture and swell; otherwise you'll soon be repeating the process once again. You can use this same technique to identify binding areas on casement windows.

Q I'm installing cherry trim and can't find corner blocks to match. Can I make my own?

A You can make a plain version by cutting square blocks, then using a router bit to chamfer the edges. To create your own bull's-eye style blocks, you'll need to purchase a special rosette cutter (available at specialty woodworking stores). Use it in a drill press to cut the profile. Be prepared to spend $60 to $80 for a good carbide cutter.

Q I'm installing new hardware on an old door. The hole for the original doorknob was only 1" in diameter, but the hole for the new one needs to be twice as big. How do I enlarge it?

A You have two options:

⊙ Use your hole saw to drill a hole the size you need in a piece of ¾" plywood, then firmly clamp this to the door with the hole in the plywood positioned over the old hole. Insert the bit in the hole in your plywood jig and use that to guide the perimeter of your bit as you drill.

⊙ Cut a square block of wood a hair larger than the existing hole, then pound that into the hole. That will create a solid starting point for your pilot bit.

In both cases, make certain the door is solidly supported on the backside, so the wood around the newly bored hole doesn't splinter when the bit exits.

Q We have a 3'-wide passageway from one room to another that is simply a cased opening without a door. I'd like to hang a door in that space. How do I cut the hinge recesses?

A Use blocks and shims to temporarily wedge your door blank into the opening, then mark the locations of the three hinges on both the door blank and door jamb. (Mark the center of your door handle while you're at it.) Remove the door, position each hinge, and trace around it with a sharp pencil. Then:

1 Using a hammer and sharp chisel, follow the outline, making a series of cuts as deep as the hinge is thick.

2 Use the chisel to make another series of "hinge-deep" cuts about ¼" apart in the area where the hinge will sit.

3 Position your chisel at a low angle, and with a series of light taps, remove the wood between each score line. Position the hinge to see if it fits flush to the doorjamb surface and fine-tune the recess as necessary.

4 Use the same procedure to cut the hinge mortises in the door and the strike plate mortise in the doorjamb.

tip: Even Moldings
Need Sanding

Don't presume the moldings you buy at the lumberyard are sanded smooth and ready to install. Many have mill marks that are hard to see until you stain them. Inspect, sand, then stain.

INSTALLED HINGE

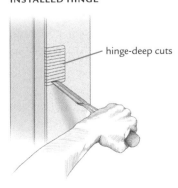

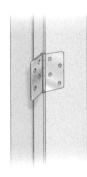

hinge-deep cuts

Base Molding

Q When I install base molding along the bottoms of my walls, what are some tips I can use for making outside corners meet tightly?

A There are two things you need to get right: the angles of the miters and the lengths of the pieces. You can figure out both by using test pieces.

1 Cut two scraps about 12" long, with a 45-degree left miter on one end and a 45-degree right miter on the other.

2 Position them at the outside corner and make a light L mark on the floor where the long points of the miters meet. This will give you the long-side measurement for each piece.

3 Now look at how the miters meet at the corners of your test pieces. If they're slightly open on the outside, cut your miters at 46 degrees. If they're open on the inside, cut them at 44 degrees. You can keep 44- and 46-degree test blocks around to pre-check those angles.

Q I consistently get gaps on inside corners where two pieces of base molding meet. It seems like the 45-degree miters should meet nice and square, but they rarely do. What am I doing wrong?

A The drywall tape and joint compound that are applied to inside corners of walls create corners that are no longer square. The solution is to run one piece of baseboard squarely into the corner, then cope the second piece so it can butt up snugly against the first. The best way to do this is to cut a 45-degree angle on the second piece of baseboard, then use a coping saw to cut the profile. Back-bevel the cut a little so the "pointier" front of the coped cut will fit snugly against the first piece.

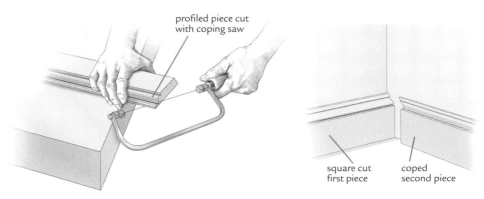

profiled piece cut
with coping saw

square cut
first piece

coped
second piece

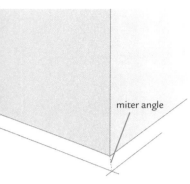

miter angle

Q We have walls that meet at odd angles in our living room. How do I figure out what angle to cut the miters for the baseboard?

A Place a scrap 1×4 or 2×4 along each side of the angled walls, and mark the outer edges so the lines intersect. Draw a line from these intersecting lines to the actual corner of the wall. This will give you the angle of the miter. You can figure out the degree of the cut by using an angle finder to copy the angle and then transfer the angle to your miter saw.

Q Another problem I have when installing base moldings is getting them to lie flat against the wall, especially a few inches out from the corners. What's the fix?

A Thin base moldings and the cap of 3-piece moldings are usually flexible enough to conform to wall bulges and waves, but thicker one-piece moldings aren't. If you're painting your trim, applying a bead of paintable caulk to fill the gap is your easiest option. If you're using natural wood base, set it in place and use a sharp razor knife to score the drywall and compound along the top edge where the wall bulges outward. Replace the molding with a 2×4 block and give it a few good whacks to indent the drywall just below your score line. This is often enough to flatten the bulges to get the molding to lie flat. If that doesn't do the trick or your walls are plaster, you may have to belt-sand the back of the molding to make it conform.

Q We just put a huge addition on our home and I need to install base molding in five rooms. Any tricks for getting the job done faster?

A One trick is to use a system where you always work clockwise around the room. That way, all of your inside-corner coped cuts will be on the "left" end of the base, and you'll become very adept (and fast) at making that particular cut.

tip: Close-Shave Stud Finder

Another way of locating wall studs is to run your electric razor across the wall. Where the pitch changes from low to high you should find a stud.

Q We finished our basement and hung new drywall with the panels running horizontally. The base moldings lean in at the bottom because of the taper along the bottom edge of the drywall. How do I get the moldings to stand upright?

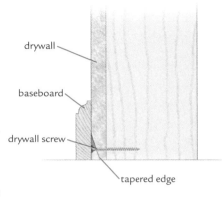

A That tapered edge provides an indented area so drywallers can apply their tape and compound without creating a bulge. To compensate for the taper on the bottom edge, drive in drywall screws every couple of feet so the heads are flush with the main surface of the drywall. This will prevent the bottom edge of the molding from tilting in.

Q I know I should nail base molding to the studs. Is there an easy way to locate them without a stud sensor?

A There are a number of clues that will help you locate your studs:

⊙ Look closely at the drywall near the floor. Often, you can spot the heads of the screws or nails used to secure the drywall to the underlying studs.

⊙ Outlet boxes also provide clues, since they're usually secured to the side of a stud. Turn off the power, remove the cover plate and carefully probe with a finish nail on both sides of the box to locate the stud. Cold-air return grills are usually flanked on each side by a stud.

⊙ Try rapping the wall with a knuckle. You'll hear a solid, versus hollow, thump when you're over a stud.

Once you've found the center of one stud, you'll most likely find the centers of others spaced in 16" (or less frequently, 24") increments.

Q I have 24'-long walls and 16'-long base moldings. What's the most seamless way to install the moldings?

A Here's what you do:

1 Locate and mark your wall studs.

2 Set a long length of base molding in place, and make a tick mark on the molding near the end to indicate the middle of a stud.

3 Cut a 30-degree angle at your tick mark so the long part of the miter is against the wall. Install that piece.

4 Measure for your second piece and cut a 30-degree angle on the one end so it will overlap the angled end of the first piece.

5 Apply glue to the ends of the two pieces, then nail them securely to the underlying stud at the seam. The overlapping piece will hold the end of the other piece flat against the wall and, if the seam does open up, the angled cuts make the gap less noticeable.

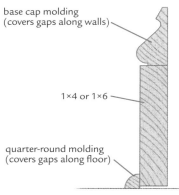

base cap molding
(covers gaps along walls)

1×4 or 1×6

quarter-round molding
(covers gaps along floor)

3-PIECE MOLDINGS

Q Does three-piece base molding serve any function beyond looking nice?

A Yes. The large 1×4 or 1×6 part of the molding is rigid and won't conform easily to wavy walls or floors. But the thinner, more flexible base cap molding can easily conform to irregularities in the wall, and the thinner cove or base shoe molding can easily follow any humps or dips in the floor. The result is an attractive baseboard that covers most gaps.

Q I'd like to make my own 1"-tall base cap molding using a router bit. How do I keep my router balanced on that skinny piece while routing?

A The best way is to start out with a wide board (say, a 1×12), rout the profile on both edges of that wide board, then rip the pieces to their final 1" width on your table saw. The wide board gives your router base a wide surface to ride on so it's less likely to tip. You should be able to repeat this process three or four more times before your stock becomes too skinny to provide proper bearing for your router.

Q I'm going to be carpeting a room. Do I butt the base molding tight to the floor or leave it up a little?

A Leave it up about ⅜" so the person laying carpet can "tuck" the edge of the carpet underneath the base. If you're installing ranch-style base molding (the stuff that's about ⅜" thick), use scraps of that as spacers between the floor and the base.

tip: Install Now, Finish Later

If you like to leave all of your painting and staining until the end of a project, here's a way to make it go faster. Cut long lengths of waxed paper into 4" strips. Pinch the waxed paper between the edge of your trim and wall as you install your moldings, leaving a couple of inches exposed. When it's time to paint and stain, flex the waxed paper toward the trim as you paint your walls, and flex it towards the walls as you stain or paint your trim. When everything is dry run a sharp razor blade lightly along the edge of the moldings to trim off the exposed waxed paper. You'll have crisp, clean lines with no drips or bleed-through.

Crown Molding

Q I'm going to make my first attempt at installing crown molding in our living room. Got any planning tips?

A Take five minutes to make a graph paper sketch of the room. You'll be able to use this for both estimating materials and creating a game plan. Here are a few more tips:

⊙ Try to avoid multiple lengths of molding that require coping on both ends. Coping is one of the trickiest, most time-consuming tasks. If a piece with a double cope winds up being too short, you've perhaps wasted lots of time and material.

⊙ Be systematic. Work clockwise around the room so you only need to cope one end of each molding — and that end will normally be the left end. In a square room, your last piece may need to be coped on each end, so plan your layout so that piece is in the least conspicuous part of the room, in case you're off a little.

⊙ Plan your layout so you begin and end at an outside corner (if there is one). Many people find it easier to fine-tune outside corners than inside corners.

⊙ Before you start, snap chalk lines along the walls (white chalk is the easiest to remove) to mark the bottom edge of the crown molding, then make small tick marks to indicate the position of each underlying stud.

Q I love the look of crown molding but don't feel my carpentry skills are good enough to make the mitered cuts and copes for the corners. Is there a simpler system?

A Yes. You could use the PAP, or point-and-pay, system (point to what you want done, then pay someone else to do it). Or, you could use a corner block system (see Resources). The latter system consists of pre-built inside and outside corners that you nail in place, then you fill in the space between with lengths of crown molding that are cut square on each end. If you have long walls, there are "splice blocks" that, again, allow you to butt square-cut sections of moldings to each side.

Most of these are complete kits where the profiles of the blocks and crown molding match. They're usually available in oak, pine, primed MDF, and polyurethane foam. The corner blocks add to the cost of the project and provide an ornate look not everyone loves, but it's a system nearly anyone can install successfully.

Q Are there any tricks for making the outside corners of crown molding line up evenly and meet squarely?

A There are two things you can do. Cut a scrap piece of molding with outside corners on each end, and butt this test piece up to the first corner piece to check the angle and length before nailing it in place. Second, don't nail either stretch of crown molding within the last 2' of the end, initially. That will give you a little play to slightly twist, raise, or lower the moldings so the corners meet properly. Once everything fits tightly, carefully glue and nail the ends.

Q My ceiling has a heavy "popcorn" texture that will prevent my crown molding from lying flat against the ceiling. What's the solution?

A Figure out how far your molding will project from the wall, cut a block of wood to match that width, then run the block around the edge of the room to scrape off the texture. It will come off easier than you might suspect. One word of caution: Ceiling texture installed prior to 1978 (and even a few years after that) may contain asbestos (see Resources for information on safe removal).

tip: Banish and Burnish Outside Corners

Sometimes you can't get rid of a hairline gap at an outside corner, no matter how many times you fit and recut the pieces. You can disguise that gap by burnishing. Take the side of a screwdriver blade and rub it up and down along the corner. This will slightly crush the corners inward and make the gap disappear. This works for base moldings, too.

Q What's the safest and most accurate way to cut crown molding on a standard power miter saw?

A Upside down. It will help you envision things if you think of the upright fence of your saw as the wall surface and the horizontal table as the ceiling.

First, determine the angle at which the molding sits in relationship to the ceiling; the most common angles are 45 degrees and 52 degrees. Position a small piece of crown molding upside down on your saw and move it to and fro until the flat faces on the back of the molding rest flat against the fence

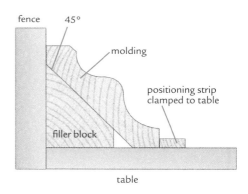

fence 45°

molding

positioning strip
clamped to table

filler block

table

and table. Clamp scrap strips of lumber to the bed of your saw so they'll position your crown molding at that angle while you cut. For extra solidity you can rip a block of wood at the appropriate angle to back up the crown molding when you cut it.

Q I've heard it's easier to cut crown molding on a compound miter saw. Is that true?

A It's easier because you can cut the crown molding with it lying flat on the table. This involves adjusting both the tilt and angle of the saw. For instance, to cut outside corners on 45-degree crown molding, you adjust the miter angle to 35.3 degrees and tilt the blade to 30 degrees. The settings for 52-degree crown molding are a 31.6-degree angle and a 33.9-degree tilt. Even with a compound miter saw, some people prefer the "upside down" method described in the preceding question, because it offers clearer visual orientation.

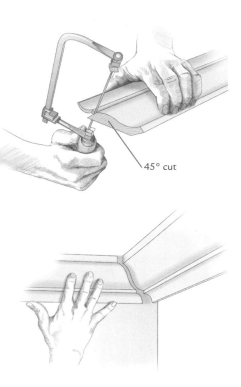

45° cut

Q What's the best way to cut and install inside corners of crown molding?

A Since most inside corners aren't truly square, you'll get the tightest fit by coping one piece and butting that to a length of molding you've previously run all the way into the corner. To create a profile of the shape you need to cut with the coping saw, begin by cutting the end of the piece as you would a 45-degree inside corner. Use your coping saw (or jigsaw) to follow the cut edge that's been created, holding the saw at an angle to create a back bevel. Once you've cut the piece, use a file and sandpaper to fine-tune the profile.

Slide the coped piece against the installed piece to check the fit and fine-tune as necessary. To make the pieces fit better, leave the end of the first piece (the one butted into the corner) unfastened for now, so you can move it as needed to fit it with the coped piece. Also, make sure your coped profile fits tight before marking the other end of the molding and cutting it to final length.

Q I overheard a couple of woodworkers at the lumberyard talking about making their own crown molding on a table saw. Is that possible?

A Yes. It may not be worth your time if you're trying to reproduce oak or pine crown molding that's similar to the stuff you can buy off the shelf, but if you need crown molding of an exotic species, size, or profile, you can create it. It will involve a good bit of trial and error to arrive at the right size and curvature, but it can be done.

Start by installing a 60- to 80-tooth carbide crosscut blade in your table saw and crank it up about ½". Now the head-scratching begins, because there are several variables, including:

⊙ What angle to set your guide fences in relationship to the blade. This angle will determine the radius or curvature of the cove. The greater the angle, the greater the radius.

- ⊙ Where and how far apart to set your guide fences. This will in part be determined by the eventual size of your molding. For a symmetrical molding, your fences need to be set equal distances from the leading and trailing edges of the blade.
- ⊙ How high to set the blade. This will determine how wide and deep the coved part of the molding will be.

The best way to figure out the variables is by experimenting. Make your best guess, clamp your two fences down, and adjust the blade to about 1/16" above the table. Turn the saw on and use push blocks to guide your test piece over the blade. Keep raising the blade in 1/16" increments and checking the shape of your curve. Adjust the angles of your fences, their distance apart, and blade height until you create the right profile for the cove. Rip the edges to the proper angle (yet another variable to figure out). When all looks good, go into mass production mode. Make your very last pass by raising the blade just a whisker; this will reduce the amount of sanding you'll need to do. **NOTE:** This procedure requires the removal of the blade guard and splitter, so extra caution is required.

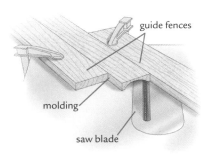

guide fences

molding

saw blade

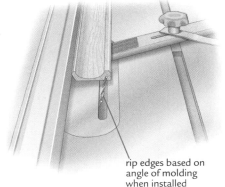

rip edges based on angle of molding when installed

Wainscot and Paneling

Q Is there a "correct" height for wainscoting and chair rails?

A In rooms with 8' or 9' ceilings, the recommended heights are 32" and 60", give or take a few inches. Avoid heights in between; otherwise, the room may seem weirdly cut in half, or you may feel like you're sitting in a playpen. If you're in doubt, find a discarded appliance box, cut cardboard panels from it of the height you're considering, install your mock wainscot, then live with it for a few days to see how it feels.

Q I'm installing wainscoting made from plywood panels and applied moldings. Without using nails, is there a good way to secure the moldings to the vertical surface so they don't slip (I hate filling nail holes!)?

A You can use a pneumatic "micro pin nailer"; the holes it creates are so small that the primer and paint will fill them. But you have other options: Masking tape will hold short, light pieces of molding in place while the glue sets. For heavier pieces try this: Run a thin bead of yellow glue on the back side of the molding, then add a drop of quick-setting cyanoacrylate (CA) glue every 6" to 8" (it's okay if the CA glue touches the white glue). The CA glue will cling to the vertical surfaces immediately and hold the molding in place until the white glue cures.

You can also use hot-melt glue in conjunction with the yellow glue, but make sure to press the piece tightly against the wall right away. Dabs of hot-melt glue that have hardened can hold your molding away from, rather than against, the wall.

Q I'm installing wainscoting in a room. How do I handle where the wainscoting meets the existing door trim?

A One way to deal with the situation is to apply a thicker band of trim around the existing door trim to give the edges of the wainscot something to "bump into." If your wainscot is 1" thick, add a band of 1¼"-thick trim around the door. If this looks odd (and it might if your door trim is thin), you can round over the edges of the wainscot where it meets the door trim.

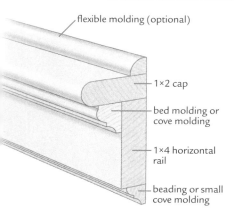

flexible molding (optional)

1×2 cap

bed molding or cove molding

1×4 horizontal rail

beading or small cove molding

Q I'd like to install a chair rail to create a dividing line between paint on the lower third of the wall and wallpaper on the upper two thirds. What's a simple design?

A You can install your own built-up chair rail using off-the-shelf moldings from a lumberyard or home center. There are dozens of options, so experiment until you find a look and size you like.

Install the horizontal rail to create the starting point for your chair rail. Since this is the "foundation" for all the other moldings you install, make certain to nail it securely every 16" to the underlying studs, using 2½" finish nails. Then apply the cap piece and other moldings. If your wall is bowed or wavy, use a small, flexible molding on top of the cap to cover gaps between the cap and the wall. That molding can also help cover the lower edge of the wallpaper after it's been installed.

Q What are people referring to when they talk about "blind-nailing" tongue-and-groove paneling?

A Blind-nailing refers to driving nails through the base of the tongue at an angle, so the groove of the next board covers the nail heads in the preceding board. You don't have to nail the grooved edge, since the tongue it slides over has already been secured, and it in turn holds the groove in place. Since there's no tongue to hold the groove of the very first board in place, that edge needs to be face nailed as shown.

There's another benefit of blind-nailing: Since one edge is nailed and the other more or less floats, wide boards can expand and contract easily without cracking. These are the same reasons why flooring is blind-nailed.

Q If I want to install tongue-and-groove boards only halfway up a wall that already has drywall on it, what do I nail the tops to?

A The bottom of each board can be nailed to the horizontal 2×4 wall plate on the floor, but, you're right, the tops will have only an occasional stud for solid nailing. To secure the tops, do these two things:

1 Apply a bead of construction adhesive to the drywall near the tops of the boards to adhere them to the wall. Your angled blind nails will hold them flat against the wall until the adhesive dries.

2 Install horizontal panel cap, a molding with a notch in the back that "hooks over" the top of the wainscoting. The panel cap covers the tops of the boards and, since it's nailed to the studs every 16", ensures the boards are held tight and even against the wall.

face-nail edges of boards in corners

panel cap

construction adhesive

Extraordinary Wainscoting
Using Ordinary Materials

Few projects do as much to jazz up a dining room, den, or family room as wainscoting — and you don't have to be a master craftsperson to create it. Here's one simple way to add an attractive wainscoting; use the basic ideas shown here to design your own.

1 Rip ½" MDF to a width of 30" to 36", then use construction adhesive and finish nails to secure it to the wall.

2 Install a horizontal 1×6 for the base and a 1×4 even with the top of the MDF for the top rail. Determine the size and position of your vertical stiles and install them between the base and top rail.

3 Secure ½"-thick MDF "raised panels" in the center of each frame using yellow glue and finish nails.

4 Picture-frame the outer edges of the raised panels with panel cap molding.

5 Picture-frame the inner edges of the frames with cove molding or other molding. Install a 1×2 cap to conceal the top edge of the MDF panel and 1×4 top rail, and add a piece of molding below that to conceal any gaps.

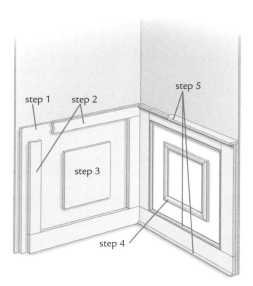

step 5

step 1   step 2

step 3

step 4

Your project will look better and go together easier if you plan ahead. Arrange the seams of your MDF panels (step 1) so they're hidden behind the vertical stiles. Make a small mockup of one section of wainscoting so you can determine the right size and proportions for your inner raised panel and the moldings.

Stairs, Railings, and Columns

Q I need to install a handrail for our basement stairs. What height should it be, and how do I install it parallel to the stairs?

A Stairways are one of the most dangerous areas of the home, so, for safety's sake, building codes are very specific in regard to handrails. A handrail must be 1¼" to 2" in diameter, and there must be a gap of at least 1½" between the handrail and the wall. The ends must be "returned" to the wall to prevent injury or snagging of clothes.

As for height, the top of the railing must be 34" to 38" above the nose of the tread. To position a handrail, measure 34" to 38" above the nose of your top and bottom treads (use the lesser measurement if you have kids), then snap a chalk line. (White chalk can be removed the easiest.) Measure down from that chalk line, taking into account the heights of your handrail and handrail brackets, and snap a second line to represent the bottom mounting holes of the brackets. Locate the underlying studs along the lower chalk line, mark the lower screw holes, then install the brackets.

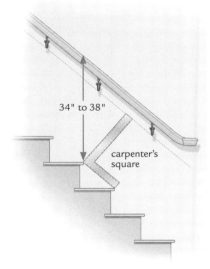

34" to 38"

carpenter's square

An old carpenters' trick that eliminates a lot of measuring and chalk marks is to rest the 16" leg of a carpenter's square (framing square) on two nosings and make a mark at the end of the 24" leg. That mark usually gives you the perfect position for the lower screw of the bracket.

Q Yesterday I was looking at one of those fancy baluster railings at a friend's house and wondering if I could build one. Could I?

A It all depends on how fancy the railing is. Some staircases and railings are more works of art than they are house parts, but there are systems available that allow someone with average woodworking or carpentry skills to build a traditional railing with balusters.

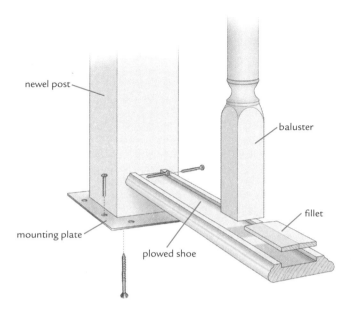

Perhaps the easiest system is one that uses plowed shoes and hand-rails designed to accommodate balusters and filler pieces called fillets. It involves installing the handrail and bottom shoe between newel posts and/or walls, then positioning and securing balusters and fillet pieces in the plowed-out section. You can get these systems along with instructions at most lumberyards and home centers. Some parts may be special-order.

Q The newel post on our staircase has become dangerously wobbly. Is there an easy way to make it sturdy again?

A You should definitely fix it, but since the original fasteners used to secure the newel post are almost certainly hidden, inaccessible, or "eccentric," it probably won't be easy. Here are some things to try:

⊙ If you can access the area from below, look to see if part of the newel post extends through the floor. If so, it was probably stabilized origi-nally by bolting it to the joists or with blocking. Try tightening or adding bolts, or adding more blocking.

⊙ In some cases, you may see a threaded rod extending through the floor that's secured to a metal plate with nuts and washers. If so, try tightening the nut.

⊙ Check the base of the newel post for wooden plugs that might be concealing mounting bolts that secure it to the stair's framework. You may be able to drill out the plugs and retighten the bolts or add new bolts.

⊙ If none of these methods work, you can remove the newel post (no easy task) and secure it back to the floor with a newel post mounting plate that screws to the bottom of the post and the floor (see illustration on opposite page). If you use this method, you'll have to find some way of covering the plate after installation.

Q I need to build a 54"-tall octagonal column to run between a half-wall and the ceiling. How do I juggle all the pieces while assembling them?

A Cut your eight sides, making sure they're all the same length, width, and angle. Apply a 2"-wide strip of tape along both edges of your first piece, leaving about 1" of tape extending beyond each edge. Apply a strip of tape to one edge of the second piece, and position the nontaped edge tightly against the first piece so it's lying on the tape. Continue doing this until all eight boards are laid out.

Apply glue to each beveled edge, then stand the pieces up (you'll be smart to have a helper for this part). Shape them into an octagon, then apply three or more band clamps to hold the pieces together while the glue sets.

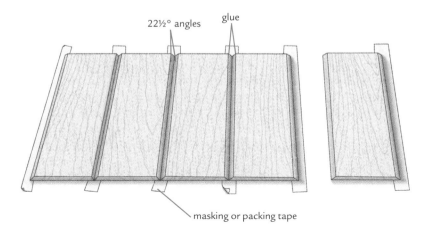

22½° angles   glue

masking or packing tape

11 | Other Projects, Inside & Out

Always do right; this will gratify some people and astonish the rest.

— MARK TWAIN

Some woodworking projects, such as installing wood flooring, remodeling a basement, or building a gazebo, don't fit neatly into any of the other chapters in this book. This chapter is sort of an "everything but the kitchen sink" affair. That said, many of the topics and projects in this chapter are the most-often tackled, and most useful, projects people take on. Building picture frames, closet organizers, and decks are hugely popular — practical, too. We divided this chapter into inside and outside projects; we'll start indoors.

Flooring

Q When discussing wood floors, a disagreement arose over which wood was the hardest: oak, Douglas fir, or maple. Who was right?

- ◎ White pine — 400 pounds
- ◎ Douglas fir — 710 pounds
- ◎ Black cherry — 950 pounds
- ◎ Red oak — 1,290 pounds
- ◎ White oak — 1,360 pounds
- ◎ Sugar maple — 1,450 pounds

A Wood hardness is measured via a procedure called the Janka hardness test. This involves measuring how many pounds of force are required to embed half of a 7/16" steel ball into a board's surface. If you want a floor that's virtually indestructible, use ipe, which requires 3,680 pounds of force to embed the test ball. See the box for ratings of some common flooring woods.

Q I want to install 1×4 tongue-and-groove maple flooring in our 12' × 14' bedroom. How much material do I need?

A You need to cover an area that is 168 square feet, but you'll need more than 168 square feet of flooring. For starters, 1×4 solid-wood flooring, by the time it's been milled and had the tongue and groove cut into it, will have an exposed face of about 3". Since each lineal foot of 3"-wide flooring will cover 0.25 square feet of area, divide 168 by 0.25 to get the total lineal footage you'll need; in this case, 672 lineal feet.

If your room is a simple rectangle, add at least 5 percent to this number for waste and cutoffs. If it has jogs or weird angles, add 10 percent. If possible, order a few lengths of 1×6 flooring; that way, if you wind up with a 4" space in your final row, you can rip a single 1×6 to that width rather than ending with a skinny 1" strip. Thin strips are apparent, especially if a room is out of square and the last board needs to be taper-cut.

Q Engineered wood floors come presanded (no dust) and prefinished (no smell), and they snap together (less labor). Why would anyone install ¾" solid wood flooring?

A Both kinds of flooring have their pros and cons.

Solid wood, ¾"-thick flooring can last hundreds of years and can be resanded and refinished up to 8 times (or until you sand down to the tongue and groove). It can be stained any color you choose and, to most homeowners, it has more character and a more solid feel.

Engineered wood flooring has all the attributes you mention. It's also vastly easier to install over a concrete surface and doesn't create as much height variation between adjoining floor surfaces. But since it's usually composed of a ¹⁄₁₆"- to ¼"-thick veneer secured to a plywood substrate, it usually can be sanded only once or twice at most (and then only *very* carefully), and it may have a hollow sound, feel, and look. Floors with rotary-cut veneers, which are peeled off the log like paper towels, tend to look more "plywood-y" and artificial than those with veneers that are flat-cut, or cut from the log like real lumber.

Q I'm installing solid wood flooring and debating whether I should spend the money to rent a floor nailer or simply nail it down by hand. What do you suggest?

A Rent a flooring nailer. It's time and money well spent. There are several types. Some drive staples, others cleated nails; some are pneumatic-driven, others operate more by brute force. Regardless of the type, they all do the two things you want a nailer to do: snug the boards tightly together while installing the fastener. The fasteners are driven at an angle through the back part of the tongue and are covered by the next board so the nail heads are concealed. Flooring nailers eliminate the guesswork as to what angle to drive the fastener, and they minimize the chance of damaging the floor with a misplaced hammer blow. Your arm will get a workout but your floor will be properly installed.

Q It seems like a flooring nailer would jostle the boards out of alignment when installing the first row. Do I butt the first row of boards against the wall to brace them?

A No. If your wall is wavy or out of square, using the wall as a starting point will create an entire floor that's wavy or out of square. It's critical to:

⊙ Start straight so the rest of the flooring follows suit.
⊙ Start rock-solid, since the flooring nailer packs such a wallop that it will jar loosely nailed boards out of position.

Snap a straight line about ½" away from the wall, then align the grooved edge of the first row of boards with your line, and face-nail them straight down to the underlying joists. Install the second row tightly against the first row, and nail this row by either face-nailing or carefully blind-nailing them by hand through the tongue. Make sure not to jar the first row out of position, and stagger the end joints by at least 2'.

With the first two rows solidly locked together and in place, you can then proceed to use the nailer without fear of jarring boards out of alignment. Since the nailer won't fit into the space for the last few rows, you'll need to face-nail or blind-nail them by hand. When the floor is done, set any exposed nail heads in the first rows below the surface, and fill the holes with putty.

Q How do I deal with the transitions between the hardwood floor I'm going to install in the living room and the kitchen and bathroom floors it will butt into? The vinyl kitchen floor will be much lower and the tiled bathroom floor about the same height.

A There are special moldings to accommodate most situations and height differences, though sometimes you have to modify them slightly to get a precise fit. A "hardwood flooring reducer" tapers from ¾" down to almost nothing to deal with the slight step down to the vinyl kitchen floor. A "T" or "transition molding" has recesses along both bottom edges so the top edge can slightly overlap and hide the edges of both floors. This might be the best molding to use at your bathroom door.

Remodeling Basics

Q I'm trying to rescue and reuse some old window molding, but when I pound the old nails out, big chunks of paint and wood come out with them. How do I salvage the wood without wrecking it?

A Pull the nails out through the backside of the molding. Grab the nail as close to the molding as you can with an end nipper or end cutter, then pry using the back of the molding for leverage. It may take a few tries to develop just the right pressure; if you grab the nail too tightly, you'll snip it off. You can also try pulling with a locking pliers. A less elegant approach is to pound the nails through and out the backside with a nail punch.

Q My neighbor installed 4×8 sheets of dark wood paneling in his basement. In the winter, you can see thin strips of the underlying white drywall where the seams have opened up. How can I avoid this when I panel my basement?

A Plywood paneling will expand and contract slightly with changes in humidity, and basements are particularly prone to wide swings. Before installing your paneling, apply a 2"-wide swath of paint that matches the paneling in the area where the seams will fall. If a gap opens up, it won't be as noticeable.

Q It seems like when I measure and mark outlet openings in paneling, I get them in the wrong position. Is there a foolproof tip for doing this?

A Rather than measuring and transferring dimensions, mark the back of the panel in place. Rub lipstick around the perimeter of the electrical box, then position the paneling and press it against the wall. The lipstick will "kiss" the back of the panel and create a "can't be wrong" outline for the electrical box. This will work only for boxes where the actual outlet hasn't been installed yet.

Q The previous owners of the house we just bought painted the beautiful oak millwork white. What's the best product for stripping the paint, now that we're living in the house?

A You need a stripper that:
- Clings to vertical surfaces
- Doesn't emit hazardous or annoying vapors
- Is safe and easy to work with

The best product may be a soy-based stripper. You need to leave it in place for several hours or overnight for it to work, but it's extremely safe to use. At first glance it seems expensive, but since it doesn't evaporate like other strippers, you only need one thick coat. Plus, you can reuse it by moving the scraped gunk to another part of the molding and letting it work again. Water-based strippers are another good option.

Q I'm installing larger windows and doors in our living room. The manufacturers list "rough opening" sizes. What are those?

A The manufacturer's literature will usually list a "frame size" or "unit dimension." This is the actual dimension of the window or door. The "rough opening" (RO) is the size you should make the framed opening that the door or window will fit into. Usually, the rough opening is ½" larger than the actual window or door (or "unit dimension"). This provides space for the shims used to plumb and level the unit in the opening (chances are the opening will be slightly out of whack).

Pay attention to the RO. If you make it too small, your window or door may not fit properly (or fit at all). If you make it too big, you'll need to add lots of shims and spacers, which can make for a less secure (and less weathertight) installation.

Q I'm remodeling our basement. The guy who's hanging the drywall told me not to forget the "backing." What's that?

A Backing is underlying wood blocking that needs to be there so something can be secured to it. That "something" commonly includes:

- ⊙ **Drywall.** There needs to be backing where walls intersect each other and the ceiling, so the ends and edges of the drywall have something to be secured to.
- ⊙ **Fixtures and accessories.** If you'll be installing grab bars or a wall-mounted sink in the bathroom, a flat-screen TV bracket, a large light fixture, or anything else heavy, you should install backing so the mounting screws have something solid to bite into.
- ⊙ **Shelving.** If you plan on mounting shelves, install backing to support the cleats or brackets.

Storage and Shelving

Q I'm designing a closet organizing system with shelves, drawers, and hanging rods. How much space should I designate for different articles of clothing?

A Here are some rules of thumb on space allotment per article:

- ⊙ Dresses — 72" vertical space, 1½" rod space
- ⊙ Shirts — 40" vertical space, 1½" rod space
- ⊙ Hanging slacks — 48" vertical space, 1½" rod space
- ⊙ Suits, jackets — 40" vertical space, 2½" rod space
- ⊙ Women's shoes — 7"–8" shelf width
- ⊙ Men's shoes — 9"–10" shelf width
- ⊙ Folded clothing — 10" wide × 12" deep
- ⊙ Folded sweaters — 12" wide × 16" deep × 3" height

Q I'm having trouble envisioning the most space-efficient design for my closet organizer. Any tips?

A Clear out your closet, then use ¾"-wide masking tape to mark out imaginary shelves, rods, drawers, and cubbyholes on the back wall. This visual aid will help you determine the most space-efficient layout, make sure shelves and rods are within proper reach, and check whether closet doors will interfere with any drawers or doors you plan on building.

Q How can I prevent melamine-coated shelves from chipping when I cut them with my circular saw?

A Use a 60- or 80-tooth carbide blade and adjust the blade so it protrudes only ⅛" beyond the material as you cut. Support the shelf on 2×4s so the melamine doesn't splinter when the scrap falls away. Cut the shelf "good-side-down," because that side will splinter less, and the surface won't be marred by the shoe of your saw.

Q I'm installing ¾" laminate shelving in our closet. What's the farthest apart I can put the brackets without the shelves sagging?

A You should install shelf support brackets no more than 32" apart. Your shelves will be even less prone to sagging if you install a horizontal board along the wall to support the back edge.

Q I read one article that said aromatic cedar was a natural moth repellant and another that said this was a myth. I'm building a clothes storage closet. Will it do any good to line it with aromatic cedar?

A It's the larvae, not the adult moths, that enjoy snacking on your clothes. The good news is that vapors from aromatic cedar, when confined in a small, well-sealed area, will indeed kill hatching moth larvae. The bad news is those vapors have minimal effect on the eggs and adult moths. Also, in large spaces such as clothes closets, the vapors are so diffuse they may not affect the hatching larvae either. Some people maintain that the tight construction of cedar closets and cedar chests has more of a role keeping out moths and larvae than the cedar within.

That said, if you enjoy the smell of aromatic cedar and the aroma it imparts to your clothes, use it. It can't hurt and it might help. Never paint, stain, or clear-coat the wood; it will negate any beneficial effects. Give the cedar a light sanding every year or two to rejuvenate and unlock the aroma.

Picture Frames and Accessories

Q I'm making several large picture frames that need to support the weight of the picture, mat, and double-strength protective glass. How can I strengthen the joints?

A There is a smorgasbord of things you can do:

⊙ Apply extra glue to the miters. The open pores on the end grain of a miter mean there's less actual long-grain wood for the glue to adhere to, and the pores themselves tend to suck up glue, making matters worse. Counteract this by using more glue than normal, or by using an epoxy-type glue.

⊙ Cross-pin the corners by driving brads in from each direction. Predrill the holes or use a pneumatic brad nailer, or you'll jar your corners out of alignment.

⊙ Reinforce the joint. If your frame is thick enough, use biscuits, corrugated fasteners, dowels, or pocket screws to add strength.

Q The picture frame moldings at home centers and craft stores are expensive. Can I make my own?

A Yes, and if you have a router or router table, you have hundreds of options. You'll get the best results routing long strips of wood first, then cutting and assembling your frame pieces. Here are the basic steps:

1 Measure the thickness of your mat, artwork, glass, and backing, then use your router and a rabbet bit to cut a rabbet deep enough to accommodate the combined thickness of these materials.

2 Use the router and desired bits to shape the profiles along edges of the strips.

3 Measure the outside dimensions of your mat or picture, then cut your frame pieces to length, allowing an extra ⅛". (You need to measure and mark the inside corner of the rabbet.)

4 Apply glue, then clamp or nail the corners of your frame together.

ROUTER-CRAFTED FRAME

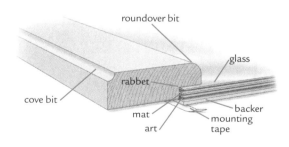

roundover bit

glass

rabbet

cove bit

mat

art

backer

mounting tape

Another option is to create your frames from built-up moldings. You can glue up long lengths of moldings, then cut them to length and glue up the frames, or build your frames stick-by-stick.

BUILT-UP MOLDING FRAME

1×3

glass, mat, art and backer material

cove molding

door stop

Q I've tried using corner clamps when gluing up picture frames, but they're awkward to use and don't seem to apply enough pressure. What's a good method of clamping corners?

A You can make your own corner clamps using strips of ½" plywood and triangular blocks. Construct at least eight of the jigs as shown. To use them:

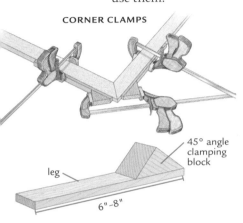

CORNER CLAMPS

45° angle clamping block

leg

6"–8"

1 Clamp the "leg" of a corner jig near the mitered end of each board.
2 Apply glue to the mitered ends and position the pieces.
3 Use a third clamp to pull the clamping blocks toward each other to tighten up the miter.

Secure all four corners and leave the clamps in place for at least an hour. You can use the same basic technique for clamping corners of boxes, window trim, and other projects with mitered corners.

Q How difficult is it to make a round picture frame?

A It may be easier than you think. Just think of your picture as a large pie with the frame as the outer crust.

1 On a scrap piece of plywood, use a large compass (or measuring tape hooked over a screw) to draw the two circles representing the inside and outside edges of the frame.
2 Draw one line through the center, then divide the circle into six or eight equal pie-shaped slices; the larger the frame, the more slices you need. Imagine the frame as the crust of the pie (a wide crust), and measure to determine the board width you'd need to make the crust for each piece. (In our example, we need eight 1×8s cut at 22.5 degrees on each end.)
3 Use a miter saw to cut the eight pieces, then use glue and biscuits or dowels to join them end-to-end to make an eight-sided frame. Once the glue has dried, find the center, then use your compass or tape measure to mark the inside and outside perimeters of your frame once more.

4 Finally, use a jigsaw, scroll saw and/or a bandsaw to cut out your round frame. Cut the rabbet around the back interior edge for housing the glass, mat and artwork by using a router and rabbeting bit.

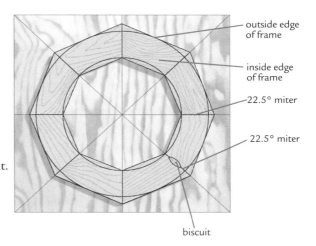

outside edge of frame

inside edge of frame

22.5° miter

22.5° miter

biscuit

tip: From Spring Coil to Corner Clamp

There are dozens of jigs and clamps you can buy for assembling picture frames, but there are also dozens you can make. Perhaps the simplest are those made from an upholsterer's coil spring. To make them, use a hacksaw to cut nearly-complete loops from a coil spring, then use a belt sander or grinder to sharpen the ends. Apply glue to the mitered ends of the frame, then pull the ends of the coil spring loops apart and position them so they bite into the wood while exerting pressure on the joint.

sharpened ends

coil spring

Toys

Q Is there a standard size or scale for building dollhouses and furniture?

A The standard scale is 1:12 (one inch equals 12 inches). Given that scale, a typical room would be about 10" × 10", a bed about 4" × 6", a chair about 2" × 2", and an adult "occupant" about 6" tall. You can build a larger- or smaller-scale house, but most furniture and accessories you can buy fit the 1:12 scale.

Q I sent away for full-size plans for a cutout child's toy. What's the best way to transfer it onto the plywood?

A Try using transfer paper, which is basically gigantic carbon paper (without the mess). It usually comes in 1'- or 2'-wide sheets, in lengths of up to 16', and can be reused dozens of times. You can buy it at most craft or fabric stores or online. Tape the paper to your wood, place your pattern over it, then trace over your pattern to transfer it to the wood.

Q I'm building a toy chest for my daughter. How do I build a safe one?

A Toy chests pose three possible dangers. All can be avoided with the proper design and hardware:

- Pinched fingers and slamming lids can be avoided by using "soft close" hinges with mechanisms that hold the lid open at 75 to 85 degrees. Some operate by friction; others use a piston or spring.
- Suffocation can be prevented by including slots or vent holes on the back or sides of the chest. Another common design incorporates a wide cutout or dip along the top of the front panel that provides both a vent and a space for the hand when opening the lid. Never put a latch or locking mechanism on a toy chest for holding it closed.

Q I want to build my granddaughter a rocking dinosaur for her birthday. What are some of the safety considerations to keep in mind?

A The U.S. Consumer Product Safety Commission has a list of guidelines for child toy design. You can find some of that information online (see Resources). A few of the most important guidelines include:

- Round off sharp wood edges. Eliminate or cover exposed threads and sharp edges of bolts and screws.
- Use nontoxic finishes.
- Limit the length of any cords or ropes to 6" or less to prevent strangulation.
- Avoid small parts that might break off or become unglued (a swallowing hazard).
- Avoid mechanisms or openings that could pinch or entrap fingers.

With your rocking dinosaur, you'll want a design that minimizes flipping and tipping.

Q What's a safe clear finish to apply to some hardwood toys I'm making for my nephew?

A A salad bowl finish, designed for use on kitchen implements, is a sure bet. Mineral or walnut oils are also safe. Most other finishes are considered safe after curing for 30 days.

Decks, Porches, and Gazebos

Q I'm replacing an older, smaller gazebo made of treated lumber with a new, larger one. Can I burn the wood from the old deck?

A No. If your structure is more than a few years old, chances are it was constructed using wood treated with chromated copper arsenate (CCA), and the smoke and ashes can contain toxic chemicals. When you demolish the old deck, wear gloves and a dust mask to prevent inhalation of dust. If you can find a good way to repurpose the wood by using it as garden edging or a storage structure, do it. Otherwise, dispose of it via your local trash collection. Call your hauler to find out how it handles the materials and situation.

Q I'm expanding the porch on our old house and want to mimic the existing railing. The balusters are flat with a decorative profile. What's the best way to reproduce 40 of them?

A Remove one of the existing balusters and carefully trace the profile onto a piece of ¼" hardboard. Very carefully cut out the profile and sand the edges. This is your template, so it's worth taking the time to be exact; any flaw (or perfection!) will be repeated 40 times.

Place your template on one of the boards and trace around it with a pencil. Use a jigsaw or a bandsaw to rough-cut the profile, staying ⅛" to ¼" *outside* the line. Use clamps or a few screws to secure the template back onto the board, then trim the baluster to its final shape using a router with a top-bearing-guided straight bit. You can try skipping the rough cutout stage and doing all the cutting with your router, but it will tax your router, your bit, and you.

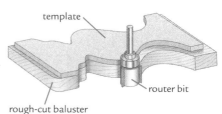

template

router bit

rough-cut baluster

tip: Don't Dig It

Gas, electric, telephone, water, and cable lines are buried in the most surprising places. Don't get a nasty surprise when you start an outdoor project. Whether you're installing a fence, building a deck, planting a tree, or tackling any other project that involves sticking a shovel in the ground, call 811 first. It's the national Call Before You Dig hotline. It will route you to a local agency that will arrange to have a locator come out to mark all your underground utilities. It sometimes takes a few days, so plan ahead.

Q How far apart should I space the pressure-treated top boards on my new deck?

A With wood that's been thoroughly kiln- or air-dried, the standard spacing is "16d nail thickness" apart. But most treated wood has a high moisture content because of the chemical treatment it receives. You can let the boards air-dry for a few weeks, but chances are warping will occur. Your best bet is to butt the boards tightly together; as the wood dries, the proper gap will appear.

Q Does it matter whether I install my new deck boards bark-side-up or bark-side-down?

A This debate has gone on for decades, and there are pros and cons to both sides of the argument (and board). But at the end of the day the best advice is to lay your deck boards with the best-looking side facing up. Be on the lookout for wane (edges of boards where there is loose or missing bark) and shelling or shake (areas of the face, most often on the non-bark side, where the growth rings are separating from one another). Your boards will cup and twist less if you apply your finish of choice to the bottoms and edges of all of the boards before installing them.

Q My building inspector asked me whether the joists for the deck I'm building were going to be 16" or 24" on center. What does she mean?

A She was referring to the distance from the center of one joist to the next. There are two factors that you need to take into account:

   1 the strength and span of your joists

   2 how much support your top deck boards require so they don't sag

In general, the larger the deck, the more support that's required, and the closer together the joists need to be. In regard to the second factor, the thinner the top board, the more support that's required, and (again) the closer together the joists.

An 8' × 8' deck with pressure-treated top boards 1½" inches thick would most likely have joists spaced at 24" centers. A 16' × 16' deck with 1"-thick top boards most likely would need hefty joists at 16" centers. Species of the wood, number of support beams, snow load, and other factors also come into play. The good news is that most lumberyards and home centers will calculate this for you.

Q What's the best type of fastener to use for installing deck boards?

A There are lots of choices, but most deck builders will tell you to use screws rather than nails, and to use stainless steel, galvanized, or coated versions (see page 251). All have their pros and cons.

Whichever type of screw you use, install them with care. Drive the heads only slightly below the surface of the wood so as not to create deep pockets for water to sit in, which can accelerate rot. If you don't like the sight of hundreds of screw holes, you can purchase systems that use special mounting strips, clips, or biscuits for securing the boards to the joists.

Yard and Garden

Q What are some good woods — and good guidelines — for building birdhouses?

A Cedar or cypress, used rough-side-out, are good wood choices, but pine or plywood painted on the outside (but not on the inside) can also be used. A few other points to remember:

- Size it right. Different birds prefer different sizes of houses and holes and different distances above the ground. Several excellent websites have detailed charts and information (see Resources).
- Create some form of ventilation. Leave either a 1" gap between the walls and eaves, or drill a series of ¼" holes around the tops of the walls.
- Create some form of drainage. Small holes in each corner and one in the middle of the floor will usually suffice.

⊙ Create the right entry. Carve a few grooves or rough up the wood under the opening to give the new occupants a good foothold. But leave off the perches; they only give predators a convenient place to lurk.

⊙ Keep it clean. Create a clean-out door so nesting material can be removed and the house rinsed out after each nesting season.

Q My 7¼" circular saw can't cut all the way through a 6×6 fence post. What's the best way to cut through a large timber?

A Measure and mark your 6×6, then use a square to draw lines on all four sides of the timber. By the time you "circumnavigate" the timber, your first and last line should meet at the corner. If not, check to see if there are any knots or large splinters that are skewing your square. Set the timber on a pair of sawhorses with the part to be cut off hanging over one end. Set your circular saw to cut as deeply as it can (most standard circular saws can cut about 2" deep), and make cuts through all four sides. When you're done, use a handsaw or reciprocating saw to cut through the remaining inner nub.

If you have a large project, such as a timber retaining wall, consider renting a 14" circular saw for a day. It can cut through a 6×6 in one pass and can speed up the project if there are lots of angled cuts.

Q What's the best type of wood for fence posts that will be buried? Is there any way to make them last longer?

A The two most widely available options are cedar and treated wood. Cedar posts aren't as strong as treated wood posts, but they're less likely to twist and bow, they age to a nice silvery gray, and they're easier to tote around and nail into. (They'll also drain your checkbook faster.) Only the heartwood of the cedar tree is naturally rot-resistant, so when you select your posts, avoid those with lighter sapwood streaks in them.

If you elect to go with treated posts, be certain to purchase those rated for "below-ground contact" (not "above-ground use," "treated to refusal," or other designations). The below-ground version has a higher concentration of preservative and will last longer. If you need to cut them, always install the uncut end in the ground. You can add an extra measure of rot resistance by letting the post stand in a five-gallon bucket of wood preservative — the longer the better — before installing it.

Q I'm building a picnic table and have run into several types of exterior screws. Will one perform better than the others?

A There are lots of choices, but you can lump them into three categories, each with their own pros and cons:

- ⊙ **Galvanized** screws are coated with zinc, which protects the screw from moisture and the tannic acids or preservatives found in many exterior woods. Hot-dipped screws (those with a rough texture) will hold up better than those that have been electroplated. Galvanized screws are the least expensive of the three options.

- ⊙ **Stainless steel** screws are an alloy of steel, nickel, and chromium and are the most corrosion-resistant (and expensive) of the outdoor screws. They're also the softest and most likely to snap or have the heads strip out during installation. Always predrill holes, especially in harder woods such as teak.

- ⊙ **Coated** screws — available in gray, tan, and other earth tones — are protected by a ceramic or plastic coating. Price wise, they fall between galvanized and stainless. Some screw manufacturers provide a special bit intended to prevent damage to the coating during installation.

Q I'd like a clear finish on the cedar patio table I just built. Can I use regular varnish?

A No, you should use a product formulated for outdoor use. Marine and spar varnishes and exterior urethanes remain flexible when dry, have UV blockers and, while expensive, are your best choice for outdoor furniture and projects. For best protection, apply the recommended number of coats.

Q What's the best type of glue to use for the Adirondack chair I'm building?

A There are several options, but the two most weather-resistant and widely available glues are:

- ⊙ **Polyurethane glues,** such as Gorilla Glue, are waterproof and will adhere to most materials. It has a longer "open time" than other glues, so it provides more working time to assemble and position the parts. It's paintable, stainable, and sandable. On the downside, it foams up in reaction to the moisture in the wood, and any glue residue will cling tenaciously to your hands, tools, workpiece, or any-thing else that gets in its way (keep some denatured alcohol around for cleanup).

⊙ **Waterproof PVA glues**, such as Titebond III, are another good form of exterior glue. You use them like regular yellow carpenter's glue, they clean up with water, and they're less expensive than polyure-thane glues. They don't stain as well as polyurethane glues, but if your joints are tight this isn't a large factor.

Two-part epoxies and **polyurethane construction adhesives** are two other options for your project, but the epoxies can be messy and the construction adhesives remain somewhat flexible, making them less than ideal for chair construction.

Q I spotted my neighbor using a hot-melt glue gun to build wood patio chairs. Isn't that stuff only good for crafts?

A There are now polyurethane hot-melt adhesives available that are excellent for exterior use. They're super strong and work almost instantly. They can also fill gaps and are waterproof. The downside? They're expensive and difficult to stain, and they're a bear to sand once they've cured.

Q Is oak a good wood to use for outdoor projects?

A White oak, yes. Red oak, no.

⊙ **White oak** (the wood used to make barrels) is incredibly strong, straight-grained, and rot-resistant. The end grain is filled with tyloses (see page 50), which minimize absorption of moisture through the end grain. The two main drawbacks are cost and workability (you'll need to predrill for screws or nails).

⊙ **Red oak** is equally strong but has end grain that sucks up moisture like a straw (in fact, you can blow bubbles in a glass of water through a short piece of red oak). Red oak is much less rot-resistant and not well suited for outdoor use.

tip: Longer-Lasting Outdoor Furniture

When the end grain of a chair or table leg sits on a damp patio, deck, or lawn, the rot process accelerates dramatically. Keep moisture at bay and make your unfinished furniture last longer by mixing up a solution of half exterior glue and half water, and brushing it on the end grain of the legs or feet. Epoxy glue also works.

Sanding & Finishing

*The best preparation for good work
tomorrow is to do good work today.*
— ELBERT HUBBARD

For some people, applying the finish is their favorite part of woodworking. After all their hard work and preparation, they get to watch the grain of the wood dance and come alive. For others, it can be a nightmare, to watch all their hard work and preparation go down the drain after applying a finish that wound up blotchy or dark. Finishing may be part science and part art, but with the right tools and know-how, you can get the results you're looking for. There are hundreds of products, opinions, and variables out there, but one can simplify the decision-making process by answering two simple questions: How do you want the piece to look and feel? And what level of protection is needed? We'll try to help you answer these and other questions.

Sanding

Q It seems like I often discover deep sanding scratches after I've stained, and by then it's too late. What can I do to locate scratches before I start the finishing process?

A Hold a reflector light or portable trouble light near the surface of the board, then view the board from the opposite side at a low angle. The low angle of the light will make any ridges and swirls more apparent by the mini-shadows they cast. Perform a quick surface check each time you move to a finer grit of sandpaper to prevent having to backtrack to get rid of coarse scratches.

Q I'm building a table where the instructions suggest sanding the top with 80-grit paper, then progressing through three finer grits. Wouldn't I save time and sandpaper by skipping a couple of grits?

A The process of sanding is simply replacing deep, wide scratches with smaller and smaller scratches until the scratches become hard to detect with the naked eye. When you skip grits, you simply make more work for yourself by making a finer-grit paper do the work of a coarser-grit paper that would remove the scratches far faster.

Q What are the advantages of using a sanding block instead of just holding the sandpaper in my hand?

A A sanding block helps distribute pressure evenly. When you don't use one, you risk rounding over edges. Instead of removing dips and waves, you'll simply make smoother dips and waves. Your sandpaper — and your arm — will both last longer and work more efficiently with a sanding block.

tip: A Better Sanding Block

If you hate the hassle of loading sandpaper onto a rubber sanding block, make your own. Cut some ¾" × 4" × 5" blocks out of MDF, coat each side with spray adhesive, then stick quarter-sheets of sandpaper to each side; the papers can be of the same or different grits. You can sand by moving your block over larger workpieces or by setting it on your workbench and moving smaller workpieces over it. When your paper is worn out, heat it with a hair dryer, peel it off, and apply a new sheet.

Q One friend told me I should only sand with the grain, while another friend said this is poppycock. Who's right?

A Your last sanding should always be with the grain, but you'll get smoother results faster if earlier passes are made at an angle slightly diagonal to the grain. If you start with 80-grit paper, work with a right slant. When you switch to 120-grit, work with a left slant, then change direction back again for your 180-grit pass. Make your final pass with 180-grit or 220-grit paper, moving with the grain.

Q My woodworking store stocks three kinds of sandpaper: the standard stuff, wet-dry, and stearated sandpaper. What's the difference?

A **Standard aluminum oxide and garnet sandpapers** are inexpensive and work quickly because of their friable grits, which constantly fracture to expose fresh new cutting edges. Aluminum oxide is the tougher and harder of the two.

Wet-dry sandpapers usually are made with fine grits of silicone carbide and most frequently are used wet for smoothing out finishes. The water keeps the paper from clogging by washing away the sanding particles.

Stearated sandpapers (sometimes called no-load papers) are covered with abrasive grit as well as zinc stearate, a soft, soapy material that lubricates the surface as it works. It also makes the paper less likely to clog. These papers can be used for sanding raw wood but most often are used between finishes. There are mixed reports that some water-based and other specialized finishes have a strange reaction when applied to surfaces sanded with stearated paper.

Q I do my final sanding with a random orbital sander with extra-fine paper, but I still get spiral pattern marks. How do I avoid this?

A A random orbital sander can be a real time-saver during the sanding process, but you should still always do your final sanding by hand, going with the grain. Your curlicue marks are probably the result of moving your sander too fast. Shoot for moving your sander at a rate of 1 ips (inch per second) to minimize swirl marks.

Q I hand-sand small toy parts on my workbench. Is there a way of keeping them from moving around without clamping them down?

A Try placing them on a scrap of high-density carpet pad. The pad will protect the facedown side of the wood, and its rubber surface will help grip the piece. Vacuum the pad every once in a while to remove dust and maintain the pad's gripping power. Carpet pad also works well for holding small pieces while routing. For about $10 you can purchase a neoprene or woven mat that's denser and has longer-lasting gripping power. They're often sold as "nonslip router mats."

Q What's the finest grit paper I need to use before applying a finish, in order to get a smooth finish?

A It depends on the wood and the finish you're applying. If you're applying a penetrating finish, such as tung or boiled linseed oil, where the finish is absorbed into the wood, you'll want to sand down to a very fine grit, since the wood itself will be the surface you'll be touching. You may want to sand down to an extra-fine 280-grit paper, or at least down to a grit that feels smooth to the touch.

If you're applying a film-forming finish, such as varnish, polyurethane, or shellac, you don't need to sand down as far, for two reasons. First, since you're touching the finish and not the wood, the wood itself doesn't need to be as smooth (though you'll most likely want to sand the finish itself to a finer grit). Secondly, film-forming finishes need to create a mechanical bond with the wood, and small scratches provide tooth for a good bond. If you sand the wood down too far, you risk failed adhesion. For large-pore woods, such as oak, ash, and elm, you'll want to stop sanding at 150-grit. For smaller-pore woods, such as maple and birch, you may want to sand down to 220, but no further.

Q I bought some manufacturer's seconds of cove molding. It's beautiful, but boy does it need sanding. Is there an easy way to sand 150 feet of the stuff?

A With that much molding to sand, it's worth your while to create a custom sanding block. There are two options:

⊙ **Rigid foam insulation.** Trace the molding's profile onto a thick piece of rigid foam, then use a bandsaw or jigsaw to cut it out. Shape your sandpaper around the foam. As you sand, the foam will conform more exactly to the shape of the molding.

⊙ **Auto body putty.** Locate a 12" section of molding that's relatively smooth, and cover it with plastic food wrap. Mix up some auto body filler and press it firmly over the molding to create a block that's about 1" thick. Remove the material after it hardens. You now have a sanding block that conforms exactly to the profile of your molding. Wrap sandpaper around this block and sand away.

Sandpaper Cutting and Storage Station

This sanding station gives you a place to organize and store your sandpaper and has a handy blade for quickly cutting paper to size. You can easily customize the number and spacing of the shelves to meet your needs. Key construction steps include:

◆ Build the box from ¾" plywood, and the shelves and back from ¼" material. Create the shelf dadoes using either your table saw or router.

◆ Include "thumb cutouts" on the front edges of the shelves for easy access to your sheets.

◆ Use sheet-metal screws to secure a 12" hacksaw blade 1" back from the front edge of the top. Make marks 4½" and 5½" back from the cutting edge to serve as positioning lines for cutting standard sandpaper in half in both directions. Add your own positioning lines as desired. To cut paper, slip it under the blade and position it on the correct line. Give it one quick upward bend to crease it, then pull upward starting at one edge to cut the paper.

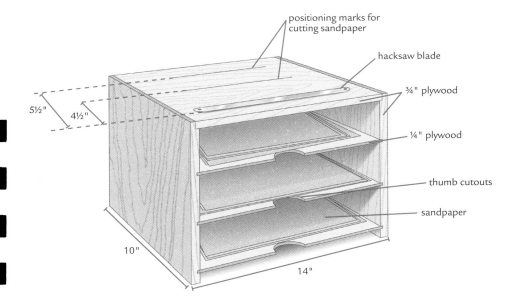

positioning marks for cutting sandpaper

hacksaw blade

¾" plywood

¼" plywood

thumb cutouts

sandpaper

5½"

4½"

10"

14"

Brushes and Spray Equipment

Q What are the differences between natural-bristle and synthetic-bristle brushes?

A They each have their own strengths and weaknesses. With either type of brush, you usually get what you pay for.

Natural-bristle brushes usually are made of hog or ox hair. The soft, hollow bristles are excellent for absorbing, holding, and evenly releasing oil-based finishes. They shouldn't be used to apply latex paints or be cleaned in water, since these same absorbent qualities will make the bristles fluffy and difficult to control over time (eventually your brush will look like the hairdo on a troll doll, and apply finish with just as much aplomb).

Synthetic-bristle brushes are made of nylon, polyester, or blends thereof. Synthetic brushes, especially inexpensive ones, won't lay down as smooth a finish as natural brushes, but they can be used for applying both water-based and solvent-based finishes.

Q My hardware store has brushes from 79 cents to $25. What are the differences between a cheap brush and an expensive one?

A High-quality brushes have split, or flagged, bristles that release paint more evenly. Also, the bristles are arranged so that the brush tapers to a chisel point, which allows for better control. A good brush should feel springy, not spongy or stiff. A good brush, properly cared for, is truly a "tool" that can last for years.

tip: Rescue Me

You can save hardened brushes from the trash can by soaking them overnight in either a store-bought brush restorer (such as Sav-a-Brush) or in your own homemade brew. To make your own brush restorer, mix together:

◇ Two parts xylene ◇ One part denatured alcohol ◇ One part acetone

Soak petrified brushes overnight, use a brush comb to remove the gunk, then rinse them in the brush cleaner one more time. Give synthetic brushes a final rinse in water and natural bristle brushes one in mineral spirits before putting them away.

Q Will my finishes look better if I spray them instead of brush them on?

A You'll be able to apply finishes faster by spraying, but not necessarily better. It's the person, not the tool, that dictates the quality of a finish. Quick-drying finishes such as shellac and lacquer are easier to apply with a spray gun; however, a brush in the hands of a patient woodworker can create a finish just as smooth and durable as that of a power sprayer.

tip: Mini Spray Paint Booth

If you have small parts you need to spray-paint, this mini spray booth will keep dust out and odors in. Set your object in a cardboard box, then slide the box into a large, clear plastic bag. Put on a glove, grab your spray can, stick your arm through the bag opening and seal it with a rubber band, then spray. Your surface may wind up a little rough since the overspray particles may stick to the tacky surface of your project.

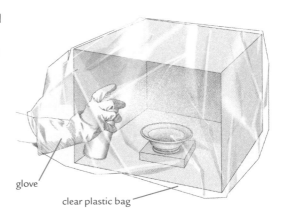

glove

clear plastic bag

Q What's the difference between a conventional spray gun and an HVLP gun?

A All spray guns have some way of atomizing finish into droplets, mixing those droplets with air then propelling the mixture toward your workpiece. There are differences in cost, portability, and a thing called *transfer efficiency* — the percentage of the amount of finish that winds up on your project rather than in your shop, in your spray booth, or on you.

A standard spray gun, which connects to a standard air compressor, can distribute any kind of finish, thick or thin, and is relatively inexpensive, especially if you already own a compressor. One of the downsides of standard spray guns is that they propel the finish so aggressively that as much as three-quarters of the finish either zips right past or bounces off the wood, resulting in a transfer efficiency as low as 25 percent.

An HVLP (high-volume, low-pressure) gun distributes air at a greater volume, but lower pressure, which creates a kinder, gentler mist. There's less overspray, and the transfer efficiency can be as high as 75 percent, which means more of the finish winds up on the workpiece (less wasted finish).

There are two kinds of **HVLP systems**. The first is a *dedicated* system consisting of a gun, hose, and turbine (to atomize the finish). These systems are small and portable but quite expensive. The second type is a *conversion* system, which converts high-pressure compressed air to a lower-pressure spray. Since these use a standard air compressor as the pressure source, the price is substantially less; however, you'll have to invest in an oil and water trap or filter to keep contaminants out of your finish.

Q Can I get good results using canned aerosol finishes?

A Yes, especially on small projects. Aerosol finishes are expensive and require the application of more coats than other methods of spraying, but you can build a smooth, durable finish. Follow the manufacturer's directions regarding the amount of drying time between coats and the distance between your project and the nozzle. Spraying too close can create bubbles. Spraying from too far away can yield a sandpaper-like finish, as the droplets dry before hitting the surface. High-quality spray lacquers have a higher percentage of solids, so they build a coat quickly.

Q I borrowed spray equipment from a friend to apply polyurethane to some cabinet doors and wound up with a finish that's thicker in some places than others. What's wrong?

A If your equipment is in good working order, chances are it has to do with your technique. Keep your gun about 8" away from your workpiece — or an inch or two farther for conventional guns, or a titch closer for HVLP guns. Then follow these three guidelines:

⊙ Begin by pointing the gun slightly off to the side of the workpiece, depress the trigger, then move the gun all the way across the workpiece at an even rate, not releasing the trigger until the spray is beyond the other edge.

⊙ Overlap the preceding pass by one-half to two-thirds its width when making subsequent passes.

⊙ Rather than swinging your arm in an arc, which positions the nozzle closer to the workpiece at the center than the edges, move your arm and nozzle parallel to the surface.

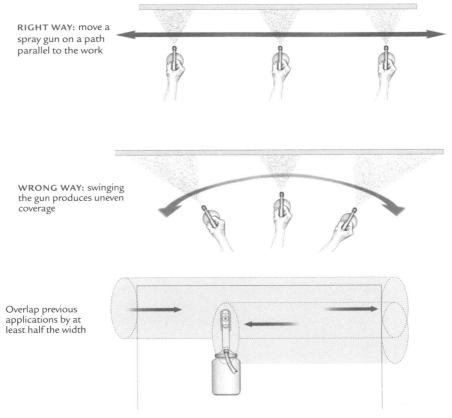

RIGHT WAY: move a spray gun on a path parallel to the work

WRONG WAY: swinging the gun produces uneven coverage

Overlap previous applications by at least half the width

tip: Latex Gloves Make Life Easier

Keep a box of cheap disposable latex gloves in your shop, and slip them on before tackling messy tasks such as gluing, staining, finishing, or cleaning up spills. You'll spend less time scrubbing your hands and will be able to switch from one task to another faster. They're also good for your health, since they can prevent solvents from entering your body via skin contact.

Fillers, Sealers, and Putties

Q I built an oak coffee table and want a surface that's as smooth as glass. The guy at the woodworking store told me to use a grain filler. What is it?

A Grain or pore filler is a substance made of binders, talc and other extremely fine particles of filler material. It's used to fill the pores of open-pored woods such as oak, teak, ash, walnut, and mahogany. When applied, it creates a smooth, level wood surface, which in turn makes it easier to achieve a smooth finish. You can use a filler that's the same color as the wood for a uniform look, or use one of a contrasting color to accentuate the open-pore grain areas.

Q Is grain filler difficult to apply?

A It's a little bit difficult — and really messy. Prior to filling the grain, seal the wood with a thin coat of dewaxed shellac (Zinsser's Sealcoat is one widely available product) and let it dry for two or three hours. You should follow the manufacturer's instructions, but the basic process involves applying the filler with a brush or putty knife, working it into the wood, scraping off the excess by wiping across the grain with burlap or a stiff squeegee, then letting it dry. Be thorough; any unfilled pores will really stand out after the finish is applied. Let water-based fillers dry for a few hours; oil-based fillers may take two or three days. Next comes a light sanding, followed by another thin coat of dewaxed shellac, stain (if desired), and a clear top-coat finish. On extremely open-grained woods, such as oak, it's a good idea to apply a second coat of filler before moving on to the top coat.

Q I built a desk using a gorgeous, wide slab of pine for the top. Part of the beauty is a large knot that the grain swirls around. The problem is, the knot is sunken and I need a smooth surface to work on. What can I do to fix this?

A Remove any loose material by nudging it with a wood chisel, then vacuum out any debris. Mix up some slow-setting, two-part epoxy and dribble a little into the dip. If it drips out the bottom, apply tape to prevent leaking. Apply the epoxy in layers, until it's slightly mounded above the surface of the wood. When it's dry, scrape and sand the area smooth. The clear epoxy will fill your dent and not detract from the beauty of your knot.

Q I filled the nail holes in an oak mirror with colored wood putty, then applied the stain and polyurethane. I wound up with blotches around the nail holes. What did I do wrong?

A The best approach when using colored putty is to stain and apply one coat of polyurethane to the wood, let it dry, fill the nail holes with putty that matches the stain, lightly sand, then apply a second coat of poly. The first coat of poly seals the wood so the oils from the putty can't bleed into the wood and create blotches, while the second coat creates a little protective barrier over the putty. That little bit of protection is critical, because most colored putties are nonhardening. There are some putties designed for use on raw wood that can be stained and sanded after they've been applied without creating blotches. Read the label on any putty you use to find out the right order of filling, sanding, and finishing.

Stains and Dyes

Q What's the difference between a stain and a dye?

A The super-simplistic answer is, stains have stuff sitting in the bottom of the can, while dyes don't. And while this is an oversimplification, it's this stuff that helps explain the difference.

Stains are made of a liquid containing ground-up opaque pigments that color the wood. While the pigments are small enough to penetrate the open surface pores of the wood, they're not small enough to penetrate deeply into the wood. In fact, these pigments are large enough actually to settle out, forming that layer of stuff in the bottom of the container.

Dyes are made of chemical colorants and molecular-size particles that stay permanently suspended in the liquid medium. Since these colorants are so fine, they penetrate deeper into the wood. Differentiating between dyes and stains can be confusing because of the ways manufacturers label their products. For example, most "penetrating oil stains" are actually dyes. Other "stains" are a combination of dye and pigment.

Q What about gel stains? They don't settle.

A You're correct. Gel stains are composed of pigments suspended in a jellylike medium that's so thick the pigments can't settle. The advantage of a gel stain is that the pigments won't penetrate as deeply or as quickly, so you have more control over the depth of the color based on how long you leave the stain on and how vigorously you wipe it off.

Q Do stains and dyes create different looks?

A Since pigmented stains settle into the open surface pores, they tend to enhance differences in grain patterns, because large pores will absorb more stain than small pores. Dyes soak more evenly into the wood, creating less contrast and a more even appearance.

tip: Glue Detector

You can discover glue smears and spots by rubbing down your piece with mineral spirits after sanding. The mineral spirits will temporarily darken the wood and reveal any hidden glue.

Q I discovered some light glue spots after I applied the stain. Can I resand and refinish those areas?

A You can remove the spots by sanding down to bare wood and restaining, but it's a royal pain in the neck — especially if you went so far as to apply the topcoat or finish. One option is to leave well enough alone and darken the glue spots using an artist's brush to apply stain to the affected areas. You can also try furniture touch-up pens or paint. Once your stain or paint has dried, apply your clear top coat to the entire piece if you haven't already done so.

Q I tried staining a rock maple side table a deep brown, but even after letting the stain sit for a while, when I wiped it off it was a wishy-washy light brown. Should I keep adding more coats of stain?

A No, chances are you're using a pigmented stain, and the pores of hard rock maple are simply too small to accept the large pigment particles. Try using a dye or dye stain, which has colorants small enough to penetrate the wood's pores. Experiment on scraps of hard maple, and adjust the amount of solvent in the dye until you get the color you want.

Q I made a toy chest for my granddaughter out of white oak boards and white oak plywood. When I applied the stain, they turned two drastically different colors. How can I prevent that from happening?

A Your white oak plywood has undergone a lot more stress and strain than your boards during its journey to the lumberyard. The plywood veneer that comes off the log has been soaked in hot water and subjected to pressure as it was cut. Then, adhesive was applied to the back, and it was pressed and heated again. All of this activity tends to clog the pores and affect the way the plywood absorbs stain.

To avoid mismatches in the future, experiment with scraps of each material to see what you can do to make the stain more uniform between the two. Try sanding each lightly before testing your stain. If it's still a mismatch, raise the grain on the plywood with a damp cloth, resand when dry, then test again. You may also want to try using a gel stain, which doesn't penetrate as deeply as other stains and is easier to control based on how long it stays on the wood and how hard you wipe it off.

Q Sometimes when I apply stain to projects, I wind up with dark sections in the corners. Even when I can wedge a rag in there, I wind up wiping the stain opposite the grain. Any tips?

A Sometimes you just need the right helper in your corner. Keep an inexpensive, stiff, short-bristled brush on hand that you can dab into the corners to absorb most of the stain, then whisk the rest away. Wipe the brush dry after each use, and clean it after the project is stained so you can use it over and over again.

Q Can I apply water-based polyurethane over an oil-based stain?

A It's usually safe to apply oil-based polyurethane over any kind of stain, but you need to be more cautious — and experiment more — if you want to apply waterborne poly over oil-based stain. You could wind up with adhesion problems. It's always safest to use a top coat and stain from the same manufacturer. Read the label to make sure the finishes are compatible. Another option is to apply a coat of dewaxed shellac over the oil-based stain, then apply the water-based poly.

Q I love the rich, dark look of fumed oak. Is there a way I can reproduce the effect on a small oak tambour table I made?

A Fuming is the chemical reaction that occurs when the tannins in wood react with ammonia. The process was used widely in finishing Craftsman and other styles of furniture, especially those made of white oak, which is high in tannin.

You can try fuming your own furniture by building a plastic tent around your table, setting pans of ammonia inside, then sealing up the tent tightly — but you must use extreme caution. Ammonia is hazardous and can wreak havoc on your eyes, skin, and respiratory system. You have to work in a well-ventilated area away from people, and wear a respirator, goggles, and rubber gloves. Don't even think about using the industrial-strength ammonia the pros use; use household ammonia, and plan on the process taking several days (see Resources for more information).

Q I've seen cherry darken when exposed to direct sunlight. I'm afraid the bookcase I'm building will darken unevenly because of the way the sun will hit it once it's in our den. Can I purposely darken the whole piece to avoid this?

A Yes. The best way is to intentionally expose your bookcase to sunlight. The best time to do this is after your final sanding, before applying your final finish. Sand the entire bookcase to 220-grit, then wipe it down with a damp cloth to raise the grain slightly. Let it dry, then hand-sand the piece to 360-grit. Place your piece in direct sunlight during the early morning or late afternoon; the intensity of the sun at high noon could promote splitting and warping. Rotate the piece every half-hour, exposing all of the surfaces uniformly. It may require several sessions to darken the entire piece. As when experimenting with any finish, first run a scrap of wood from the project through the process to see if you get the results you're looking for.

Q I built some oak speaker cases that I'd like to stain jet-black to match the other audio components. I've never gotten consistent results mixing and using aniline dyes. What else can I try?

A If you like the look of aniline dye but don't like the mixing part, you might want to experiment with leather dye. It's aniline-based but premixed, so it has excellent consistency, is colorfast, and is easy to apply. You can purchase it through leather retailers (or maybe from your friendly neighborhood shoe repairperson).

Clear Finishes

Q I hear woodworkers talk about penetrating finishes and film-forming finishes. What are they, and what are the differences?

A **Penetrating finishes** are those that absorb into the pores of the wood, leaving very little on the surface. Tung oil and boiled linseed oil are the two most common types, but there are dozens of products that combine these two products with varnishes and polyurethanes to create "wipe-on" quasi-penetrating finishes. They're easy to apply and are your best choice if you like the feel of the wood to the touch.

Film-forming finishes, as the name implies, primarily lie on the surface. Shellac, varnish, lacquer, and polyurethane fall into this category. While they're more difficult to apply, they do offer superior protection from moisture and household chemicals and solvents.

There are plenty of gray areas. If you apply enough coats of some penetrating finishes, they'll build to create a film. And if you thin some film-forming finishes enough, they'll behave like penetrating finishes.

Q What are some steps I can take to prevent drips and brush marks when I apply clear finishes?

A Try one or all of these tips:
⊙ Apply your finish to a horizontal surface whenever possible, even if it means repositioning your piece several times during the process.
⊙ Shine a light at a low angle across your surfaces and look for runs and drips as you work.
⊙ If your finish pools, unload your brush by dragging it across the edge of a container, then going back over the area to absorb the excess.
⊙ Thin your finishes by 10 percent so they will brush out better. (The downside of this is they're more likely to drip and sag.)
⊙ "Tip off" your finishes by lightly dragging the tips of the bristles across the area to help remove bubbles and level the finish.

Q Will oil-based polyurethane offer better protection than water-based polyurethane for the bar top I built?

A Both are similar in terms of durability, but since oil-based poly offers a hair more protection against heat and chemicals, you may want to go with that for a bar top. There are other factors to consider: Water-based polys are clear, dry quickly, and have low odor, while oil-based polys, with their amber tint, help bring out and accentuate the richness of the wood.

Q What is Danish oil?

A Danish oil is a "wipe on" finish consisting of penetrating oil and varnish. It's thin and easily penetrates the wood pores, giving it a natural, hand-rubbed appearance. It comes in a variety of tinted colors, and many woodworkers love it because of the ease of application. A single coat doesn't offer much protection against scuffs, moisture, or chemicals, but you can build up enough coats to increase durability.

Q I applied a cherry-tinted Danish oil to a breadboard I made, and the end-grain turned out way darker than the top. How do I avoid this in the future?

A Next time, first apply a coat of clear or natural Danish oil to just the end grain, and let it dry. Then, apply the tinted oil uniformly to all of the surfaces. The initial clear coat will seal the end grain so it doesn't absorb the darker oil as readily.

Q I opened a can of varnish the other day and discovered a trampoline-like, rubbery skin covering the top. I peeled it off, and the varnish looked okay — but is it okay to use? And how do I prevent this?

A The varnish below the skin should be fine to use, as long as you strain it first with a paint filter or old pantyhose. To make sure it's good, spread a little on a scrap of wood and make certain it dries okay.

You can prevent this in the future by spraying a few shots of an aerosol product, such as Bloxygen, into the can just before you close it. Oil-based finishes dry and harden by absorbing oxygen. Bloxygen replaces the oxygen in your half-filled can with argon to prevent this reaction from happening. At about 10 cents a shot, it can save time, material, and hassle.

tip: Tacky Idea

When you've stained and finished cabinet doors, plywood panels, and furniture parts, I bet at some point you've wished you could do both sides at once so you could finish the job twice as fast. If you have components where a perfect appearance isn't critical on one side, try this: Purchase some carpet tack strips — you know, those things that look like a yard stick with dozens of tacks hammered through them. Cut them into short lengths and keep them at the ready. Apply the finish to the least conspicuous side of the part, position tack strips so they can support it, then set it on the tack strips wet side down. You can then immediately apply finish to the other side.

Q Can I use polyurethane as a finish on salad bowls I turned on my lathe?

A Yes, but make sure the finish has fully cured before you use them, a process that takes about 30 days under normal conditions. Years ago, when lead and other powdered metals were added to finishes to promote drying, this was a safety hazard. The driers used today are considered food-safe, but appearance is another issue. Since polyurethane sits on the surface, it's more likely to show scratches. A penetrating-type finish or salad bowl oil would show fewer scratches and be easier to renew.

Q What's a good finish for a cutting board?

A Try using walnut oil. It's safe, won't go rancid like some vegetable-based oils, and, since it's non-film-forming, it's easily repaired by simply wiping on another coat.

Q I just completed building a coffee table and was told by a friend that I should apply just as many coats to the bottom of the table as to the top. Why?

A By applying finish equally to both sides of your top, the upper and lower surfaces will react similarly to humidity levels and therefore expand and contract at the same rates, preventing uneven warping and cracking.

Q If I apply enough coats of finish to a piece of furniture, can I prevent the wood from expanding and contracting entirely?

A No. A finish can minimize wood movement but not eliminate it entirely. Penetrating finishes do the least to prevent movement; film-forming finishes do the most.

tip: Avoid Finishing Fiends

If you need to get floating motes of dust out of the air so they don't land on the finish you're about to apply, try spraying the air with a plant mister. The fine droplets will make the little particles heavy enough to fall to the floor — not onto your beautiful finish.

Also, close heat vents so the air doesn't spew out or stir up more dust when the furnace or air conditioner kicks on. And if your workshop is in the basement, watch out for falling dust when people walk around upstairs. If it's a persistent problem, staple sheets of polyethylene plastic to the ceiling.

Q I like to apply lots of thin coats of clear finish rather than a couple of thick ones. How far can I thin a finish before I start getting myself into trouble?

A You can thin shellac, lacquer, varnish, and polyurethane to your heart's content without affecting durability or longevity. Since you'll be applying a higher percentage of solvents and a lower percentage of solids with each coat, you'll need to apply more coats. You should avoid thinning water-based finishes altogether, but if you must, thin them no more than 10 percent.

Q How do I avoid all those little bubbles that appear in clear finishes when I brush them on?

A A variety of things can cause bubbles, including applying a finish that's too thick, applying a finish too thickly, or working it into the wood by wiggling the brush back and forth. Shaking, rather than stirring, the finish can also create bubbles. So avoid these scenarios. If you still get bubbles, "tip off" your wet finish by holding the brush at 90 degrees to the surface and lightly drawing the tips of the bristles across the finish.

Q What is boiled linseed oil, and what kind of finish does it produce?

A Boiled linseed oil is raw linseed oil, derived from flaxseed, that's been processed to dry faster. Contrary to its name, the oil hasn't been boiled but was allowed to oxidize or had thinners added to it. Boiled linseed oil is a true penetrating finish that imparts a mellow, antique look. When buffed, it gives wood a soft, satin-like luster. On the downside, it darkens with age and offers low water-resistance. Using it requires more patience than with modern penetrating oils. It's best applied in thin coats and should be allowed to dry overnight between coats.

tip: Beware of Spontaneous Combustion!

Penetrating finishes, such as tung oil, linseed oil, and Danish oil, dry through oxidation, meaning the oils combine with oxygen to harden. This process can generate so much heat that oil-soaked rags, in the process of drying out, can spontaneously burst into flames — especially when left piled up. For safety, dispose of rags in a metal container filled with water, or by first allowing them to dry out thoroughly on the lawn or driveway. Don't be like the fussy homeowner who disposed of those "terrible looking" rags his spouse left drying on the lawn by stuffing them into the garbage can in the garage. They awoke in the middle of the night to find their garage engulfed in flames.

Q With premixed shellac so readily available, why do some woodworkers bother mixing their own?

A Brewing up your own shellac, using shellac flakes and denatured alcohol, offers several advantages. It lets you control the thickness, or "cut," of the shellac. For example, if you're wiping or spraying it on, you'll want a thinner cut than if you're brushing it on or using it to seal knots. Mixing your own also allows you to control color based on the color of the flakes you use or tints you add. It also guarantees freshness.

Q I want to use shellac on a wood lamp base I made. Is it okay to use some premixed stuff I've had on my shelf for a few years?

A Probably not. Old shellac hardens very slowly and never obtains the same hardness as fresh shellac. Try putting a drop of it on a piece of glass and letting it dry overnight. If you can dent it with your fingernail the next day, invest in a fresh can.

Paints and Painting

Q I love the old-fashioned look of milk paint, but it sounds mysterious. What is it, and how difficult is it to use?

A Milk paint is a powdered mixture of casein (a protein found in milk) and lime mixed with water. It creates a velvety yet amazingly durable coating that's been used for thousands of years (many of the artifacts in King Tut's tomb were painted with the stuff). It's available in a wide variety of vivid colors, and it adheres well to solid woods, plywoods, and even MDF (medium-density fiberboard). You can apply a single coat to create a washed look or multiple coats for an opaque finish. Since milk paint is physically absorbed into raw wood, priming isn't necessary. And, it's relatively easy to apply (see Resources for milk paint suppliers):

⊙ In powdered form, milk paint will last indefinitely, but once mixed it has a short shelf life, so mix only as much as you can use in a day. Mix equal parts powdered milk paint and water, then let the mixture slake for 10 minutes.

⊙ Use a brush to apply the first coat with the grain. It absorbs quickly into the wood, so overlap strokes and keep your brush saturated. Immediately apply a second coat to even out the coverage.

⊙ Once the paint has dried, lightly sand the surface with 220-grit sandpaper to smooth it and to remove any raised-grain "fuzz." Then continue adding coats until you achieve the look you want.

⊙ Milk paint is durable, but its flat finish is a magnet for dirt and oily fingers. If your project will be subjected to lots of manhandling and moisture, add a protective coat of wax, shellac, or polyurethane.

Q I just finished building a plant stand and would love for it to have that antique "crackled paint" look. Is there a faster way of doing this than waiting 75 years for the paint to crackle on its own?

A You can create a crackled finish on your plant stand in a single day. There are plenty of crackle finish products you can buy, but you can also make your own. Here's how:

⊙ Apply a base coat of latex paint to your plant stand. This color will eventually show through the cracks, so make sure it contrasts with the color of your topcoat.

⊙ When the paint is dry, use a sponge applicator or brush to apply a coat of liquid hide glue (available at most home centers and hardware stores). Apply the glue in a single pass in one direction; avoid the temptation to go back and rework the glue.

⊙ Let the glue dry for four to five hours, then apply the topcoat. A light coat will create thin cracks; a thicker coat, wider cracks. Again, apply the paint in a single pass, and don't go back and rework it. The finish should start crackling in just a few minutes.

⊙ Once the paint has dried, you can apply a clear finish for protection. Water-based polyurethane will have the least effect on the color.

Q Last year I installed knotty pine tongue-and-groove wainscoting in our basement. I primed the wood before painting it, but now dark circles are starting to appear around each knot. What did I do wrong?

A The knots contain resins that continue to bleed long after the paneling has been installed. Standard latex (water-based) and oil-based primers aren't effective when it comes to sealing wood knots. The best thing to do is to spot-prime each knot with dewaxed shellac or a shellac-based product (such as B-I-N Primer) before priming and painting. Both products dry quickly and can be topcoated with any kind of paint.

tip: Prepaint Your T & G

It's a good idea to paint tongue-and-groove paneling before installing it. That way, when the boards contract (usually in the dry winter), you'll see painted wood rather than bare wood at the seam. Be sure to give the tongue just a light coat of paint, and don't allow any drips in the groove. Otherwise, you'll have trouble fitting the tongue into the groove during installation.

Q We're installing all new doors in our house, and I have more than a dozen to paint. Is there a trick for painting both sides at the same time?

A Sure. Here's what you do:

1 Lay your door on a pair of sawhorses.

2 Drill two ¼" holes in the top edge, about 4" in from each end, then drill one ¼" hole in the bottom edge, near the center. Install 4"-long, ⁵⁄₁₆" lag bolts about 1" deep into each hole.

3 Spread your sawhorses apart so the head of each lag bolt is resting on the sawhorses.

4 Paint the top side and all four edges of the door, then use the two lag bolts on the top edge as handles to rotate the door (like a rotisserie), so the other side is facing up, and paint that side.

5 You can either let the door dry while it's supported by the sawhorses, or enlist a helper to stand up the door, using the lag bolts to prevent the door from touching the floor or walls. This works well for applying stain and clear finishes, too.

6 When your door is dry, remove the bolts, plug the holes with wood filler, and give them a dab of paint.

Q I built a stepstool for my granddaughter to use in the bathroom. Will oil paint offer better protection than latex?

A If you'd posed this question 20 years ago, the answer may have been "yes," but today the gap has narrowed significantly. Oil-based paints were once the product of choice for furniture and woodwork. They took longer to dry, meaning brush strokes had more time to level out, creating a smoother surface. They also offered better adhesion and durability. However, latex paint manufacturers have continued to improve their products, and today both types will do the job.

You should pay attention to the sheen. High-gloss enamel paints, available in both water- and oil-based versions, are more scrubbable and easier to keep clean, making them the best candidate. Pay extra attention to priming and painting the bottoms of the legs, so the end grain doesn't absorb moisture from the floor.

tip: Clean Shot

When you're finished using aerosol spray paint, place the nozzle on the stem of a WD-40 can, give it a shot, then put the nozzle back on the paint can. The WD-40 will clean out the nozzle and prevent it from clogging.

Furniture Refinishing & Repairs

The reward of a thing well done is to have done it.

— RALPH WALDO EMERSON

Building a piece of furniture can bring all your skills and tools to bear, but repairing an old piece does all that and more. Not only do you have to figure out how you're going to make the repair, you also need to figure out how the woodworker who originally built the piece put it together. You may encounter old-world joints, glues, woods, fasteners, and finishes. You need to be part craftsman and part Sherlock Holmes to figure out the right way to approach things. But repairing or refinishing an old piece of furniture, particularly one that's been in the family for generations, can be doubly rewarding. In the process, you'll gain not just some new skills but a family heirloom as well.

Basic Furniture Repairs

If you purchase or inherit a piece of furniture, especially one over 150 years old, do a little research before going to work on it. Period furniture, such as Chippendale, Hepplewhite, and Queen Anne, can be astonishingly valuable. A secretary bookcase made by Christopher Townsend in 1740 recently sold for over $8 million at auction. Original finishes are prized by collectors and dealers, and refinishing a rare piece can cause its value to plummet. Look for marks, dates, or labels on the back or bottom of the piece. If you think you have a gem, bring it to a furniture expert for an appraisal.

Q Is there a simple test to determine whether a chair is sturdy enough as is or needs to be reglued?

A It's a subjective call, but try this: Face the chair, plant one knee firmly on the seat, and wiggle the back in both directions. If it shifts in one direction and stays put, it's definitely time to reglue. If it springs solidly back into its original position, it's probably sturdy as is. Anything in between is a judgment call; you'll need to make your decision based on how often and how vigorously the chair is used and whether you're gearing up to reglue other chairs in the set anyway.

Q I bought an antique chair at a garage sale and am having trouble regluing the wobbly old thing. Any tips?

A New glue simply won't adhere to old, dried glue, so your first mission is to remove the old glue. Here's how:

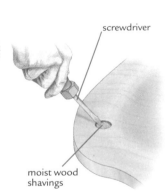

screwdriver

moist wood shavings

1 Label all the parts with masking tape, snap a picture of the chair, then disassemble it.

2 To dissolve and remove the dried glue (which most likely is hide or yellow glue) from the tenons, soak them in warm water or vinegar until the glue softens. Then, use a coarse cloth to scrub each tenon clean.

3 To clean the mortises, pack wood shavings into them, pour in a small amount of warm water or vinegar, wait 15 minutes, then swirl the mixture around with the tip of a screwdriver or dowel. The shavings will scrub the walls of the mortise and absorb the loosened glue.

4 Let all the parts dry out and return to their original size, then test-fit the parts. If they fit snugly, reassemble the chair using yellow or hide glue. If there are gaps, use epoxy or some other type of gap-filling glue (though these glues will make future repairs more problematic).

Q I have a perfectly solid chair with just one severely cracked spindle. Are there any tricks for replacing it without taking the chair apart?

A Remove the damaged spindle by sawing it in two, then remove the halves. Scrape the glue from the mortises, and use a drill to deepen the mortise in the top hole or backrest an extra ½". To install the new spindle, apply glue to both ends, push the upper end as far up into the deep upper mortise as you can, then push the lower end of the spindle into the chair seat mortise.

Q I have a chair with one loose leg, but all the other parts seem to be solid. Is there some way to fix this without taking the whole chair apart?

A If it's an everyday chair, you can try fixing the leg by drilling an angled ⅛" hole near the joint, then use a glue syringe to inject either a slow-setting epoxy (which will fill open spaces around the joint) or a product such as Chair-Loc (which swells the fibers to hold the parts in place). That said, serious restorations on older pieces usually involve disassembling the loose part along with others directly attached to it, then making the repair. Epoxies and fiber swellers don't always do the trick, and they're a mess to clean out when someone finally gets around to doing a "correct" restoration. You can free the loose parts by injecting hot water (around 140 degrees) into the joints with a syringe, then twisting things apart, cleaning off the old glue, letting the wood dry out, then regluing with hide or yellow glue.

Q I'm trying to disassemble an antique chair, but I can't get the leg out of the seat socket. There are no screws, pegs, or nails holding it, and I can twist it, but it just sits there laughing at me. What's going on?

A There's a good chance the chairmaker used a blind-wedged tenon. To make one, a kerf was cut in the end of the leg tenon, a wedge was partially inserted into the kerf, glue was applied, then the assembly was pounded into the mortise. The wedge expanded the tenon as it was driven in. The mortise was most likely undercut so the expanding tenon really became locked in.

BLIND-WEDGED CHAIR TENON

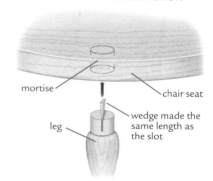

Your best bet is to add a drop or two of water to the joint to lubricate it, then give the chair bottom a few sharp whacks with a rubber mallet while holding the leg in a wood-jaw vice. Once it's disassembled, scrape out the old glue and let everything dry out. When it's time to reassemble the chair, fit a new wedge in the slotted tenon, apply glue, and tap the leg back in while the wedge expands the tenon. (And let the next person who restores it scratch his or her head when the time comes.)

Q I have a side table with an oak top that's cracked down the middle. The crack is straight, but the edges are jagged and the gap is filled with years of gunk. How do I reglue something like that?

A If the crack is relatively straight, your best bet probably is to cut the tabletop in half, then glue the freshly sawn edges back together again. Remove the top, and use a circular saw and a straightedge guide (see page 97) so the blade cuts right down the center of the crack. If it's a wide crack, it might require two passes of the blade. Test-fit the halves to make sure the newly cut edges fit tightly together, then apply yellow glue and clamps.

To prevent future splits, secure the top to the table base using a method that allows the wood to expand and contract freely without cracking (see page 181).

Q I inherited an old table, and over half of the veneer is missing from the top. How do I get the rest of it off without damaging the underlying wood?

A Lift the edges of the loose veneer and squirt or spray some moisture between it and the substrate. Cut open a brown paper bag and lay it over the veneer. Glide a clothes iron set at medium heat over the paper until the glue liquefies and the veneer loosens. Then, use a putty knife to gently pry off the veneer as you go. Repeat as needed.

If you want to save the veneer for later use or for repairing a matching piece, use warm vinegar, sandpaper, and a scraper to remove the old glue. Then, place the old veneer between two pieces of plywood and clamp it flat until you need it.

Q How do I repair an end table that has a small damaged section in the veneer top?

A Purchase a piece of veneer that matches the grain and color of the original veneer as closely as possible. You may want to experiment first with finishes on a scrap piece of this veneer to see how close you can come to a color match. Then, proceed as follows:

1 Place the veneer patch over the damaged area, align the grains as closely as possible, then tape it in place.
2 Use a ruler and sharp utility knife to cut a diamond shape through BOTH the veneer patch and the damaged veneer on the tabletop.

It will take several passes. Set the patch aside.

3 Use a sharp chisel or utility knife to remove the damaged veneer from inside the scored cutout on the tabletop. Scrape off any glue, then fill any dips or gouges with wood filler.

4 Test-fit the patch and use sandpaper to fine-tune the fit. Apply yellow or hide glue to the back of the patch, then position and press it in place. Use a damp cloth to remove excess glue, then place waxed paper on top of the patch and weight it down with books (your Kindle won't be heavy enough).

5 Remove the books after a few hours, and lightly sand the patch so it's flush with the veneer of the tabletop.

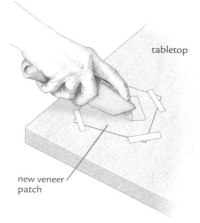

tabletop

new veneer patch

REPLACING DAMAGED VENEER

Q **I'm trying to remove the legs of an old dining room table to make repairs, but six screws have stripped heads and I can't get them out. What's the solution?**

A If they're protruding from the surface (a long shot), grab the heads with locking pliers and twist them out. Otherwise, try this:

1 Use a rotary tool with a small grinding disc to cut a new slot in each screw head, perpendicular to the old one; the deeper the slot, the better.

2 Plug in a soldering iron or hot-melt glue gun, let it warm up, then touch the tip of the tool to the screw for 30 to 60 seconds. The heat will help loosen the wood fibers and melt any glue surrounding the screw.

3 Apply downward pressure on a straight-slot screwdriver, then back out the screw.

If that doesn't work, try using a screw extractor (a tapered rod with reversed threads). Begin by using a drill bit to bore a small hole in the head; a standard bit will work with most old screws. Insert the proper size of screw extractor in the hole and turn it counterclockwise to remove the screw.

Q I dropped a pipe clamp on the top of a wood filing cabinet and created a half-moon indentation. Is filling it with putty my only out?

A Putty might be a good solution for repairing a gouge or a chip, but it sounds like you're dealing with crushed, not missing or torn, wood fibers. Grab your clothes iron and set it to its highest temperature. While it's warming up, apply a few drops of water to the dent. When that water has absorbed add a few more drops. Cover the dent with a wet towel, and press the tip of your iron over the spot. The fibers should expand and regain most of their original shape. Repeat the procedure if necessary. There's actually a chance your dent will turn into a slight bulge. If so, once the area is dry, sand the area with fine sandpaper and a sanding block until it's level with the surrounding surface.

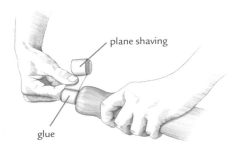

plane shaving

glue

Q I'm repairing a stool, and two of the mortises for the legs have become enlarged over the years. How do I create a tight-fitting joint again?

A Create a larger tenon. Find a thin wood shaving (or create one using a hand plane), apply glue to one side of it, and wrap it tightly around the tenon. Give it as many wraps as you need to build it up to the right size. When the glue has dried, use sandpaper or a file to reshape the new tenon, then glue it in place.

Q I need to reproduce 18" of molding that's missing from a sideboard I'm restoring. How can I do this simply and quickly?

A If you had miles of molding to reproduce, it would make sense to have a router or shaper bit custom-made for milling the molding. Another option would be to figure out some combination of standard router bits or standard moldings that might do the trick. But since it's just a short piece, try this technique (which is neither simple nor quick):

1 Trace the profile of an existing piece of the molding onto the ends of two strips of wood. One of these will be your test piece, the other will be your actual piece. The wood strips should be at least ½" wider than your finished molding so you have legs to support it while you make the cuts.

2 Set the fence of your table saw the correct distance away and the blade at the right height for one end of your profile. Run your test strip into the blade to see if the kerf just "kisses" your layout line. If it does, run the actual piece through.

3 Adjust the distance of the fence and height of the blade for the next cut, make a test cut, then cut the workpiece. Repeat this process until you've roughed out the profile.

4 When you're done, flip your molding over and run it through your table saw to remove the support legs.

5 Use carving gouges, chisels, and sandpaper to smooth the molding to its final shape.

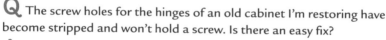

profile

legs

table saw blade

Q The screw holes for the hinges of an old cabinet I'm restoring have become stripped and won't hold a screw. Is there an easy fix?

A Add a dab of white glue to each screw hole, then jam in toothpicks until the holes are filled. Once the glue has dried, use a razor knife to remove any toothpick ends extending beyond the hole. This will create enough new material for the threads of the screws to bite into. For really large holes, try gluing and tapping in golf tees.

Q The caned seat of my grandmother's old rocking chair has finally worn through. Is this something I can fix?

A If the chair is less than 60 years old, there's a good chance you can. First, look at the seat. If individual strands of cane have been woven through individual holes drilled in the wood frame, it's a job for a pro (or for someone who wants to learn the art of caning). But if the seat is made of sheet cane held in place with a flexible spline pressed into a groove around the perimeter of the opening (like your window screens), you can tackle the job.

There are many excellent books and videos available to guide you through the process (see Resources), but see the next page for what the job involves in a nutshell.

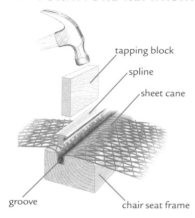

tapping block

spline

sheet cane

groove

chair seat frame

- Use a chisel to pry out the old spline and sheet cane, then clean out the groove.
- Cut the new sheet cane oversize, soak it in warm water for an hour, then use caning wedges to force and hold the edges of the sheet cane into the groove.
- Soak the spline, apply glue, then remove the wedges one-by-one while pressing and tapping the spline and edges of the sheet cane into the groove.
- Trim the excess cane.

Stripping Furniture

Q My local hardware store sells over a dozen different furniture strippers. How do I figure out which one to use for the chair I'm stripping?

A There are pros and cons to every stripper. Some work fast but have potentially flammable or harmful vapors. Others are safer to use but work slowly as the tradeoff. Strippers can be grouped into three broad categories:

Liquid refinishers work quickly by breaking the bond between the wood and the finish. But there are drawbacks. They don't cling well to vertical surfaces, some are flammable, and those containing methylene chloride emit harmful vapors.

Solvent mixtures, often in semi-paste form, work slower than liquid refinishers but are also safer and will work on most finishes. They'll cling to vertical surfaces as they work, so they're good for projects like your chair. They can damage wood if left on too long, so follow the directions carefully.

Water-based strippers are the safest but slowest-acting of the lot, taking up to 24 hours to do their job. They're very effective at removing oil-based paints and some oil-based finishes but aren't as effective with lacquer or shellac. Since they're water-based, they tend to raise the grain (easily remedied by sanding) and in some instances can loosen veneers (not so easily remedied). Since their vapors are not harmful, these strippers are the perfect candidates for stripping millwork and moldings in place.

Q What type of safety precautions should I take when using chemical furniture strippers?

A Read the directions and follow them. They may seem overly cautious, but this is an area where being overly cautious is wise. Also keep in mind these general guidelines:

⊙ Work outside in a shaded area, if possible. The fumes will dissipate faster and there's less danger of creating an explosive situation if vapors build up. If you can't work outdoors, work in a very well-ventilated area.

⊙ Wear the proper respiratory equipment. The best is the type that supplies fresh air, rather than filters room air (see page 31). Read the label for information on the required safety equipment. A dust or particle mask will NOT offer adequate protection.

⊙ Wear splash-proof goggles designed to deflect liquid splashes.

⊙ Wear an old pair of long pants and a long-sleeved shirt with an apron on top.

⊙ Wear thick neoprene gloves with the cuffs rolled outward to "catch" any stripper that might spurt outward or droop downward.

⊙ Set the project on newspapers or plastic on a surface that allows you to work comfortably and clean up easily.

Q It seems like the stripper I'm using evaporates almost as quickly as I apply it. What am I doing wrong?

A You may be skimping on the amount of stripper you're applying. Glop it on with an old natural-bristle brush, then cover your workpiece with a garbage bag or wrap it in plastic sheeting. This will help contain the vapors to minimize evaporation and maximize the effectiveness of the stripper.

Q What's the best way to remove the dissolved gunk from all the curves and indentations of a turned table leg?

A Try rubbing coarse wood shavings or sawdust around the leg using a gloved hand. The small particles will help gently scrub the wood and absorb the gunk as you work.

tip: Get a Leg Up on Strippers

When refinishing chairs, tables, or anything else with legs, place a disposable pie pan under each leg to catch the stripper as you scrape it off. Your cleanup task will be easier, and you can often reuse the stripper you gather.

Q I'm stripping an old carved picture frame I found at a garage sale. I'm having trouble getting the paint out of the hundreds of little nooks and crannies with my putty knife. What's the solution?

A You need to get creative. Reapply the stripper. Then, while it's working, walk around and look for things that might do the job. You can use plastic potato scrubbers, twine, barbecue skewers, nail heads, popsicle sticks with whittled ends, dental tools, or anything else that will conform to the indentations and protrusions. Avoid objects so sharp that they'll gouge the wood.

Q I inherited six formerly beautiful walnut chairs that my sister, in a fit of inspiration, spray-painted bright blue. I dread the thought of stripping them. What are the pros and cons of having them professionally dipped and stripped?

A Done correctly, dipping is a fast, effective way of removing paint. Done incorrectly, it's a fast, effective way of ruining a piece of furniture. Dipping involves giving furniture a bath (or, in some cases, a shower) in refinishing solution, followed by a thorough rinsing. Two dangers of dipping are weakening the glue joints and loosening veneers. But refinishers with the right equipment and experience can circumvent these problems. Another drawback is cost. Be prepared to spend $100 or more per chair for the service. If you want to go the dipping route, visit a couple of refinishers and ask to see some recently completed projects to get a feel for their proficiency.

Q I hate using chemicals. Can I use a heat gun to remove paint from an old kitchen table?

A Yes, heat guns work well on painted furniture, especially pieces with large flat surfaces. As you work, remember:

⊙ Work outside or in a garage, where you can clear the area of combustible materials. Keep a fire extinguisher nearby.

- ⊙ Wear an organic cartridge or supplied air respirator (SAR) designed for use with heat guns and goggles (see page 31), as well as protective clothing and cloth gloves.
- ⊙ Lay down a canvas drop cloth to catch paint scrapings; plastic drop cloths can melt and paper can catch on fire.
- ⊙ Hold the gun 5" to 6" away and fan it back and forth in a small arc until the paint bubbles. Use a putty knife (slightly round the corners to avoid gouging the wood) to scrape the softened paint. Once you get the hang of it, you'll be able to soften the next patch of paint with one hand while scraping with the other.
- ⊙ Scrape the peelings onto the drop cloth or into a metal container; otherwise they can reattach themselves to the furniture as they cool.

Take care not to scorch the wood as you work; it will impact how the wood accepts stains, paints, and other finishes. Heat guns actually work better on thick layers of paint than thin ones. If your table has lots of curves and carvings, or if you have trouble removing the last coat of finish, put the heat gun away and complete the process using a chemical stripper.

Furniture Refinishing and Touch-Ups

Q I found an old wood bookshelf in the back of our attic. It looks like all it needs is a good cleaning. What's the best way to do this?

A You can remove most built-up wax and grime with good old mineral spirits. It's an effective cleaner and safe to use on any finish. Dampen a clean, coarse rag with mineral spirits (about the same dampness as a healthy dog's nose) and rub away. Keep changing cloths as they become dirty. Use cotton swabs to get into ridges and crevices. When your rag no longer picks up dirt, give one final pass with a clean rag dampened with mineral spirits.

Q My reckless uncle left a glass of iced tea on a side table without a coaster under it. When we discovered it the next morning, we found a white ring in the lacquer finish. Do we need to refinish the whole table?

A Probably not. Wick up any remaining water and let the area dry. Dampen a clean, soft cloth with denatured alcohol, and lightly rub the area in a tight circular motion. Repeat until the ring disappears. If this doesn't work, create a mild abrasive by mixing cigarette ashes (your uncle probably left those behind, too) with vegetable oil, and rub this over the area with a cloth. If this leaves a dull spot in the finish, restore the luster by rubbing the area with a high-gloss automotive polishing compound or light coat of finish.

Q A neighborhood kid used our dining room table as a racetrack for his toy cars and left hundreds of light scratches on the surface. Do I have to refinish the top?

A If the scratches are only in the finish — not in the stain or wood — you may be in luck. Find an inconspicuous area and lightly rub the surface with superfine (No. 0000) steel wool dipped in natural Danish oil. If this helps eliminate or disguise the scratches in your test spot, use this procedure for the entire top. Take it easy near corners and edges, where it's easy to rub through the finish. When the oil has dried, lightly wipe down the top with mineral spirits. To add an extra layer of protection, apply a light coat of clear aerosol lacquer. And the next time your neighbor visits, give him a jigsaw puzzle to play with.

Q Several of our dining room chairs have acquired nicks and scratches over the years. What's the simplest way to make them disappear?

A You can easily disguise light scratches using felt-tipped furniture touch-up markers, available at hardware stores and home centers. Dab the area with the marker, then wipe the surrounding area with a paper towel to remove excess stain. Buy two or three markers of varying shades, and apply the lightest stain first. If that's too light, apply the next darkest tone until you've found a good match.

Deep scratches and nicks are most easily disguised by filling them with wax sticks (which look and operate like large crayons). Rub the fill stick over the area until the gouge is filled, then use the edge of a credit card to scrape off excess wax around the nick. Finish by burnishing the area with a dish towel.

In a pinch, you can use standard felt-tip markers and crayons to make the repairs.

Q How do I determine what kind of clear finish is on an antique dresser I just bought?

A Find an inconspicuous spot on the dresser and try these simple tests:

- Dampen a clean rag in denatured alcohol and rub a small area. If the finish immediately starts dissolving or becomes tacky, it is most likely shellac.
- Dampen another rag in lacquer thinner and rub another small area. If that dissolves or becomes tacky, the finish is most likely lacquer.

If neither test yields positive results, the finish is most likely varnish or polyurethane.

Q I'd like to apply another coat of finish to an old dresser but don't want to strip off the old finish. What product should I use, and how do I make sure it will stick?

A If you can't determine the existing finish, you can still move ahead with your project:

- Remove the drawers and hardware, then clean all of the wood surfaces with mineral spirits to remove any wax or polishes.
- Lightly sand all surfaces with extra-fine sandpaper until the sheen is gone. This will also provide "tooth" for the new finish to cling to.
- Find a small, inconspicuous test spot and apply a thinned coat of dewaxed shellac (or a product such as Zinsser Sealcoat) and let it dry. Apply a small amount of the new finish to the test spot.
- Visually check your test spot after a few days to make certain it's adhered. If so, use a sharp utility knife to etch a small tic-tac-toe shape into the test finish. If the edges of the finish still adhere well, chances are your finish will work.
- Apply thinned dewaxed shellac and then your final finish to all of the surfaces.

Q How do I remove tarnish from the brass drawer pulls on the dresser I'm refinishing?

A Dip superfine (No. 0000) steel wool into white vinegar and scrub. For tight spaces and corners, use a toothbrush. Rinse the hardware with water when you're finished.

Q How do I age new brass hardware pulls so they match the patina of the old hinges?

A The easiest way is to use a brass aging or darkening solution, available at woodworking stores. Submerge the items in the liquid, then remove them when the right shade or patina has been attained. If you don't like your results, clean the pulls with a scouring pad and try again.

There are other methods for those who like homespun techniques. You can suspend the hardware from the lid of a glass jar, pour ammonia in the jar, then put the lid in place. Remove the pulls and rinse when the right color has been attained. Though not everyone's cup of tea, you can also submerge the items in urine, an ammonia-rich substance, to attain the right look. Horse urine is rich in ammonia and will work fast, but as for the best way of collecting it, we leave that to your imagination.

Whichever method you use, before aging your brass hardware, place it in a container of lacquer thinner, then scrub to remove any protective lacquer.

tip: Make a Mini-mallet

To make a mini-mallet for getting into tight spaces when assembling and disassembling furniture, try this. Slip a rubber foot or crutch tip onto the cylindrical end of a ball peen hammer head. It creates a mar-proof hammer that will be just the right size for many tasks.

Resources

GENERAL INFORMATION AND SUPPLIES

The sources listed below cover a wide array of woodworking skills and projects. You'll find thousands of other great resources for woodworkers on the Internet. For specific references mentioned in the text, see Resources by Chapter starting on page 290.

Magazines

All magazines listed here have excellent web-sites packed with excellent information.

American Woodworker, New Track Media, LLC,
  www.americanwoodworker.com
  Great resource for woodworkers of all skill levels

The Family Handyman, Home Service
  Publications, Inc.,
  www.familyhandyman.com
  Tons of information on projects and repairs, both inside and outside the house

Fine Woodworking magazine, Taunton Press,
  www.finewoodworking.com
  One of the most respected magazines for serious woodworkers. Its tagline "For woodworkers, by woodworkers" explains the publication's slant.

Popular Woodworking Magazine, F+W Media,
  www.popularwoodworking.com
  Geared to all levels of woodworking

Shop Notes, August Home Publishing Co.,
  www.shopnotes.com
  Great illustrations and projects for the intermediate to advanced woodworker

Wood Magazine, Meredith Corporation,
  www.woodmagazine.com
  One of the oldest and largest woodworking magazines around. Geared to all levels of woodworking.

Woodworkers Journal,
  www.woodworkersjournal.com
  Good all-around magazine for those who love wood and woodworking

Woodsmith magazine, August Home
  Publishing Co.,
  www.woodsmith.com
  Detailed plans for furniture and other woodworking projects, plus tons of tips

Books

Bird, Lonnie, Andy Rae, Thomas Lie-Nielsen, Jeff Jewitt, and Gary Rogowski. *Taunton's Complete Illustrated Guide to Woodworking.* Taunton Press, 2005.
  Over 300 pages of solid, indispensable woodworking know-how by the best in the business

Engler, Nick. *Nick Engler's Woodworking Wisdom: The Ultimate Guide to Cabinetry and Furniture Making.* Rodale Press, 1997.
  Good overall look at woodworking tools and techniques

Korn, Peter. *Woodworking Basics: Mastering the Essentials of Craftsmanship.* Taunton Press, 2003.
  This book's title says it all.

Rae, Andy. *The Complete Illustrated Guide to Furniture & Cabinet Construction.* Taunton Press, 2001.
  A master craftsman (who knows how to teach and write) covers basic and advanced techniques.

Tolpin, Jim. *Jim Tolpin's Woodworking Wit & Wisdom.* Popular Woodworking Books, 2004.
  A master craftsman offers advice in many areas of woodworking, in a light-hearted tone.

Online

StartWoodworking.com, Taunton Press,
  www.startwoodworking.com
  Created by the publishers of *Fine Woodworking* and geared to beginners

Women in Woodworking,
  http://womeninwoodworking.com
  Designed especially for the growing number of women woodworkers

WOODWEB, Inc.,
www.woodweb.com
Discussion forums, project galleries, classifieds, and more

Woodwork Forums,
www.woodworkforums.com
Great discussion boards about every woodworking topic

WoodWorkers Guild of America,
www.wwgoa.com
Woodworking videos, classes, online forums, and information for woodworkers of all levels. Midwest-based and run by woodworker extraordinaire George Vondriska

woodworking.com, Rockler Press,
www.woodworking.com
Information on products and techniques, plus extensive online forum

Supplies and Services

Highland Woodworking,
www.highlandwoodworking.com
Hand and power tools and woodworking supplies

Proven Woodworking,
www.provenwoodworking.com
Woodworking guilds and clubs are a great place to learn, share, and socialize. Nearly every state has a few. This website has an extensive list.

Rockler Woodworking and Hardware,
www.rockler.com
Online catalog and retail outlets nationwide offer a complete line of woodworking hardware, tools, and finishing supplies. Stores offer classes and seminars.

Woodcraft Supply, Inc.,
www.woodcraft.com
Online catalog and over 80 stores offer 20,000 tools and products for woodworkers of all levels.

Woodworker's Supply, Inc.,
www.woodworker.com
Online catalog and three brick-and-mortar stores for all your woodworking needs

RESOURCES BY CHAPTER

The following resources are more specific to the task at hand and contain further information about topics covered in each chapter.

CHAPTER 1: Setting Up Shop

Books, Magazines, and Online Resources

Editors of *American Woodworker* Magazine. *Workshop Dust Control: Install a Safe, Clean System for Your Home Woodshop.* Fox Chapel Publishing, 2010.
Full of tips, information and great illustrations to help you figure out the best dust-collection system for your shop and how to install it

Landis, Scott. *The Workbench Book: A Craftsman's Guide to Workbenches for Every Type of Woodworking.* Taunton Press, 1998.
A professional woodworker looks at other people's workbenches and offers plans for yours.

Nagyszalanczy, Sandor. *Setting Up Shop: The Practical Guide to Designing and Building Your Dream Shop*, rev. ed. Taunton Press, 2006.
Information on shop size, location and equipment, geared to professionals and hobbyists alike

Supplies and Services

Air Handling Systems,
www.airhand.com
Complete line of dust collectors, ductwork and supplies

Center for Furniture Craftsmanship,
www.woodschool.org
Classes, workshops, as well as 12-week and 9-month programs in furniture making, carving, turning, marquetry and finishing. Based in Rockport, Maine.

Conney Safety Products,
www.conney.com
Complete line of personal safety equipment and first aid kits

Fine Woodworking magazine, Taunton Press,
www.finewoodworking.com
Extensive list of woodworking schools and programs listed by state and country

Marc Adams School of Woodworking,
www.marcadams.com
Dozens of weekend and weeklong classes in a wide variety of subjects, taught by some of the best in the business. Based in Indiana.

Oneida Air Systems, Inc.,
www.store.oneida-air.com
Complete line of dust collectors, ductwork, and supplies

Peachtree Woodworking Supply, Inc.,
www.nosawdust.com
Complete line of dust-collection equipment and ductwork

W. W. Grainger, Inc.,
www.grainger.com
Safety equipment and repair parts for all sorts of equipment

CHAPTER 2: Wood & Plywood

Books, Magazines, and Online Resources

Carlsen, Spike. *A Splintered History of Wood: Belt-Sander Races, Blind Woodworkers & Baseball Bats.* HarperCollins, 2008.
Fifty-five "short stories" dealing with the unusual, fascinating, and vital role of wood through the ages. Created by the author of the book you're now reading!

Denig, Joseph, Eugene M. Wengert, and William T. Simpson. *Drying Hardwood Lumber,* USDA Forest Service, 2000.
Download a free copy by visiting www.fpl.fs.fed.us/documnts/fplgtr/fplgtr118.pdf

Hoadley, R. Bruce. *Understanding Wood: A Craftsman's Guide to Wood Technology,* rev. ed. Taunton Press, 2000.

Walker, Aidan, ed. *The Encyclopedia of Wood.* Quarto Publishing, 2005. First published 1989.
Full-color photos of hundreds of woods, along with explanations of their uses and properties

Supplies and Services

Ancientwood, Ltd.,
www.ancientwood.com
Supplier of 50,000-year-old kauri wood

Hearne Hardwoods, Inc.,
www.hearnehardwoods.com
Imported and domestic hardwoods, natural-edge slabs

International Wood Collectors Society,
www.woodcollectors.org
Publication (*World of Wood*), conventions, and information for those interested in collecting and working with woods from around the world

States Industries,
www.statesind.com
Manufacturer of ApplePly veneer-core panels. Carried by many hardwood retailers; visit the company's website to find an outlet near you.

Talarico Hardwoods,
www.talaricohardwoods.com
Imported and domestic hardwoods, amazing natural-edge slabs

CHAPTER 3: Hand Tools

Books, Magazines, and Online Resources

Burch, Monte. *Tool School: The Missing Manual for Your Tools.* Popular Woodworking Books, 2008.
Down-to-earth information on stationary and handheld power tools. Good diagrams.

Rae, Andy. *Choosing & Using Hand Tools.* Lark Books, 2008.
Great hands-on information about using hand tools

Tolpin, Jim. *The New Traditional Woodworker: From Tool Set to Skill Set to Mind Set.* Popular Woodworking Books, 2010.
A comprehensive guide to using hand tools; includes projects and information on finishing.

Vintage Saws, *www.vintagesaws.com*
Complete information on sharpening handsaws

Supplies and Services

Lee Valley Tools Ltd. and Veritas Tools, Inc.,
www.leevalley.com
Top-of-the-line hand tools and power tools

CHAPTER 4: Portable Power Tools

Books, Magazines, and Online Resources

Anthony, Paul, ed. *Working with Power Tools.* Taunton Press, 2007.
How to choose and use portable and stationary power tools

Burch, Monte. *Tool School: The Missing Manual for Your Tools.* Popular Woodworking Books, 2008.
Down-to-earth information on stationary and handheld power tools. Good diagrams.

Supplies and Services

Darex, *www.drilldoctor.com*
Produces the Drill Doctor; probably the best-known manufacturer of reasonably priced drill bit sharpeners

eReplacementParts.com, Inc., *www.ereplacementparts.com*
Millions of replacement parts (including brushes and cords) for power tools, along with articles on how to make common repairs and replace common parts

Gator, Inc., *www.gatorgrip.com*
Sanding supplies and conversion kits for random orbital sanders

Seven Corners Hardware, Inc., *www.7corners.com*
Online and mail-order tools at great prices

ToolPartsDirect.com, *www.toolpartsdirect.com*
Replacement parts for cordless, electric, and pneumatic power tools (including brushes and replacement cords), along with thousands of tool schematics to help you order the right part and install it correctly

CHAPTER 5: Stationary Power Tools

Books, Magazines, and Online Resources

Alan Lacer Woodturning, *www.alanlacer.com*
DVDs, classes, woodturning tools, and DVDs, including his *Woodturning: Getting Started Right!*

American Association of Woodturners, *www.woodturner.org*
Publishes *American Woodturner* magazine; sponsors shows; gallery space and information

Anthony, Paul, ed. *Working with Power Tools.* Taunton Press, 2007.
How to choose and use portable and stationary power tools

Scrollsaw Association of the World, *www.saw-online.com*
Information for those interested in fretwork, marquetry, and intarsia; quarterly newsletter, events and information

Tibbetts, Malcolm J. *The Art of Segmented Wood Turning: A Step-by-Step Guide.* Linden Publishing, 2003.
One of the world's most accomplished segmented woodturners explains the process from start to finish

Supplies and Services

Rockler Woodworking and Hardware, *www.rockler.com*
Seller of "zero clearance" inserts for table saws and bandsaws

CHAPTER 6: Glues & Fasteners

Books, Magazines, and Online Resources

Bailey, Anthony. *Success with Biscuit Joiners.* Guild of Master Craftsmen, 2006.
Techniques and projects for using this simple, versatile tool

Proulx, Danny. *The Pocket Hole Drilling Jig Project Book.* Popular Woodworking Books, 2004.
Step-by-step information on how to use a pocket hole jig, plus 11 projects you can build using this simple system.

Supplies and Services

Kreg Tool, *www.kregtool.com*
Wide array of pocket hole screw jigs, bits, and fasteners

McFeely's, *www.mcfeelys.com*
Every type of screw and fastener imaginable, plus tools and books

CHAPTER 7: Joints & Special Techniques

Supplies and Services

Franklin International, *www.titebond.com*
Manufacturer of Titebond Cold Press for Veneer glue

Highland Woodworking, *www.highlandwoodworking.com*
Better Bond cold-press veneer adhesive

VeneerSupplies.com, *www.veneersupplies.com*
Better Bond cold-press veneer adhesive

Also see General Information and Supplies on page 89.

CHAPTER 8: Building Furniture

Books, Magazines, and Online Resources

Hurst-Wajszczuk, Joe. *Furniture You Can Build: Projects That Hone Your Skills.* Taunton Press, 2006.
Good, solid projects for solidifying your furniture-building skills

Rae, Andy. *The Complete Illustrated Guide to Furniture & Cabinet Construction.* Taunton Press, 2001.
A master craftsman (who knows how to teach and write) covers basic and advanced techniques.

Supplies and Services

Adams Wood Products, Inc.,
www.adamswoodproducts.com
Manufactures and sells wood furniture components; specializes in legs and feet.

Natural-Edge slabs available through Talerico Hardwoods, Hearne Hardwoods, and Ancientwoods, Ltd., listed in the Resources section for chapter 2. Find other sources online by searching with the words "natural edge slabs" and "wavy edge slabs."

CHAPTER 9: Cabinets & Countertops

Books, Magazines, and Online Resources

Engler, Nick. *Nick Engler's Woodworking Wisdom: The Ultimate Guide to Cabinetry and Furniture Making.* Rodale Press, 1997.
Great basic information for the beginning and intermediate cabinetmaker and furniture builder

National Kitchen & Bath Association,
www.nkba.org
Information and guidelines on kitchen and cabinet design

Schmidt, Udo. *Building Kitchen Cabinets.* Taunton Press, 2003.
Loaded with pictures, tips, and simple building techniques

Supplies and Services

Outwater Plastics Industries, Inc.,
www.outwater.com
Don't let the name fool you; Outwater sells a huge array of columns, corbels, moldings, hardware, and kitchen accessories.

Rockler Woodworking and Hardware,
www.rockler.com
Custom cabinet door and drawer program

CHAPTER 10: Windows, Doors, & Trimwork

Books, Magazines, and Online Resources

The Family Handyman, Home Service Publications, Inc.,
www.familyhandyman.com
Both website and magazine contain tons of useful information on projects and repairs, for inside and outside the house.

Supplies and Services

"Asbestos in Your Home," Environmental Protection Agency,
www.epa.gov/asbestos/pubs/ashome.html
Information on safe removal of ceiling texture containing asbestos

Outwater Plastics Industries, Inc.,
www.outwater.com
Don't let the name fool you; Outwater sells a huge array of corner block crown molding systems, stair rail systems, columns, corbels, moldings, hardware, and kitchen accessories.

CHAPTER 11: Other Projects, Inside & Out

Books, Magazines, and Online Resources

Bird Bath and Beyond,
www.birdbathandbeyond.com
Guidelines for building birdhouses, with detailed charts and information

Kistler, Vivian Carli. *The Complete Photo Guide to Framing & Displaying Artwork.* Creative Publishing International, 2009.
Complete information on how to design, mat, and frame artwork

Parks, Andy. *The Picture Framing Handbook: Matting, Mounting, and Framing Techniques for Professional Results.* Watson-Guptill, 2009.
How to frame anything with professional-quality results

United States Consumer Product Safety Commission,
www.cpsc.gov
Provides guidelines for child toy design

Wild Bird Watching,
www.wild-bird-watching.com
Guidelines for building birdhouses, with detailed charts and information

Supplies and Services

framingsupplies.com,
www.framingsupplies.com
Moldings, mats and everything else you need to frame pictures

CHAPTER 12: Sanding & Finishing

Books, Magazines, and Online Resources

Allen, Sam. *The Wood Finisher's Handbook,* rev. ed. Sterling Publishing, 2007.
All the basics, from wood preparation to the final coat. Includes information on French polishing, faux wood graining, and other techniques.

Dresdner, Michael. *Wood Finishing Fixes.* Taunton Press, 2003.
One of the best finishing experts around solves your wood finishing dilemmas in a Q & A format.

Jewitt, Jeff. *Taunton's Complete Illustrated Guide to Finishing.* Taunton Press, 2004.
Information on sanding, staining, and finishing, including a section on fuming

Supplies and Services

Klingspor's Woodworking Shop,
www.woodworkingshop.com
Every sanding supply you'll ever need for hand- or power sanding

Old Fashioned Milk Paint Co., Inc.,
www.milkpaint.com
Milk paint information and supplies

The Real Milk Paint Co.,
www.realmilkpaint.com
Milk paint information and supplies

CHAPTER 13: Furniture Refinishing & Repairs

Books, Magazines, and Online Resources

Black & Decker Corp. *Finishing & Refinishing Wood: Techniques & Projects for Fine Wood Finishes,* rev. ed. Creative Publishing International, 2006.

Editors of *Family Handyman. Complete Do-It-Yourself Manual,* rev. ed. Reader's Digest, 2005.
Information on furniture repair (and how to repair just about anything else)

Hingley, Brian D. *Furniture Repair & Restoration.* Creative Homeowner, 2010.

Wicker-Works Cane Specialists,
www.wickerworks.com.au
Great step-by-step information on installing pre-woven cane, as well as links to material suppliers

Supplies and Services

Chair Caning and Supplies LLC,
www.chaircaningandsupplies.com
Supplies and information on caning

Constantine's Wood Center,
www.constantines.com
Complete refinishing supplies, plus veneers and lumber

INDEX

italic = illustration
bold = chart

Other Storey Titles You Will Enjoy

Compact Cabins, by Gerald Rowan.
Simple living in 1,000 square feet or less — includes 62 design
interpretations for every taste.
216 pages. Paper. ISBN 978-1-60342-462-2.

HomeMade, by Ken Braren & Roger Griffith.
An ideabook of 101 easy-to-make projects for your garden,
home, or farm.
176 pages. Paper. ISBN 978-0-88266-103-2.

The Kids' Building Workshop, by J. Craig & Barbara Roberston.
These projects bring parents and children together to teach
essential skills and build 15 fun and useful items.
144 pages. Paper. ISBN 978-1-58017-488-6.

PlyDesign, by Philip Schmidt.
Distinctive plywood projects for every room in the house.
320 pages. Paper. ISBN 978-1-60342-725-8.

Rustic Retreats: A Build-It-Yourself Guide, by David and
      Jeanie Stiles.
Illustrated, step-by-step instructions for more than 20 low-cost,
sturdy, beautiful outdoor structures.
160 pages. Paper. ISBN 978-1-58017-035-2.

The Vegetable Gardener's Book of Building Projects.
Simple-to-make projects include cold frames, compost bins,
planters, rasied beds, outdoor furniture, and more.
152 pages. Paper. ISBN 978-1-60342-526-1.

These and other books from Storey Publishing are available
wherever quality books are sold or by calling 1-800-441-5700.
Visit us at *www.storey.com*.